One Man's Terrorist

One Man's Terrorist

*A Political History
of the IRA*

Daniel Finn

VERSO
London • New York

First published by Verso 2019
© Daniel Finn 2019

All rights reserved

The moral rights of the author have been asserted

1 3 5 7 9 10 8 6 4 2

Verso
UK: 6 Meard Street, London W1F 0EG
US: 20 Jay Street, Suite 1010, Brooklyn, NY 11201
versobooks.com

Verso is the imprint of New Left Books

ISBN-13: 978-1-78663-688-1
ISBN-13: 978-1-78663-691-1 (US EBK)
ISBN-13: 978-1-78663-690-4 (UK EBK)

British Library Cataloguing in Publication Data
A catalogue record for this book is available from the British Library

Library of Congress Cataloging-in-Publication Data
A catalog record for this book is available from the Library of Congress

Typeset in Sabon by MJ & N Gavan, Truro, Cornwall
Printed in the UK by CPI Group (UK) Ltd, Croydon CR0 4YY

Contents

IRELAND

Introduction

For thirty years, Northern Ireland was the site of a war without parallel in modern European history. There were no sieges, no battles, no aerial bombardments. The British Army faced an enemy that lurked in the shadows, wearing denim, not khaki, armed with light weapons and homemade explosives. The casualty figures – just under 3,500 deaths and 48,000 injuries – may not seem very high when compared to the bloodshed in countries like Bosnia or Lebanon. But they were the equivalent of 125,000 deaths and nearly 2 million injuries in Britain, or half the British death toll during the Second World War. The same calculation for the US would yield a figure of 600,000 deaths and almost 9 million injuries – much higher than the country's losses in WWII, and nine times the US casualty rate in Vietnam.[1] Of those killed, 70 per cent were civilians. This devastating conflict unfolded in a highly developed West European state with a reputation for political stability. From Wilson and Heath to Thatcher and Blair, a whole generation of British prime ministers had to grapple with an unprecedented security challenge in their own backyard.

The main protagonist throughout that conflict was the Irish Republican Army (IRA), which was responsible for nearly half of all deaths. According to Martin McGuinness, one of the IRA's most senior commanders, at least 10,000 people belonged to the organization at some point during the Troubles. As Brendan O'Leary pointed out, that plausible figure 'suggests that an extraordinarily high proportion of Northern Irish working-class Catholic males who matured after 1969 have been through IRA ranks'.[2] For obvious reasons, public support for an illegal organization is difficult to quantify. But when the IRA's political wing, Sinn Féin, had a policy of unconditional support for its armed campaign, it regularly won between 30 and 40 per cent of the Catholic-nationalist vote. It was that degree of sympathy or toleration among Northern Irish Catholics that made it possible for the IRA to sustain a guerrilla war for so long against one of Europe's most powerful states.

In a survey for the Pentagon, the RAND Corporation described the IRA as 'one of the most ruthless and capable insurgent forces in modern history'.[3] During the 1970s and 80s, Northern Ireland and West Germany were the two most important theatres for the British Army. British generals often preferred to downplay the significance of Operation Banner, as their Northern Irish campaign was known. In fact, the conflict was far more typical of the Army's experience after 1945 than its preparations for a hot war on the German front that never came. From the decolonization struggles of the 1950s and 60s, to the occupations of Iraq and Afghanistan, British forces have usually found themselves pitted against irregular combatants who wage war with rifles and car bombs rather than tanks and artillery. In belated recognition of that fact, high-ranking officers have started referring to the lessons of Operation Banner, claiming that recent wars in the Middle East demonstrated 'the particular techniques and the levels of expertise learnt through hard experience, both on the streets and in the fields of Northern Ireland'.[4] From a very different standpoint, critical historians of the war on terror have begun to recognize the importance of Northern Ireland for any serious account of the British state's record.[5]

Developments elsewhere have also made it easier to place the Troubles in a wider context. In the 1970s, Tom Nairn insisted that Northern Ireland should be seen not as a relic of the past, but as a portent of things to come.[6] The resurgence of national conflicts in post-communist Europe and further afield has driven the point home. From Crossmaglen to the Caucasus, the ingredients of such conflicts are easy to identify: frontier disputes, divided populations, self-interested meddling by powerful states. Nationalism and imperialism, two of the most powerful and ubiquitous forces in modern history, are what set neighbours at each other's throats, not atavistic hatreds. Ancestral voices do not call out to people from beyond the grave: they have to be summoned by the living to legitimize a present-day political stance.

As the title suggests, the main focus of this book is on the political movement that developed alongside the IRA in opposition to British rule. I have concentrated on the period between the first civil rights protests in 1968 and the Good Friday Agreement that drew a line of sorts under the conflict three decades later. Before reaching that point, I have included a short overview of Irish history from the late eighteenth century to the 1960s that should be helpful for those with little or no grounding in the subject. In the final chapter and epilogue, I have also addressed the period since 1998, which as yet scarcely qualifies as history.

The Irish republican movement had two main components, an underground armed wing and a legal political party, formally separate although they were often led by the same people. At the beginning of the conflict, the movement split into two rival camps, known as the Provisionals and the Officials. The Provisionals were by far the most important republican faction: in general, when referring to Sinn Féin or the IRA without any adjectives, they are the tendency I have in mind. But I will also be looking at the history of the Officials – who had their own splinter group, the Irish Republican Socialist Party – and addressing the role played by People's Democracy, a small left-wing group that had an outsized influence on political events. In the 1970s, activists often referred to the 'anti-imperialist movement' as a phenomenon embracing various groups and individuals that could be said to share a common purpose. That concept offers a useful line of approach – even if the rivalry between different sections of the 'movement' was bitter and sometimes murderous.

There are a number of recurring themes in republican politics that transcend organizational boundaries. One is the relationship between political activity and guerrilla warfare. 'Politics' should be understood here in a broad sense, as something much wider than what happens in parliaments or voting booths. Malcolm X's famous dichotomy between the ballot and the bullet has its Irish counterpart in the supposed polarization between 'constitutional' and 'physical-force' nationalism. In fact, many episodes of the struggle for national independence could not be slotted neatly into either category, from the Land League of the 1880s to the general strike against conscription in 1918, and the same can be said of more recent events.

The protest guru Gene Sharp adopted the term 'civil resistance' to describe his preference for Gandhian forms of agitation, but it was already commonly used by activists who prioritized mass action over armed struggle during the Troubles. Civil resistance in this sense need not be non-violent in a way that Gandhi or Sharp would have recognized, but it does not involve creating a specialized military force with its own weapons. There were three moments when civil resistance reached a peak – 1968–69, 1971–72, 1980–81 – all of which proved to be of decisive importance. The self-image of Irish republicans has often been profoundly elitist: they saw themselves as a courageous, self-sacrificing vanguard, winning freedom for the masses. In practice, it was only when republicans and others were able to mobilize those masses as a force in their own right that their efforts left a permanent mark on Irish history.

The successive attempts to blend the republican tradition with socialism form another theme. Writers have often presented Northern Ireland as a region where the writ of Marxism simply does not run. There is no question that communal identities were more important than class consciousness in shaping its political life. However, this would have come as little surprise to a Marxist as orthodox as Lenin, who dismissed the idea that national disputes would simply melt away, even in the white heat of socialist revolution: 'By transforming capitalism into socialism the proletariat creates the *possibility* of abolishing national oppression; the possibility becomes *reality* "only" – "only"! – with the establishment of full democracy in all spheres, including the delineation of state frontiers in accordance with the "sympathies" of the population.'[7]

Soon after Lenin wrote that sentence, in a pamphlet that identified Ireland as 'the touchstone of our theoretical views' on national self-determination, the British government established new state frontiers on the island without taking the wishes of local inhabitants into account. It was entirely predictable that those frontiers would remain in contention, greatly weakening the impact of class politics. Nonetheless, socialist ideas and activism had a very tangible impact on the region's history, and some of the most important developments stemmed from the effort to combine republican and socialist ideologies.

Influenced by Marxist perspectives, left-wing republicans had to address some fundamental questions. Was the struggle for national independence synonymous with the battle for socialism, or did one take priority over the other? How should Northern Ireland's Protestant working class be understood – as fellow proletarians to be won over, or as settler-colonists to be defeated? The answers they supplied have lasting relevance to modern political debates.

There is always a danger of 'presentism' when discussing events on the island. At a time when question marks still hang over Northern Ireland's political status, the difficulty of holding recent developments in a long-term historical perspective should be obvious. Of course, it is easier to identify this pitfall than to avoid it. I have tried to keep speculation about the region's future trajectory to a minimum, and the approach I take to its past may help guard against an overly deterministic view of what comes next. When writing about the modern republican movement, it is only proper to give central importance to the Provisionals and their most enduring leadership team, composed of men like Gerry Adams, Danny Morrison and Martin McGuinness. But I have also kept an eye on the paths not taken, and the individuals who came to the fore at various points before exiting the stage: Cathal Goulding and Seán Garland, Seán Mac Stíofáin and Ruairí Ó Brádaigh, Michael Farrell and Bernadette McAliskey, Seamus Costello and Ronnie Bunting. Northern Ireland's history need not have been as it was, and its future will depend on conscious political choices as well as long-term structural constraints.

Note on terminology

Traditionally, Irish nationalists and republicans have preferred to speak about 'the North of Ireland' (or simply 'the North'), rather than 'Northern Ireland', because they feel the latter term confers unwarranted legitimacy. I have used these names interchangeably throughout the text. Northern Ireland has existed in its present form for a century, and the refusal to accept its official title now seems quixotic. This does not imply approval of the way Northern Ireland was established by the British government in 1920–21, or any particular view of how its future should be determined. I have referred to Northern Ireland's second-largest city as 'Derry', not 'Londonderry', in line with the majority preference of those who live there.

1

The Long War

In December 1956, weeks after Fidel Castro and his comrades landed on the Cuban coast, a much older revolutionary movement on another small island was getting ready to complete some unfinished business. During the early hours of 12 December, the Irish Republican Army launched a series of attacks on police and military targets throughout Northern Ireland, aiming to dislodge Britain's last foothold on Irish soil after centuries of foreign rule.

Six years later, Castro had taken power in Havana, seen off the Bay of Pigs invasion, and was about to take delivery of Soviet nuclear missiles, thrusting his country to the forefront of global attention. But the IRA had not been able to attract the interest of its own people, let alone the outside world. A statement in February 1962, announcing the end of the movement's latest campaign, looked forward hopefully to 'a period of consolidation, expansion and preparation for the final and victorious phase of the struggle'.[1] The *New York Times* derided 'a few score of young toughs' who had used 'a grand and famous name' to exalt their feeble efforts: 'The Irish Republican Army belongs to history, and it belongs to better men in times that are gone.'[2]

Illustrious Ancestors

The IRA had documented the progress of its failed uprising in a newspaper called the *United Irishman*, named after a group of eighteenth-century separatists whose most famous leader was Wolfe Tone, a Protestant lawyer from Dublin. Every year, Irish republicans made the pilgrimage to Tone's graveside at Bodenstown to hear the movement set out its vision for an Ireland that had changed beyond recognition since his death. Products of a revolutionary age, the United Irishmen took inspiration from Tom Paine and the French Jacobins in their struggle for an Irish Republic. Armed with such Promethean ambitions, they set out to bridge the gap between descendants of Catholic natives and Protestant settlers, turning the page on the sectarian wars of the seventeenth century: 'We have thought little about our ancestors – much of our posterity. Are we forever to walk like beasts of prey over fields which these ancestors stained with blood?'[3]

Remarkably, it looked as if they might succeed. The discrimination suffered by Presbyterians at the hands of an Anglican establishment helped the United Irishmen to carve out a popular base in Ulster, the heartland of Protestant settlement. Their middle-class, Protestant leadership struck up an alliance with the Defenders, a movement of artisans and small farmers with an eclectic ideology that was mostly supported by Catholics.[4] Although the founders of the United Irishmen were archetypal bourgeois revolutionaries, and the initiative still lay with middle-class radicals like Tone, the society's membership became increasingly plebeian after the British authorities drove it underground.[5] In pursuit of mass support, United Irish leaders spiced up their political manifesto by promising to reduce the burden of taxes, tithes and rents.[6] In 1797, one British general warned that his government's position in the country rested on sand: 'The loyalty of every Irishman who is unconnected with property is artificial.'[7]

The administration at Dublin Castle responded with savage repression, while the leaders of the movement held their fire in the hope of receiving French military aid. When a French expeditionary force did land on Irish shores in 1798, it was already too late to make a difference. Hamstrung by informers, the United Irishmen saw their plan for a national rebellion miscarry in almost every case, with the exception of Wexford, where a month-long struggle ended in a crushing defeat for the rebels. Captured by British forces, Wolfe Tone took his own life in prison to evade the hangman's noose. He became an inconvenient figure for those who sought to identify Irishness with Catholicism: the 'Irish-Ireland' polemicist D. P. Moran later dismissed him as 'a Frenchman born in Ireland of English parents', and some Catholic ideologues tried to write Tone and his disciples out of the nation's history altogether.[8]

The role played by Ulster Presbyterians in the revolt was just as troublesome for those who associated the Protestant faith with loyalty to Britain. There was no sequel to this episode: the loyalist Orange Order, founded in the 1790s, proved to be a far more enduring presence in the world of Protestant Ulster than the United Irishmen. Over the course of the nineteenth century, the barrier between Anglicans and 'Dissenters' melted away, leaving the movement for national independence to draw its support almost exclusively from the Catholic population. The memory of 1798 saddled that movement with a pledge to overcome sectarian boundaries that was more honoured in the breach than the observance. At a time when the Catholic Church increasingly sought to monopolize Irish identity, such well-intentioned failure still counted for something.

In the aftermath of the rebellion, William Pitt's government pushed through an Act of Union between Ireland and Britain that came into effect in 1801. Pitt abandoned plans to combine the Act of Union with the repeal of legislation that discriminated against Catholics, and 'Catholic emancipation' became the rallying cry for a decidedly unrevolutionary politician, Daniel O'Connell, in the 1820s.

Having won the vote for propertied Catholics, O'Connell turned his attention to the Union itself, but retreated in the face of a government clampdown. The year after O'Connell's death in 1847, during one of the most catastrophic famines in modern European history, a group of radical nationalists who called themselves Young Ireland tried to join Europe's 'springtime of nations'. However, the British authorities had no trouble suppressing their revolt.[9] The Great Famine decimated the lower ranks of the Irish peasantry, and spawned a vast Irish-American diaspora that would provide future struggles for national independence with a vital source of moral and material support.

James Stephens, a veteran of France's revolutionary underground, founded a new organization, the Irish Republican Brotherhood (IRB), in 1858. Unlike the United Irishmen and the Young Irelanders, the IRB established a lasting presence on the Irish political scene, surviving well into the twentieth century. Its supporters became popularly known as the Fenians. Backing for the movement came predominantly from the working and lower-middle classes, giving it a strong egalitarian flavour, although the movement's radicalism was largely pre-socialist, pitting the people against the aristocracy, not the proletariat against the bourgeoisie.[10] The Catholic Church responded to the Fenians with ferocious hostility, and they were the nearest thing to an anti-clerical force in a deeply religious society. However, in contrast to the French republicans who had inspired James Stephens, the IRB tried to avoid a head-on clash with the Church.[11]

The IRB's Irish-American allies pressed hard for an uprising against British rule, and even mounted raids of their own into Britain's Canadian possessions: the first time a military force calling itself the 'Irish Republican Army' went into action. In 1866 the American branch accused Stephens of foot-dragging and ousted him from the leadership. Yet after another failed insurrection the following year, the IRB's Supreme Council decided to adopt a more cautious strategy.[12] A revised constitution published in 1873 promised that the organization would 'await the decision of the Irish nation, as expressed by a majority of the Irish people, as to the fit hour of inaugurating a war against England', in the meantime offering its support to 'every movement calculated to advance the cause of Irish independence'.[13] For the rest of its history, the IRB had one foot in the world of conspiracy, and the other in the realm of open mass politics.

The IRB's main rival in the latter sphere was the Irish Parliamentary Party (IPP), founded by Isaac Butt in 1874, but given real impetus by Butt's successor Charles Stewart Parnell, a Protestant landowner who deployed his aristocratic hauteur to good effect against Britain's ruling class. It later became customary to refer to two different strains of Irish nationalism: the 'constitutional' and 'physical-force' parties. However, those labels obscured some basic facts about Irish political life. The reformist, parliamentary approach favoured by the IPP ran up against two main obstacles. Restrictions based on class and gender prevented the majority of Irish men and women from voting, even after franchise reform trebled the Irish electorate in 1885. Moreover, Irish MPs took their seats in an overwhelmingly British parliament, with no guarantee their voices would be heard. Parnell recognized as much by pursuing obstructionist tactics in the House of Commons, to the displeasure of Isaac Butt.

The IRB gave some tentative backing to Butt's party, and one member of its Supreme Council, John O'Connor Power, won a seat at Westminster for the IPP.[14] IRB activists also played a central part in the genesis of the Land League, a movement for agrarian reform founded in 1879.[15] The League spearheaded a bitter struggle against 'landlordism' in the midst of a deep agricultural depression, demanding the right of tenants to buy their plots. The British prime minister William Gladstone prohibited the League in 1881 and had Parnell imprisoned. A series of land acts went some way towards addressing the grievances of rural Ireland, enabling many tenants to become small proprietors, although agrarian discontent remained a live issue well into the twentieth century, especially in the western counties.

After his release from jail, Parnell began pivoting towards a parliamentary alliance with Gladstone's Liberal Party. He cemented that pact after the IPP's electoral triumph in 1885, when it swept the boards outside Ulster. Meanwhile the IRB wilted under the onslaught of Britain's political police.[16]

Parnell accepted a proposal for self-government within the United Kingdom that fell a long way short of what the IRB was prepared to accept. Even in this diluted version, Home Rule still faced resistance at Westminster. Gladstone's first bill in 1886 was voted down in the House of Commons; a second bill seven years later passed the lower chamber but faced uncompromising opposition from the House of Lords. In the intervening period, revelations about Parnell's private life had seen him ejected from the IPP's leadership at the behest of Gladstone and the Catholic bishops. As a consequence, the Home Rulers split, and Parnell turned back to the Fenians for support – an alliance that his followers continued for some time after Parnell's death on the campaign trail in 1891.[17]

As late as 1909, one-quarter of the IPP's parliamentary group had a background in the IRB.[18] But by the turn of the century, the Brotherhood itself was a greatly diminished force.[19] The revolutionary tradition in Irish politics appeared to have been extinguished, while the IPP's reunified caucus waited for the stars to align in its favour once again.

The Home Rule Crisis

That moment looked to have finally arrived in 1910. The Liberal Party had returned to power four years earlier after a long period of Conservative hegemony that took Home Rule off the agenda at Westminster. A snap election deprived the Liberals of an overall majority and left them relying on Irish MPs to pass legislation that stripped the aristocratic upper chamber of its veto power. In return for this support, Herbert Asquith's government reluctantly pledged to grant Ireland self-government.[20]

That happy consummation could not come soon enough for the Home Rulers and their leader John Redmond. The IPP's near-monopoly of electoral representation had left the party flabby and complacent. Its MPs rarely had to face a serious challenge at the ballot box, and their average age had risen sharply since Parnell's time.[21] If the movement began to falter, there were new forces ready to challenge Redmond's authority as national leader. The journalist Arthur Griffith, a former IRB man, led a rival party that called itself Sinn Féin ('We Ourselves').[22] Griffith called for a 'dual monarchy' on the Austro-Hungarian model as a halfway house between Home Rule and full independence, to be achieved by the abstention of Irish MPs from Westminster. A rising tide of cultural nationalism, channelled through organizations like the Gaelic League and the Gaelic Athletic Association, frequently spilled over onto the political field. The IRB also began to revive under the leadership of Young Turks like Denis McCullough, who in his own words 'cleared out most of the older men (including my father) most of whom I considered of no further use to us'.[23]

Most alarmingly for the IPP, with its conservative, Catholic stamp, the promising turn of events at Westminster coincided with a dramatic surge in labour militancy as syndicalism took root on Irish soil. The Irish Transport and General Workers' Union (ITGWU) sought to mobilize unskilled workers who could only hope to better their condition through tactical militancy and the strength of numbers.[24] The ITGWU leader Jim Larkin was a strong supporter of Irish independence who believed that the working class would be its only reliable champion.[25] Larkin's socialist ally James Connolly expressed the same viewpoint in works like *Labour in Irish History*, with such eloquence that many came to believe he had invented it from scratch.

The business tycoon William Martin Murphy saw 'Larkinism' as a mortal threat to the interests of property. He organized a lock-out of union members in 1913 that became a struggle of unparalleled bitterness and intensity. When police attacked strikers at a rally in Dublin, the ITGWU leaders formed a working-class militia, the Irish Citizens' Army, to protect their members in future clashes.[26] The lock-out ended in victory for the employers, leaving the Irish workers' movement to lick its wounds and prepare for the next round.

Murphy's appetite for the battle had been whetted by his belief that Ireland would soon have its own parliament. A strong supporter of Home Rule, he wanted his class to hold the initiative at the dawning of a new age. However, the IPP's confidence that a smooth road to self-government lay ahead proved to be disastrously misplaced.

At Westminster, the Conservative Party wanted to use Ireland as a lever to return it to government, and its leader Andrew Bonar Law threw his full weight behind Unionist opposition to Home Rule.[27] In Ireland itself, the Ulster Unionist Party began making preparations for war, pledging to establish a provisional government on the day Home Rule came into effect. With enthusiastic support from Bonar Law, the Unionist leaders Edward Carson and James Craig set up a private militia, the Ulster Volunteer Force (UVF), and armed it with weapons from Germany.[28] There was a large element of shadow-boxing in these manoeuvres, however. With the Tories on their side and regular briefings from sympathetic generals, the Ulster Unionists knew there was little danger they would have to face the British Army. This was confirmed by the Curragh mutiny of March 1914, when British officers defied orders to 'coerce Ulster'.[29]

The Tory–Unionist alliance wavered between opposing self-government for the entire country and demanding Ulster's exclusion from the new dispensation. Carson, a southern Unionist, would have preferred to block Home Rule altogether, but his lieutenant Craig was ready to fall back on the north-eastern counties, the only real stronghold for Unionism in an age of mass politics. As partition began to seem inevitable, the definition of 'Ulster' itself became rather hazy: the term could refer to the full nine-county province, where there was a small unionist majority, or a more compact area of six counties. A slimmed-down, manageable territory had obvious attractions for Unionism, although two of the six counties still had more nationalists than unionists.

Supporters of Home Rule observed these developments with fury, contrasting the indulgence bestowed on the UVF with their own rich experience of British coercion. John Redmond's inability to respond to the crisis sapped his authority, and the IRB saw a chance to intervene. Its members took the lead in establishing the Irish Volunteers as a counterweight to the UVF. Although the Volunteers formally pledged to support the IPP leader, who made sure to place his own men on their executive, the implicit challenge to Redmond's cautious parliamentary tactics was unmistakable.[30]

The outbreak of a European war in August 1914 postponed a head-on clash. Asquith's government put Home Rule on ice until the conflict was over, while the UVF enlisted in the British Army; Redmond urged the Irish Volunteers to do the same. The majority heeded his call, leaving behind a militant rump under strong IRB influence. As the war dragged on, becoming deeply unpopular, Redmond's standing among the nationalist population declined sharply.[31]

During this period, a close-knit group of IRB leaders began making plans for an uprising against British rule. They kept their scheme secret, not only from the general public, but even from the nominal head of the Irish Volunteers, Eóin MacNeill. Fearing that the socialist leader James Connolly would mount a separate insurrection of his own, the conspirators brought him into their confidence. Jim Larkin's departure for the US had left Connolly in charge of both the ITGWU and the Irish Citizens' Army. The collapse of European socialism into support for the war effort horrified Connolly, and he was desperate to strike a blow of some kind against the slaughter in the trenches.[32] In the past, Connolly had argued that the working class should lead the struggle for national independence; now he decided to join an uprising with a more ambiguous social content, leaving future generations of left-wing activists to puzzle over his legacy.[33]

The Easter Rising of 1916 lost any real chance of success when Eóin MacNeill discovered that the conspirators had tricked him and sent out instructions for the Volunteers to stand down. Knowing they would be prosecuted anyway, even if they abandoned their plan, the leaders of the rebellion decided to go ahead, in hope rather than expectation of victory, with a fraction of the manpower they had been counting on, and none of the anticipated German support. Outside Dublin, there was little action of note.[34] The capital itself saw intense street fighting that far surpassed the impact of 1848 or 1867. After six days Patrick Pearse, the rebel commander, surrendered to avoid further loss of life. Pearse became the first of sixteen men to be executed under martial law, including a badly injured James Connolly.

The steady trickle of executions helped convert a general feeling of bewilderment at the Rising into popular admiration for its leaders. Sinn Féin played no direct part in the rebellion, but Arthur Griffith's party became a channel for the new mood, winning a series of by-elections and choosing Éamon de Valera, one of the most senior rebels to have escaped the firing squad, as its leader.[35] De Valera, whose US birth and part-Spanish parentage gave him a dash of exoticism, went on to dominate Irish politics for the next half-century, combining the appearance of rigidity with a readiness to dance around awkward principles when the situation demanded it.

An attempt by the new Liberal prime minister, David Lloyd George, to impose conscription on Ireland completed the work that the Rising had begun. The anti-conscription movement, supported by Sinn Féin, the IPP and the Catholic bishops, climaxed with a general strike in April 1918 that shut down the country outside Ulster.[36]

Eight months later, the United Kingdom held the first general election since 1910, with the taste of victory over Germany still fresh. Franchise reform had nearly trebled the size of the Irish electorate, and Sinn Féin took full advantage to mobilize support. De Valera's party promised to boycott the parliament in Westminster and secure international recognition for an Irish Republic.

It won 73 of 105 seats, wiping the IPP off the electoral map. The Unionists held their own in Ulster, the only bulwark against Sinn Féin's hegemony, winning 23 of the region's 37 seats.[37] On 21 January 1919, Sinn Féin MPs gathered in Dublin's Mansion House to inaugurate a new assembly, Dáil Éireann, and declare Irish independence. After a century of disappointment, the dream of Tone and Stephens looked to have become a reality.

A Nation Once Again?

On the same day, a group of Irish Volunteers began the War of Independence with an attack on the Royal Irish Constabulary (RIC) in Tipperary. By now, the reorganized Volunteers were generally known as the Irish Republican Army. The maxim of their new campaign might have been drawn from words attributed to John MacBride, one of those executed in 1916: 'If it ever happens again, take my advice and don't get inside four walls.'[38]

Guerrilla tactics had been used before in struggles against foreign occupiers, most famously in response to Napoleon's invasion of Spain, but never in such an effective and systematic manner to achieve a political goal. The British government denounced the IRA as cowardly murderers because its Volunteers refused to meet highly trained, professional troops in open combat. The bitterness of the attacks underlined how difficult it was for a powerful state to crush a much weaker enemy that chose not to play by the rules. Anti-colonial militants in the rest of Britain's empire took careful note.

The IRA began by targeting members of the RIC, an armed police force recruited overwhelmingly from the Irish Catholic population. Many rural police stations shut down altogether, leaving much of the countryside outside government control. Fear of assassination and communal pressure combined to produce mass resignations, obliging the authorities in London to rely on outside recruits to fill the gap. Reprisals against civilians by these auxiliary troops deprived British rule of such moral authority as it still possessed.[39] In November 1920, Lloyd George boasted to a society banquet in London that his government had 'murder by the throat'. By the end of the month, the IRA had killed fourteen men it identified as British intelligence officers on a single morning in Dublin, while its 3rd Cork Brigade wiped out an eighteen-strong company of auxiliaries in an ambush at Kilmichael.[40] British troops responded to the assassinations in Dublin by opening fire on the crowd at a Gaelic football match, killing twelve. Soon afterwards, the government declared martial law in the south-west.

For the most part, the IRA fought its war in Dublin and Munster, with rural chieftains such as Seán Moylan, Liam Lynch and Michael Brennan operating at some remove from the national leadership. The relationship between the Volunteers and the IRB was never fully clarified: on paper, the Brotherhood had no input into IRA decision-making, but the last president of its Supreme Council, Michael Collins, was also one of the IRA's most charismatic and influential commanders.

Sinn Féin politicians like Arthur Griffith and Éamon de Valera did their best to maintain that the IRA took orders from the Dáil and its cabinet. In practice, the military wing of the movement paid little attention to its nominal superiors, and Sinn Féin's main contribution to the struggle lay elsewhere, in a system of 'republican courts' that by-passed the British legal system.[41] Organized labour also played a significant part in this campaign of civil resistance: there was a short-lived Soviet in Limerick to protest against martial law, railway workers blocked the transport of British soldiers, and a general strike in April 1920 forced the authorities to release hundreds of republican prisoners.[42]

Facing a choice between negotiation and wholesale repression, Lloyd George put out feelers to the Sinn Féin leadership, leading to a truce in July 1921.[43] A delegation headed by Arthur Griffith and Michael Collins went to London to discuss the terms of an Anglo-Irish Treaty.

Lloyd George had already moved to secure the Unionist position in Ulster by partitioning the island. The IRA was less active in the province than in other parts of the country. In Belfast, it had to play the role of communal defence force, facing off against loyalist militias as the city descended into a maelstrom of sectarian violence. The 1920 Government of Ireland Act created two Home Rule parliaments for a twenty-six-county 'Southern Ireland' and a six-county 'Northern Ireland'. Opposition from Sinn Féin made the first of those parliaments a dead letter, while the second took on a life of its own. The Unionist leader James Craig now saw regional self-government as a vital safeguard against the threat of British perfidy.[44]

The US president Woodrow Wilson had popularized the concept of 'self-determination' in Europe after the war, but there was no consensus between Irish nationalists and Ulster unionists about how and where that right should be exercised. The settlement imposed by the Government of Ireland Act resolved this dispute by giving the Unionist Party everything that it asked for. With backing from their Conservative allies, who were also Lloyd George's coalition partners, the Unionist leadership had decided that a six-county area was the largest chunk of territory they could safely manage. If there were any more nationalists inside the boundaries of Northern Ireland, its stability could not be guaranteed.[45]

There was no county or large town in the South where unionists were in the majority, yet two of Northern Ireland's six counties, Tyrone and Fermanagh, had a nationalist preponderance. Alternative ways of subdividing the island to establish local preferences – by Westminster constituencies, for example, or county and city boroughs – would all have assigned a smaller area to Craig's party.[46] In private, Lloyd George acknowledged that the case for his government's preferred model of partition was weak, and he sought to keep it off the agenda for talks: 'Men will die for throne and Empire. I do not know who will die for Tyrone and Fermanagh.'[47]

The Treaty negotiations concentrated on two issues: the political status of an independent Ireland, and its relationship, if any, with the area that remained under British rule. The British negotiating team offered Dominion status that would put the new Free State on a par with Britain's white colonies, Canada, Australia and New Zealand. This was considerably more than John Redmond had expected to receive a decade earlier, but under those terms the government in Dublin would still be subordinate to the British Crown.

Arthur Griffith privately agreed to accept a Boundary Commission on the status of Northern Ireland, rather than local plebiscites. He argued that the commission's findings were bound to 'give us most of Tyrone, Fermanagh, and part of Armagh, Down, etc.' Michael Collins took a similar view, believing that a truncated Northern Ireland would soon come under the authority of an all-Ireland parliament.[48]

Lloyd George hustled Griffith into accepting the draft Treaty by revealing his Boundary Commission pledge, and threats of immediate war created the right atmosphere for the rest of the delegation to sign.[49] Sinn Féin and the IRA both split over the terms of the document: the Dáil voted in favour by a slender margin, but the majority of IRA brigades were opposed.[50] A steady drift towards conflict began, during which the British government applied intense pressure on Griffith and Collins to take action against their republican adversaries.[51]

On 28 June, the new pro-Treaty army began shelling IRA units that had occupied Dublin's Four Courts, inaugurating the Irish Civil War. For many years after, conventional opinion in Britain credited Lloyd George with bringing peace to Ireland. His real achievement was to have brought peace to Westminster, for which a war between Irishmen was an acceptable price to pay.

Historians have often explained the split between pro- and anti-Treaty camps in psychological terms, as a division between realists and idealists, practical men and 'die-hards'.[52] It was certainly not a straightforward clash between opposing political blocs like the civil wars in Russia, Spain or Greece. The leading figures in the two camps had a shared nationalist outlook. Insofar as ideology played a role in the split, it was a question of 'hard' and 'soft' tendencies within the movement, which could sometimes be difficult to parse. Many observers expected Éamon de Valera to be more accommodating than Michael Collins when the negotiations began, but de Valera became the political figurehead of the 'die-hard' cause, while Collins used his position as IRB chief to promote the Treaty.[53]

The Civil War also resists any easy categorization as a class conflict.[54] However, the Treaty did receive overwhelming approval from the elites of Catholic Ireland, and there was more than a simple desire for peace behind their attitude. The War of Independence coincided with a tremendous wave of land and labour agitation that swept through the country. Membership of the ITGWU increased from 5,000 in 1916 to 120,000 four years later.[55] The Irish Labour Party, founded before the war by Larkin and Connolly, took on real substance for the first time. After Labour stood aside in the 1918 election to give Sinn Féin a clear run, the Dáil voted to accept a blueprint for social reform drafted by the Labour politician Thomas Johnson. Politicians who later deplored the 'communistic flavour' of Johnson's Democratic Programme praised it effusively at the time.[56] For the Church, the press and the business class, it was vital to establish a new authority capable of holding the line against social upheaval. The precise terms of its relationship with Britain were a secondary concern.

Such factors did not produce the Civil War, but they helped determine its brutality. One minister in the new Provisional Government, the arch-conservative Kevin O'Higgins, famously described it as being composed of 'eight young men in the City Hall standing amidst the ruins of one administration, with the foundations of another not yet laid, and with wild men screaming through the keyhole'.[57] A display of force would help those foundations to set. His fellow Treaty-ite Eoin O'Duffy urged Michael Collins to ignore talk of peace from 'the Labour element and Red Flaggers'. For O'Duffy, a glittering prize now lay within reach: 'If the Government can break the back of this revolt, any attempts at revolt by labour in the future will be futile.'[58]

In August 1922, Collins died in an ambush by anti-Treaty forces in Cork, where he was directing the war effort. Collins had been more conciliatory towards the republican 'die-hards' than most of his fellow ministers, and his death removed the last inhibitions on the Provisional Government leaders. There were seventy-seven official executions of republican prisoners, three times more than the British carried out during the earlier phase of conflict, along with an unknown number of extra-judicial killings.[59]

Facing a government that, unlike the administration at Dublin Castle, could not be stigmatized as an alien presence on Irish soil, the anti-Treaty forces soon lost the military initiative. On the eve of the Civil War, James Connolly's son Roddy went to Moscow in search of assistance for Ireland's fledgling communist movement. The Bolshevik leader Mikhail Borodin told him that the Treaty's opponents would soon be crushed: 'It is really laughable to fight the Free State on a sentimental plea. They want a Republic. What the hell do they want a Republic *for*?'[60]

The IRA's chief of staff Liam Lynch brushed aside a proposal from his imprisoned comrade Liam Mellows for a social programme that could mobilize support among workers and small farmers.[61] Mellows was dispatched to the firing squad soon afterwards. Lynch soldiered on, making no attempt to build a political movement that could explain why a struggle against the Treaty was necessary. After Lynch's death at the hands of government troops in April 1923, with the military situation clearly hopeless, his successor Frank Aiken gave the order to dump arms.[62]

'Our Question Isn't Finished'

The debate in the Dáil over the Treaty had concentrated on the status of the Free State, not the question of partition.[63] Many nationalists believed that the Boundary Commission would resolve the issue, but that confidence proved to be badly misplaced. The terms of reference for the commission required it to 'determine in accordance with the wishes of the inhabitants, so far as may be compatible with economic and geographic conditions, the boundaries between Northern Ireland and the rest of Ireland', without specifying what those conditions might be. In practice, the matter would be settled by considerations of power, not justice, and Northern Ireland's nationalist minority was sorely lacking in such clout. When the Boundary Commission completed its work in 1925, it recommended some minor territorial exchanges that would have left James Craig's mini-state substantially intact. Embarrassed by the outcome, the Irish leader William Cosgrave readily agreed to the report's suppression.[64]

There was no ideal solution to the problem of Ireland's conflicting identities, and the partition settlement made no attempt to provide one. On formal democratic grounds, the outcome was clearly illogical, as John McGarry and Brendan O'Leary have pointed out: 'A 30 per cent minority in the island (in the 1918 voting returns) was able to prevent one area from seceding, but this area in turn contained a 30 per cent minority (in the same voting returns) in favour of the secession of the whole island.'[65] However, the case for partition had never rested on such premises.

For British politicians, an unshakable conviction that 'Ulster must not be coerced' sat alongside a will to coerce the rest of Ireland into recognizing the Crown's authority – not to mention those parts of Ulster that wanted to join the new Irish state. Irish nationalists, painfully aware of this double standard, often used it as an excuse for not thinking about the challenge Northern Ireland posed to their worldview. Future historians had no trouble pointing out the blind spots in that outlook: its reliance on geography, not history, to constitute the 'Irish people', and its tacit exclusion of most Ulster Protestants from the imagined community of Irish nationalism.[66] The force of such criticisms should not obscure the one-sided character of partition, or the vital role of British power in making that imbalance possible.

William Cosgrave and his colleagues averted their gaze from Ulster and concentrated on building up the Free State. Their ruling party called itself Cumann na nGaedheal ('Band of the Gaels'). Cosgrave's ally Kevin O'Higgins dismissed the social aspirations of the revolutionary period as 'poetry', and there was a distinctly prosaic quality to Cumann na nGaedheal's rhetoric, although its very bluntness could lend it a certain aura: it would be a long time before anyone would forget Patrick McGilligan's warning that 'people may have to die in this country and die of starvation' if his government was going to balance the books.[67] Arthur Griffith's plan for a protectionist regime to build up Ireland's manufacturing base was largely forgotten.[68]

Sinn Féin refused to take its seats in the Free State parliament, and the task of opposing Cosgrave initially fell to the Irish Labour Party. But the party's leader Thomas Johnson was anxious, as he explained, to 'reassure timid people who shiver when they think of Labour in power'.[69] Johnson's cautious approach posed no real challenge to Cumann na nGaedheal. The Labour leader once acknowledged that his party might win popularity by 'disturbing and disintegrating the existing social order', while insisting that no politician 'with a sense of responsibility' would dream of following that course.[70]

Éamon de Valera had a much keener eye for the main political chance. Frustrated with the sterility of Sinn Féin's opposition to the Free State, he broke away in 1926 to establish a new movement,

Fianna Fáil ('Soldiers of Destiny'). Most of Sinn Féin's Dáil representatives followed his lead, promising to take their seats if Cosgrave's government abolished the oath of allegiance to the British Crown. After the assassination of Kevin O'Higgins by IRA members in 1927, Cosgrave brought in a law obliging all Teachtaí Dála (TDs) to take their seats on pain of forfeiture. Dismissing the oath as an 'empty political formula', de Valera led his supporters across the threshold.[71]

Five years later, Fianna Fáil took power in Dublin, inaugurating eight decades of electoral hegemony, during which the party never found itself on the opposition benches for more than one consecutive term. Contrary to legend, de Valera never uttered the words 'Labour must wait' during the War of Independence, and his party took care to incorporate social themes in its programme.[72] Those who saw Fianna Fáil as a baffling, *sui generis* phenomenon usually expected independent Ireland to have a party system that corresponded to the West European norm. In fact, the mould of southern Irish politics was perfectly normal for a post-colonial state with an underdeveloped economy. The Irish party system was different because Ireland was different. Fianna Fáil wanted to remove all traces of British sovereignty over the Free State, but it also vowed to promote economic development by returning to Griffith's protectionist vision. For workers and small farmers, it offered social reforms that, however modest in scope, still made for a welcome contrast with the grim austerity of Cumann na nGaedheal.[73]

It all made for a highly effective formula, especially when it started to deliver the goods. By the end of the 1930s, de Valera had scrapped the oath of allegiance and reduced the British governor-general to helpless impotence. A new constitution adopted in 1937 laid formal claim to the six counties of Northern Ireland and made the state a republic in all but name. De Valera also won back control of the 'Treaty ports' from Britain in 1938, enabling his government to remain neutral when war broke out the following year – the ultimate assertion of Irish sovereignty.[74]

Employment rose in protected industries, and a public-housing programme brought some relief to the working class.[75] The success of Fianna Fáil wrong-footed Labour and the erstwhile 'Free Staters', who rebranded themselves in 1933 as Fine Gael ('Tribe of the Gaels'). When the opposition parties finally came together to form a coalition government in 1948, ejecting Fianna Fáil from office for the first time in sixteen years, they completed de Valera's project by declaring a republic and taking the Irish state out of the Commonwealth.

The IRA watched these developments from the sidelines. By the late 1920s, it was already a shadow of its former self, with barely 5,000 activists: a third of the membership it possessed when the Civil War ended.[76] A faction that included such figures as Peadar O'Donnell, Frank Ryan and George Gilmore argued for the IRA to reinvent itself as a movement of the dispossessed. They drew heavily upon Connolly's writings and the prison notes of Liam Mellows to develop a socialist-republican platform in the hope of winning mass support. At their urging, the IRA launched a new party, Saor Éire ('Free Ireland'), to take the place of a largely moribund Sinn Féin.[77] But the republican leadership soon retreated when the Catholic hierarchy denounced their 'communistic' and 'anti-Christian' endeavour. In 1931, Cosgrave's government banned the IRA and its nascent political front.[78]

In 1934, O'Donnell and his comrades broke away from the IRA to form an organization of their own. The manifesto of the Republican Congress declared its belief that an all-Ireland republic could never be achieved 'except through a struggle which uproots capitalism along the way'.[79] An early split hobbled the Congress, which faded from the scene within a few years. Many of its activists departed to fight for another Republic in Spain. Their attempt to fuse republican ideology with socialism remained a historical oddity until it was rediscovered by a new generation of activists in the 1960s.

Meanwhile, the rump IRA carried on in ever-decreasing circles. Fianna Fáil lifted the ban on the movement after coming to power, but drove it underground once again in 1936, this time for good. By the end of the decade, the IRA had lost its most capable leaders and was about to enter the leanest period of its history. Bereft of all political direction, oblivious to what was happening in the wider world, the remaining stalwarts even tried to form an alliance with Nazi Germany. Mercifully they lacked the resources to make such a partnership meaningful, and the question of forming an 'Irish Republic' on the Wehrmacht's coat-tails never arose.[80]

Fearing that the IRA would compromise Ireland's neutrality, de Valera cracked down hard on his former allies, who appeared to have shot their bolt. The coalition government of 1948–51 included a new organization, Clann na Poblachta ('Clan of the Republic'), that sought to capitalize on disillusionment with Fianna Fáil. Its leader Seán MacBride was a former IRA chief of staff, who steered through the declaration of a republic as the coalition's foreign minister. Denounced by his old comrades as another renegade in the line of Collins and de Valera, MacBride had stripped the IRA of its vestigial *raison d'être*.

However, there was still one issue upon which republican purists could bring their energies to bear. MacBride's government launched a diplomatic offensive against partition in the late 1940s, to be greeted with crushing indifference by a world that had bigger fish to fry.[81] That failure inspired some to contemplate stronger methods. A younger generation of activists took over the IRA leadership and even managed to breathe some life into Sinn Féin's waxwork figurine. One of those militants, Ruairí Ó Brádaigh, later recalled his feelings as he watched Britain's empire begin to crumble after the war: 'We were the indomitable Irish that started all this off, when they controlled a quarter of the world. And now our question isn't finished and all these people have passed us by.'[82] After several years of preparation, Ó Brádaigh and his comrades set out in December 1956 to 'finish the job'.

Operation Harvest, as the IRA called it, fizzled out long before its formal conclusion. In 1957, there were 341 incidents associated with the campaign; two years later, there were just twenty-seven.[83] The internment of IRA suspects on both sides of the border struck a heavy blow against the republican movement, but its greatest problem was the lack of popular support. A statement drafted by Ruairí Ó Brádaigh to mark the end of the so-called Border Campaign deplored 'the attitude of the general public whose minds have been deliberately distracted from the supreme issue facing the Irish people – the unity and freedom of Ireland'.[84] It wasn't just the British colonies in Africa and Asia that had passed republicans by. In the eyes of most Irish people, the IRA was a movement that time forgot.

2

Fish through a Desert

Army of the People

The task of rejuvenating the IRA after Operation Harvest fell on the shoulders of its new chief of staff, Cathal Goulding, a working-class Dubliner who was about to turn forty. From a well-known republican family, Goulding already had an IRA record dating back to his teens. He had been interned during the Second World War, and watched the Border Campaign unfold from a British jail cell after being captured on a mission to steal weapons from an armoury in Essex. Like his childhood friend, the playwright Brendan Behan, Goulding combined a republican outlook with left-wing sympathies and was not afraid to call the movement's orthodoxy into question. Now he would have to draw upon all the authority bestowed by his track record, as he guided the IRA's dwindling core of faithful activists into uncharted territory.

The Belfast republican Billy McMillen later described the shattering impact of the campaign's failure upon the movement: 'The IRA had to face the fact that armed resistance to British rule in the North was getting the cold shoulder from the overwhelming mass of the Irish people.' In the immediate aftermath, McMillen recalled, many IRA Volunteers 'succumbed to the general feeling of hopelessness and despair and drifted off to attempt to build their personal lives again'. For those who remained, 'the task of rebuilding the organization in the face of paralysing apathy and lack of support from the ordinary people was a daunting one.'[1]

Confronted with this challenge, the leadership team that crystallized around Goulding decided to broaden the focus of the movement and tilt it sharply to the left. Republicans would no longer confine themselves to preparation for a guerrilla campaign against British rule in the North. In addition to their clandestine work, IRA members were now expected to take part in open political activity, performing a new role as social agitators. Their goal was to organize a mass movement among workers and small farmers that could overthrow the two Irish states, north and south, and replace them with an all-Ireland socialist republic.

The IRA's house publication, *An tÓglách*, called for a determined struggle against those 'moneylords depending on the British connection for support' who still ruled Ireland half a century after the Rising: 'The essence of Tone and Connolly's teaching is that the freedom of the Irish people can only be achieved through a complete break with the British Empire (under any name) and that the only power capable of achieving and maintaining that freedom is a National Movement led by the Irish working class.'[2] Goulding and his associates began to criticize much of the republican tradition as it had developed since 1916, with the help of survivors from the previous generation. George Gilmore, who had taken part in the ill-fated Republican Congress experiment of the 1930s, contributed a series of articles to the *United Irishman* calling for a return to the politics of James Connolly.[3]

The IRA leadership used carefully chosen quotations from Wolfe Tone and Patrick Pearse to legitimize their freshly minted socialist ideology, stressing its continuity with the republican heritage. However, there could be no mistaking their political innovations. Operation Harvest had been exclusively northern in its scope, but much of the agitational work conducted by republicans now took place south of the Irish border. Goulding insisted that confrontation with the Dublin establishment, and with the 'economic imperialism' of foreign capitalists, was just as important as the struggle against British rule in the North: 'While the IRA faced North, its sole aim being the ending of partition, the salesmen of imperialism aided by their native servants commenced a systematic takeover of Irish assets, a systematic speculation in Irish money, Irish manpower, Irish land. The Army guarded a frontier while the imperialists quietly entered by another and laid claim to Ireland.'[4]

Kieran Conway, a university student who joined the movement in the late 1960s, has described the charismatic aura of its most influential leaders: 'Cathal Goulding, Seán Garland and Seamus Costello were living, visible, here-and-now revolutionaries, who had done prison time, or carried the scars of British bullets on their bodies, unlike the dead and distant heroes of the other left-wing groups.'[5] Seán Garland, like Goulding, came from a working-class background in Dublin's north inner city. He had been seriously wounded during the Border Campaign while leading an attack on an RUC barracks in Fermanagh. Two of Garland's comrades were killed during the raid, each inspiring a celebrated folk song. His reputation for toughness, both physical and ideological, was to be greatly reinforced in the years to come. Seamus Costello was also a veteran of Operation Harvest: after leading an IRA unit on a cross-border raid as a teenager, he was nicknamed 'the Boy General', and the loss of a finger in a training accident added to his mystique. Youthful, good-looking and highly articulate, Costello became a poster boy for the movement's political turn, winning a council seat in his native Wicklow after building up a local base through energetic community activism.

The president of Sinn Féin, Tomás Mac Giolla, did not have the same military profile as Garland or Costello, although he had also been interned during Operation Harvest and now served as chairman of the IRA's central authority, the Army Council.[6] After some initial hesitation, he became a strong supporter of Goulding's left turn. As a university graduate, Mac Giolla was an exception to the rule in the IRA leadership, where self-taught men like Goulding and Garland held sway. When the Border Campaign lurched to a halt, Peter Berry, a senior official at Dublin's Department of Justice, disdainfully referred to IRA Volunteers as 'men of limited education and poor personality who have made no particular mark in their jobs and private lives'.[7] Cathal Goulding would have despised Berry's elitism, but he was keen to recruit some college-trained intellectuals who could give the movement's new platform a more elaborate theoretical foundation. Anthony Coughlan and Roy Johnston stepped forward to play that role. Johnston, the son of an Ulster Presbyterian who had taken a lonely stand against Unionism during the Home Rule Crisis, became the IRA's director of education.

Opposition to Goulding's new departure soon began to emerge. Some veterans drifted away from the movement, while other leading figures continued to oppose Goulding from within. Two of the most important dissenters were the IRA's director of intelligence, Seán Mac Stíofáin, and Goulding's predecessor as chief of staff, Ruairí Ó Brádaigh. Mac Stíofáin, born in England of part-Irish descent, had served in the Royal Air Force before joining the IRA. He was arrested in 1953 on the same arms procurement venture that had landed Cathal Goulding in jail, and got to know members of the Cypriot revolutionary group EOKA while serving time in Pentonville Prison. Ó Brádaigh had seen action during the Border Campaign and now worked as a schoolteacher in Roscommon, a poor, largely rural county in Ireland's west. Both men held positions on the Army Council.

In many cases, the resistance to Goulding stemmed from conservative political attitudes held by IRA members. Others simply believed that the IRA should concentrate on the struggle for national independence and steer clear of 'divisive' social questions. However, some traditional republicans also held the new platform responsible for a perceived slackening of commitment to armed struggle. After bubbling beneath the surface for several years, this current of opinion was forcefully articulated in July 1969 by a well-known Belfast republican, Jimmy Steele, at the reinterment of two IRA men who had been hanged in Britain during the Second World War. Steele pointedly heaped praise on those who 'went forth to carry the fight to the enemy, into enemy territory; using the only methods that will ever succeed, not the method of the politicians, nor the constitutionalists, but the method of soldiers, the method of armed force'. In Goulding's new-look IRA, he added contemptuously, 'one is now expected to be more conversant with the teachings of Chairman Mao than those of our dead patriots.'[8]

Of course, there was a certain irony in Steele's invective, as the movement led by Mao had not shown any reluctance to use force in pursuit of its objectives and was now a leading sponsor of armed struggle in the Third World. The IRA itself discreetly petitioned Mao's government for support in the 1960s, although Chinese diplomats snubbed its emissary Seamus Costello.[9] Cathal Goulding rejected claims that the movement had turned its back on guerrilla warfare. Speaking at an IRA commemoration in 1965, he gave the following assurance to supporters: 'The only way to rid this country of an armed British force is to confront them with an armed force of Irishmen backed by a united Irish people. The British forces in the Six Counties will be confronted by such a force.'[10] At Bodenstown two years later, Goulding stressed that there was no contradiction between armed struggle and political action: 'The will to use military force does not exclude the use before or at the same time of other forces both political and social, to the realization of the same end.'[11]

A similar message could be found in a confidential IRA document obtained by the Irish government when its police force arrested Seán Garland in 1966. Although Garland's paper warned that 'classic guerrilla-type operations cannot be successful', it went on to recommend a different type of insurgency in the North, with operations 'designed to inflict as many fatal casualties as possible' on the British Army: 'We must learn from the Cypriots and engage in terror tactics only.'[12]

The movement's ideological baggage made it harder to discuss such matters without confusion. For many republicans, after the apostasy of Michael Collins, Éamon de Valera and Seán MacBride, 'politics' was a dirty word, and only those who bore arms for the Republic could be trusted to follow the right path. Garland's blueprint may have been partly designed to appease men like Seán Mac Stíofáin, who worried that the movement was drifting away from its true vocation. Mac Stíofáin would still have been troubled by the document's stress on the need to build a political movement 'with an open organization and legal existence' as the precursor to any 'extra-legal' action.[13]

Ruairí Ó Brádaigh was more sympathetic to the idea of political agitation as a complement to the IRA's traditional role. He had stood for election to the Dáil during the Border Campaign and won a seat on an abstentionist platform. But Ó Brádaigh personified a type of republican for whom abstention from the assemblies in Dublin, Belfast and London was not merely a tactic but a sacrosanct principle. From his perspective, the IRA's right to wage war derived from its claim to represent strict legal continuity with the Second Dáil of 1921. Whatever leeway might exist for tactical innovation in other fields, there could be no flexibility on this point.

As a result, when Goulding and his allies broached the question of taking seats in parliament, there was bound to be a strong backlash from traditionalists. Seamus Costello was one of the strongest voices calling for the policy of abstention to be discarded. Goulding and Garland later argued that he was needlessly abrasive, alienating people who might otherwise have been won over.[14] But Costello combined this view with a firm belief in the necessity of armed struggle, as he made clear when speaking at Bodenstown in 1966: 'To imagine that we can establish a republic solely by constitutional means is utter folly. The lesson of history shows that in the final analysis, the robber baron must be disestablished by the same methods that he used to enrich himself and retain his ill-gotten gains.'

For Costello, it was essential to maintain 'a disciplined armed force which will always be ready to strike at the opportune moment'.[15] Seán Garland had a similar message at Wolfe Tone's graveside two years later, where he urged the IRA to embrace a new role. The movement's open, political wing was expected to function as 'a bridge between the underground activities of the army and the people', while the IRA itself provided the necessary muscle: 'It must be ready to defend a revolution in the making, to defend the people who are agitating for their rights.'[16]

The Orange State

For all the bombast of its leaders, Goulding's new model army was more of an irritant than an existential threat to the ruling class in Dublin. Its supporters took part in direct action of various kinds, from 'fish-ins' on the property of foreign landowners to the occupation of vacant buildings.[17] There was a gradual increase in IRA membership in the South as it recovered from the low point of the early 60s, rising from 657 in 1962 to 1,039 four years later, according to police estimates.[18] However, Goulding had no illusions about the movement's overall strength: 'A famous revolutionary once said: "A guerrilla must move through his people like a fish moves through water." We, I think, moved through our people like fish through a desert.'[19]

The internal debate on abstention had not been resolved in time for the Irish general election of 1969. Even if it had, Sinn Féin would have struggled to make an impression. Popular opinion in the South did shift towards the left in the late 1960s, but only to a limited extent, and in any case the Irish Labour Party was harvesting the fruits of that turn, having shed some of its rhetorical timidity and promised to break the mould of Irish politics. Labour won its highest-ever vote share in the 1969 election, but Fianna Fáil still comfortably outpaced its rival after a red-baiting campaign.[20] At a time when political turbulence rocked much of Western Europe, the Republic of Ireland appeared to be an oasis of stability.

Its northern neighbour presented a very different prospect. The political system in Northern Ireland was much less flexible, and the potential for republican agitation to disrupt the status quo much greater. The Unionist Party had held power at Stormont, the regional assembly, without interruption for almost half a century: between 1920 and 1969, there were just four prime ministers, two of whom served for twenty years each. When Basil Brooke took the helm in 1943, he warned that a post in the Northern Irish cabinet 'is not, and should not be, a life appointment', but did little to dispel that impression over the years that followed.[21] There was no clear line of demarcation between the Northern Irish government, the Unionist

Party and the Orange Order. Between 1921 and 1969, all but three cabinet ministers and all but eleven of the ruling party's MPs were Orangemen at the time of their election.[22] The first Unionist prime minister, James Craig, abolished proportional representation for elections to Stormont in 1929, having already done so for local councils in 1923. His aim, openly stated, was to ensure that every regional poll would be a referendum on partition, with all other questions pushed to one side.[23]

In local government, Unionists made extensive use of gerrymandering to maintain their control in areas like Fermanagh and Derry City where there was a nationalist majority.[24] The restriction of the local-government franchise to property owners served as another barrier to nationalist participation, as Catholics were more likely than Protestants to rent their homes. When the Nationalist Party put down a motion at Stormont calling for universal suffrage in 1958, the Unionist politician Brian Faulkner remarked in a private conclave that it was 'quite obvious' why such reforms were unacceptable, although the sectarian logic could not be stated openly: 'The real reason behind it is Derry, Tyrone and Fermanagh.'[25]

If opposition developed outside the electoral field, the Special Powers Act of 1922 gave Northern Ireland's government the authority to ban newspapers and demonstrations, and to intern suspects without trial. The Act even gave Stormont's home affairs minister the power to criminalize any act 'not specifically provided for in the regulations' that he considered to be 'prejudicial to the preservation of the peace'.[26] A part-time force known as the B Specials backed up the full-time Royal Ulster Constabulary (RUC). In the late 1960s, the RUC was nine-tenths Protestant, the Specials almost exclusively so. Both were armed.[27]

Protestants had a much greater share of professional, managerial and skilled-manual jobs, while Catholics tended to occupy unskilled posts if they were employed at all. In 1971, Catholic men were two-and-a-half times more likely to be out of work than their Protestant counterparts.[28] Less than 5 per cent of the workforce in Belfast's iconic shipyards was Catholic.[29] Unionist politicians regularly issued warnings that the minority should be kept out of sensitive posts. In 1933, the future prime minister Basil Brooke boasted to supporters that as a businessman, 'he had not a Roman Catholic about his place', urging his fellow employers to remain vigilant against those who 'were endeavouring to get in everywhere and were out with all their force and might to destroy the power and constitution of Ulster'.[30] Emigration levels reflected the economic disparity: between 1926 and 1981, the annual rate of departure for Catholics was more than twice that for Protestants.[31] This had the happy effect, from the Unionist perspective, of counteracting a higher birth rate among Catholics, otherwise their share of the population would have been almost 5 per cent greater.[32]

The law that established the machinery of government in Northern Ireland made it clear that ultimate jurisdiction lay with Westminster. However, British politicians preferred to overlook this clause and leave the Unionists free to govern as they saw fit. For many years it was the convention at Westminster to ban all discussion of Northern Irish affairs. Britain's political class had the best of both worlds, with full control over Northern Ireland's territory – which proved to be of vital strategic importance during the Second World War – but no responsibility for its day-to-day affairs. When the Irish state left the Commonwealth in 1949, Clement Attlee's government quickly passed a bill guaranteeing there would be no change in Northern Ireland's constitutional status against the will of Stormont. It made no attempt to push through local government reform as a quid pro quo from the Unionist administration, claiming, wrongly, that such matters lay beyond its remit. A group of backbench Labour MPs, the Campaign for Democracy in Ulster, set out to disrupt this consensus in the 1960s, but Harold Wilson ignored their calls for intervention after his accession to Downing Street.[33]

The most significant challenge to the Unionist Party at the ballot box came from the Northern Irish labour movement. Communal divisions had not squeezed class conflict out of the picture altogether. In the 1930s, a communist-led movement of jobless workers briefly forged a pan-sectarian alliance to demand action against unemployment. During the Second World War, Northern Ireland accounted for 10 per cent of all working days lost to strikes, despite having just 2 per cent of the UK's total workforce.[34] That surge left its mark on the first post-war election, when the vote for Labour candidates jumped from 7.5 per cent in 1938 to almost 32 per cent seven years later.[35] Working-class discontent drove Basil Brooke to accept the social reforms introduced by Attlee's government after 1945, at a time when some Unionist politicians wanted to loosen ties with Westminster so they could maintain the pre-war status quo.[36] The challenge to Unionist hegemony faded during the 1950s, but started to recover again in the last years of Brooke's premiership. In 1962, the Northern Ireland Labour Party (NILP) won four seats in Belfast with over 40 per cent of the vote.[37]

Unlike Nationalist politicians, whose support came exclusively from the Catholic minority, the pro-union NILP could eat into the Unionist Party's support among working-class Protestants if it played its cards right. With regional unemployment well above the UK average, Basil Brooke's languid approach to government was becoming a liability. In 1963 the Unionist hierarchy eased Brooke out of his position, to be replaced by Terence O'Neill.

If the NILP's electoral growth had enabled it to supplant the Unionist Party, its willingness to tackle discrimination against Catholics was open to question. Paddy Devlin, who was elected to Stormont as an NILP candidate in 1969, later described the party's record on civil rights issues as 'scandalous'.[38] But by the time Devlin won his seat, the question of what a government led by the NILP might do was purely academic. After Brooke's departure, the Unionist leadership worked hard to project a more dynamic image to Protestant voters, promising 'a social and economic revolution' that would 'make Ulster a place where every man's head is held high'.[39] That proved to be enough to banish the spectre of defeat.

One facet of Terence O'Neill's modernizing image was an apparent willingness to venture out of the Orange bunker. He welcomed the Irish Taoiseach Seán Lemass on a visit to Stormont in 1965, and arranged some photo ops with Catholic nuns to show his ecumenical spirit. But that was about as far as such gestures went. O'Neill dismissed charges of systematic discrimination against Catholics as 'baseless and scurrilous', and certainly showed no appetite for sweeping reform.[40] With the electoral road blocked and Harold Wilson's government reluctant to intervene, opponents of Unionist rule now began to explore another path. O'Neill's administration soon faced the challenge of a civil rights campaign in which Goulding's IRA played a central part.

'Where would unionism be then?'

In January 1967, a meeting in Belfast set up the Northern Ireland Civil Rights Association (NICRA). NICRA wanted a clean-up of local government, with fair electoral boundaries and no restrictions on the franchise, and an end to discrimination in housing and employment. In principle, none of these demands posed a direct challenge to the Union: indeed, their effect would be to bring Northern Ireland into line with British practice. However, many Unionist politicians insisted that a subversive conspiracy lurked behind NICRA's respectable facade. Terence O'Neill's home affairs minister, William Craig, dismissed the civil rights campaign as 'bogus and made up of people who see in unrest a chance to renew a campaign of violence'.[41] This view informed Craig's handling of civil rights demonstrations when the movement took to the streets.

Hard-line Unionists could certainly point to a substantial republican element in the civil rights campaign. Gerry Adams, then a young militant in Belfast, described the first NICRA meeting as having been 'packed by republicans, who wielded the biggest bloc vote'. The commander of the IRA's Belfast Brigade, Billy McMillen, confirmed that the meeting was 'attended in strength' by republican activists, to the point that its decisions 'could have been completely dictated by their votes'. However, both men went on to complicate this picture of NICRA as an IRA proxy by explaining that their comrades were instructed to vote for a broad-based committee.[42] In any case, the fact that republicans had the strongest presence at NICRA's launch does not prove that they remained in control over the next two years as the campaign developed into a mass movement.

The civil rights association brought together a wide range of political forces around its call for reform, from Con and Patricia McCluskey, founders of a Dungannon-based lobbying group called the Campaign for Social Justice, to Nationalist politicians like Gerry Fitt and Austin Currie. None of these individuals had any interest in using NICRA as the platform for an uprising against the state, as their subsequent political trajectories clearly showed. But we still need to ask why republicans had chosen to involve themselves in a project of this kind at all. Was it simply, as Craig insisted, the prelude to a new IRA campaign? Or did it represent a break with tradition?

However much the IRA might have transformed itself since the Border Campaign, it was still unclear what Goulding's strategy meant for republicans in the North. According to Billy McMillen, the Belfast IRA was slow to embrace the new thinking: 'We used to spend hours at meetings trying to conjure up ideas and excuses as to why we shouldn't become involved in this type of political activity, and to tell Dublin GHQ why they were wrong.'[43] McMillen eventually signed up to Goulding's agenda and became a staunch ally for the leadership in Dublin, but other veterans like Joe Cahill, Seamus Twomey and Billy McKee dropped out of the IRA altogether.

The movement's first notable venture after the failure of Operation Harvest came in 1964, when McMillen ran as a candidate for West Belfast in the UK general election. Republicans displayed an Irish tricolour in the campaign office on Divis Street, flouting legislation that prohibited such emblems. The fundamentalist preacher Ian Paisley demanded that the RUC remove the flag or he would do so himself. When police officers broke into McMillen's office and took down the offending item, it provoked several days of rioting on the nationalist Falls Road.[44] For McMillen, the Divis Street confrontation had proved that there were still 'embers of patriotism' among the city's nationalists, needing only 'a good strong Republican wind' to spark a conflagration. But he also admitted that, in practical terms, the IRA only gained a couple of dozen new recruits on the back of the disturbances.[45]

It was some time before the IRA leadership devised a plan of action for northern republicans that was informed by their new ideology. Tomás Mac Giolla made an early contribution with his speech at Belfast's Easter parade in 1965, where he announced that republicans would soon begin a campaign for universal suffrage in local government elections. Mac Giolla was keen to stress that the movement could raise such demands without compromising on its ultimate goal: 'The conduct of this campaign will not in any way distract Republicans from their primary objective which is to enforce the evacuation of British troops and British administration from Irish territory, to unite the whole people of the nation and to develop the resources of the nation in such a manner as to benefit the mass of the Irish people and not a limited capitalist class.'[46] This was a foretaste of the ideological tensions that would become apparent when republicans lined up with the civil rights movement.

By the time NICRA was founded, the *United Irishman* had published a detailed blueprint for republican involvement in civil rights agitation. It called for a campaign of protest that would put the Unionist leadership under intense pressure, confronting O'Neill's administration with 'popular demands from the disenfranchised, the gerrymandered, the discriminated against, the oppressed Catholic and nationalist minority within the North'. If the campaign was successful, it would lead to 'the destruction of the machinery of discrimination to the maximum, the unfreezing of bigotry to the greatest extent, the achievement of the utmost degree of civil liberties possible, freedom of political action, an end to the bitterness in social life and the divisions among the people fostered by the Unionists'.

This was certainly a very ambitious vision for political change when set against the realities of Northern Ireland at the time. But it still fell short of the republican demand for an end to British rule, and there was no mention of any role for the IRA as the spearhead of resistance. Indeed, the blueprint implied that partition would remain in place for some time to come, even if the civil rights movement was an unqualified success: 'If things change too much the Orange worker may see that he can get by alright without dominating his Catholic neighbour. The two of them may in time join forces in the labour movement, and where would Unionism be then?'[47]

For some of Cathal Goulding's supporters, NICRA's reform programme was a realistic platform that could be put into effect if it brought enough pressure to bear on the governments in Belfast and London. By compelling the authorities to grant such reforms, republicans would create a more hospitable environment in which to work for their long-term objectives. Goulding's young protégés Anthony Coughlan and Roy Johnston were the main advocates of this perspective in republican circles. The thinking of Desmond Greaves, a Marxist historian who had recruited them to the Connolly Association when they were living in Britain, strongly influenced the two men.[48] Arguing that a civil rights campaign could undermine Unionist hegemony in Northern Ireland, Greaves worked tirelessly in the British labour movement to highlight discrimination against nationalists under Stormont rule. From his standpoint, there was no question of ending partition in a single bound: Northern Ireland had first to be reformed and democratized before it could unite with the South.[49]

Greaves was a member of the Communist Party of Great Britain, and saw the Irish communist movement as the main vehicle for progressive politics on the island. Irish communism, which had never been a substantial force, was divided into two organizations: the Communist Party of Northern Ireland (CPNI) and the southern Irish Workers' Party. Although its membership was small, the CPNI did have some influence in Northern Ireland's trade unions, with figures such as Betty Sinclair and Andy Barr occupying senior positions. Speaking at a party conference back in 1952, Barr had urged the labour movement to unite behind demands for franchise reform, repeal of the Special Powers Act, and 'the removal of all forms of discrimination directed against the nationalist minority'.[50] This was the NICRA programme in embryonic form, almost two decades before the civil rights movement got off the ground.

Republicans were keen to get the CPNI on board, seeing its trade union base as a potential route into the Protestant working class, and Betty Sinclair became NICRA's first chairwoman, with the help of republican votes. Sinclair proved to be one of the most cautious figures in the civil rights movement. She wanted NICRA to emulate Britain's National Council for Civil Liberties by taking up individual cases of discrimination and lobbying politicians at Westminster, and opposed a decision to begin organizing street demonstrations in the summer of 1968.[51]

Sinclair was old enough to remember both the tentative cross-sectarian unity forged in the struggle against unemployment during the Great Depression, and the vicious communal rioting that followed a few years later.[52] Anything that brought sectarian passions to the fore threatened to split Northern Ireland's trade unions down the middle. But with other avenues seemingly blocked, Sinclair's NICRA allies decided to go ahead with a campaign of protest, beginning with a march from Coalisland to Dungannon in August 1968.

Class and Creed

It was hardly surprising if Unionist politicians like William Craig fell back on traditional stereotypes as they got to grips with the civil rights movement. A campaign that had the IRA demanding equal rights under British rule, while their communist allies pleaded for caution and restraint, was bound to confuse its adversaries. Craig's bewilderment would have been shared by many IRA activists as they tried to absorb the new line on civil rights. For republicans, the tactics now being urged upon them were as unconventional as NICRA's plea for reform.

The *United Irishman* told civil rights activists to study the experience of their US counterparts and challenge the Unionist government by defying its laws: 'The secret of effectiveness in acts of civil disobedience is careful planning, well-prepared publicity and the avoidance of undisciplined, provocative actions which would alienate rather than increase public sympathy and support.'[53] Of course, republicans had no problem with the idea of breaking the law, but they had not been trained to turn the other cheek when they encountered violence from the state and its agents.

If the reformist civil rights strategy prevailed in the long run, it was difficult to see what place it would hold for the 'Army of the Republic'. But NICRA's programme could also be seen in a very different light, as a way for republicans to expose the true character of the Northern Irish state and prepare the ground for its destruction. According to this line of thought, the nationalist population would not support a direct military challenge to that state, but could be mobilized to take part in demonstrations calling for its reform. If the authorities responded with hostility and repression, nationalists would then be open to more radical ideas, and the IRA might once again come to the fore, this time with the popular support that had been lacking in the 1950s. Gerry Adams later spoke about the civil rights movement in precisely these terms, describing it as 'a means of confronting an apartheid state, exposing its contradictions and building popular opposition to them and to the state itself'.[54]

In a 1970 interview, Cathal Goulding implied that he had been thinking along similar lines. For Goulding, physical force could not be the starting point of a successful movement, as the US experience showed: 'We first had to try to inject some militancy into ordinary people who wouldn't join a violent struggle but would support a peaceful one, people whom you could organize to march, to demonstrate, sit-in, and things like that. It was this peaceful activity that really brought the situation to a head in the Six Counties.'[55]

This does not mean that Craig's suspicions about the movement were correct. At the time, such distinctions were not as clear-cut as they might appear in hindsight, and it was quite possible for individuals to waver between the two perspectives on civil rights agitation. According to Adams, a junior figure at the time, his own view took shape gradually as the struggle gathered momentum. He believed that the IRA leadership had embarked on 'a serious attempt to democratize the state', during which 'the national question would be subordinated in order to allay Unionist fears'.[56]

To complicate things further, the proposal to begin a campaign of street marches came not from the republicans in NICRA but from the Nationalist MP, Austin Currie.[57] Currie had already organized a protest against housing discrimination in Dungannon in June 1968. Another Nationalist politician, Gerry Fitt, delivered a fiery speech from the platform on that occasion, calling for civil disobedience to undermine the Unionist government. Fitt even hinted that he would be willing to go further if the need arose: 'If a day came when we had to fight in the street for the protection of our future, for the protection of our wives and children, then that day can't come soon enough.'[58] However, both Currie and Fitt proved to be staunch opponents of republican violence in the years to come.

One thing soon became obvious. Neither republicans nor the wider civil rights movement would be able to discuss these questions at their leisure without taking account of the response they encountered from the Unionist state and its Protestant supporters. Terence O'Neill was already under pressure from Unionist hardliners for alleged backsliding before NICRA had started its campaign, and Ian Paisley continued to nip at the heels of the Unionist establishment after his role in the Divis Street riots of 1964.[59]

Paisley was a larger-than-life character in more than one sense: with a booming voice and a mountainous physique, he could deploy his rhetorical skills and encyclopaedic knowledge of scripture in defence of traditional Unionist values. If NICRA took its cue from Martin Luther King, Paisley looked to King's opponents for inspiration, brandishing an honorary doctorate in theology from Bob Jones University, a bastion of the segregationist cause. He kept up a steady stream of religious publications throughout his career – including the imperishable *Sermons with Startling Titles* – but did not hesitate to use more robust methods when the situation required, greeting the Irish premier Seán Lemass with a hail of snowballs on his ground-breaking trip to Stormont.

In 1966, the Orange Order's Grand Master, George Clark, warned that Paisley and his supporters might 'succeed in doing what the IRA failed to do in Northern Ireland at Easter', by 'attracting television cameras and newsmen from all over the world to Ulster'.[60] To many observers of the Northern Irish scene, Paisley seemed like a farcical throwback, with his doom-laden rhetoric evoking a conspiracy between Moscow and Rome against the Protestant way of life. But the journalist Jack Bennett warned readers of the *United Irishman* that he should be taken very seriously indeed: 'The Paisleyites are not the wild men on the outskirts; they are the hard core of Unionism *per se*. Nothing Paisley preaches is offensive to the spirit of Unionism; rather it is the pure essence of Unionist Party ideology as nourished in local Unionist associations throughout the Six Counties.'[61]

Paisley's rhetoric helped inspire a British Army veteran called Gusty Spence to organize a new paramilitary group, the Ulster Volunteer Force (UVF), which took its name from Edward Carson's militia.[62] Spence had fought in Cyprus against the EOKA guerrillas whose campaign inspired the IRA commander Seán Mac Stíofáin. The UVF leader and his associates wanted to assassinate a republican activist in Belfast, but only managed to kill three civilians in the space of two months in 1966. O'Neill's government banned the UVF after the murders, and Spence received a life sentence. Paisley's *Protestant Telegraph* disclaimed any responsibility for the killings, blaming the 'hell-soaked liquor traffic' instead.[63]

Many writers have accused Cathal Goulding and his comrades of woeful naivety about the potential for class politics in Northern Ireland. Conor Cruise O'Brien was willing to grant that the IRA leadership was 'sincerely committed to an anti-sectarian policy', albeit one grounded in sheer fantasy: 'It thought that, if class issues were emphasized, and a revolutionary situation created, the "false consciousness" of the Protestant proletariat would be eliminated, and all the workers would join together in the attack on the political and industrial establishment and on British imperialism.'[64] In his own critique of the Goulding line, Gerry Adams recalled a modest attempt by republicans in Belfast to organize a pan-sectarian campaign that was scuppered by the intervention of Unionist tub-thumpers: 'If the state would not allow Catholics and Protestants to get a pedestrian crossing built together, it would hardly sit back and watch them organize the revolution together.'[65]

Some comments made by republican leaders during this period do lend substance to the charge of reckless myopia. Tomás Mac

Giolla let his imagination run free when he addressed Sinn Féin's annual conference at the end of 1967: 'There is welcome evidence of change among the Protestant community of the North. They are beginning to think for themselves. Once they open their mind to new ideas, no one will be more receptive than they to Republican principles.'[66]

But the reformist strategy put forward by Roy Johnston and Anthony Coughlan did not count on any sudden and dramatic shift in the political consciousness of Northern Ireland's unionist majority. According to their arguments, the change sought by left-wing republicans would have to come about in stages.

First, the civil rights demands were to be won through a peaceful but militant campaign of protest. Northern Ireland's political system would be democratized, its unorthodox features swept away. That would open the way for the second stage, during which the republican movement and others would struggle to bring class politics to the fore. Only when this had been achieved and left-wing forces had come to power on both sides of the Irish border would it be possible to dissolve the border between the two states and establish an all-Ireland workers' republic.[67] The real flaw with this blueprint was not that it anticipated support from Protestants for the civil rights platform. Rather, it was the tacit assumption that the unionist population would remain largely passive as NICRA set about winning those demands.

The realism of this political vision can be measured on two different timescales, long and short term. If the civil rights programme had been carried out in full, the political class at Stormont would have been constrained in a number of ways. From below, universal suffrage and fair electoral boundaries would have resulted in areas such as Fermanagh and Derry City passing out of Unionist control altogether. From above, a Bill of Rights guaranteed by Westminster would have blocked discrimination by the Unionist Party against its political opponents. Any regional government would have found itself partly 'defanged', having lost its most important legislative tool of repression, the Special Powers Act, and its access to a paramilitary police force. The assembly itself would have been opened up to some extent by the adoption of a new voting system – or to be precise, the restoration of an old one, the PR system abolished by James Craig in 1929. Under such conditions, a transformation of Northern Ireland's political life would surely have been the result, whether or not the final outcome was in line with republican hopes.

But that scenario required time and patience, two commodities that were in short supply as the civil rights movement began to pick up steam. The NICRA leadership was satisfied with its first public outing, from Coalisland to Dungannon in August 1968, which brought 2,000 people onto the streets. However, the police redirected the march from its original route after Ian Paisley and his associate Ronald Bunting threatened to obstruct the marchers with a demonstration of their own. Gerry Fitt denounced the RUC as 'bastards' from the platform, and claimed that he would have led the marchers into police lines 'but for the presence of women and children'.[68] Fitt's rhetoric contrasted sharply with the nature of the protest, as the stewards worked hard to prevent any clashes with the police.[69]

The tactics deployed by Paisley and Bunting could be expected to come into play at any subsequent demonstration. Sooner or later there would have to be a clash, whether with loyalist ultras or the police. In that case, another assumption underpinning the civil rights strategy would be put to the test. If the Unionist Party proved unwilling to reform the sectarian state, Westminster could, it was argued, be forced to act over their heads. In effect, once the civil rights campaign got going in earnest, there would be a race against time: the British government would have to intervene and take the heat out of the situation before the sectarian pot came to the boil. When NICRA announced its plan to march through Derry's city centre in October 1968, the countdown to crisis had begun.

3

Points of No Return

Paris, Derry and Berlin

5 October 1968 can justly be ranked as the second most important date in twentieth-century Irish history, surpassed only by the Easter Rising.[1] The protest held that day is best seen as one moment in a sequence that culminated in the civil rights march from Belfast to Derry three months later. The two demonstrations did more to unsettle the politics of Northern Ireland than anything that had happened since partition, forcing the British government to abandon its policy of non-intervention. This cycle of protest, the work of left-wing radicals who took their bearings from international youth culture, brought Stormont to its knees. Of all the movements that challenged the status quo that year, none had a greater impact on its own country than Northern Ireland's (frequently neglected) contribution to the 'spirit of '68'.[2]

Unionist hardliners saw every NICRA protest as a challenge to legitimate authority, but the symbolism of a Derry march lent it particular force. The city had long occupied a central place in Northern Ireland's political culture. In 1689, its Protestant garrison held out for three months against the Catholic army of King James, enduring terrible hardship before a Williamite force relieved them. A loyalist marching order, the Apprentice Boys of Derry, marked

the end of the siege every summer with a parade that most nationalists saw as an exercise in sectarian triumphalism.

Over the course of the nineteenth century, Catholic immigra-
tion transformed the city's demographics, and its council briefly fell
under Nationalist control during the War of Independence. Unionist
leaders, determined to avoid any repeat of that trauma, made sure
to rig the local election boundaries in their favour. The year before
NICRA's march in 1968, Unionist candidates won half as many
votes as their opponents yet still had a majority of seats.[3] To add
to the sense of nationalist grievance, Derry was one of the poorest
regions in Northern Ireland, an unemployment blackspot that had
received little of the investment solicited by Terence O'Neill's government in the 1960s. By the time NICRA announced its plan to
march through Derry, there was a rich seam of local discontent
ready to be tapped.

A local activist group, the Derry Housing Action Committee
(DHAC), had been trying to do just that for the previous year.
The DHAC brought together republicans enthusiastic about
Goulding's move to the left with another group of militants who
had taken over the local branch of the NILP. Prominent figures in
this milieu included Eamonn McCann, Terry Robson and Johnnie
White.[4] McCann, who came from a working-class family in the
city's Bogside, had passed the eleven-plus exam to win a place
at St Columb's, a Catholic grammar school whose other graduates included the Nobel laureate Seamus Heaney. He went on to
attend university in Belfast and achieved some renown as a student
debater before moving to London, where he joined a Trotskyist
organization called the Irish Workers' Group (IWG). Gery Lawless,
a veteran of the Border Campaign, was the IWG's dominant figure,
and McCann became the editor of the group's newspaper, the *Irish
Militant*, where he and Lawless first honed their journalistic skills.[5]
On returning to Derry, McCann quickly made an impression with
his eloquence and force of personality, but the DHAC had little
success with its first attempts to rally the city's working class.

The modest turnout on 5 October suggested that this NICRA-
sponsored protest might also prove to be a flop. While estimates

vary, there may have been fewer than 1,000 marchers on the day.[6] Significantly, the crowd included the Westminster MP Gerry Fitt, who had invited three colleagues from the British Labour Party to witness the day's events.

Meanwhile, the unionist Apprentice Boys, taking their cue from Ian Paisley, claimed that they were planning a traditional march along the same route as NICRA, and at the very same time. In response, Stormont's home affairs minister, William Craig, hastened to ban the NICRA demonstration from Derry's city centre. A civil servant at Craig's ministry, writing to his counterpart in London on the eve of the march, dismissed NICRA's aims as 'largely Nationalistic, although these are cloaked by other alleged pretensions'. He claimed that NICRA's proposed route trespassed upon areas that were the 'traditional preserve' of Derry's unionists.[7]

The IRA leader Billy McMillen believed that Craig's decision was a blessing for the civil rights campaign: without it, NICRA 'would have died a quiet and natural death that day as had so many similar anti-Unionist movements before it'.[8] When the marchers reached Duke Street and received orders to disperse, a section of the crowd refused to budge, ignoring a plea from Betty Sinclair. Eamonn McCann's uncompromising speech fortified their resolve, and Sinclair later said that she would never share a platform with McCann again.[9] The RUC then tried to clear the street with a chaotic baton charge that a television crew from the Irish state broadcaster recorded on camera. Gerry Fitt was one of those injured in the fracas: as McMillen gleefully recalled, Belfast republicans had been given orders to push dignitaries like Fitt into the police ranks if the RUC stopped the march.[10]

What the demonstration lacked in numbers, it quickly made up for in impact. As word spread through Derry about what had happened, angry locals converged on the city centre to confront the RUC, and three days of rioting ensued.[11] But the footage of police officers swinging their truncheons with reckless abandon posed a much greater problem for the authorities in Belfast. Harold Wilson also received an eyewitness report from the Labour MPs who had attended the march that was scathingly critical of the RUC. Terence

O'Neill soon had to face unwelcome questions from his political superiors about what had happened in Derry, and about his plans for reform.

Seemingly oblivious to such pressures, William Craig congratulated the police at Stormont for handling the marchers with 'a tolerance which some members of this House may feel was undeserved'. He dismissed the civil rights movement as an IRA front and angrily reproached the opposition MPs who had boycotted the debate: 'Perhaps the real reason for their absence today is that they know they are guilty.'[12] In private, O'Neill took a more circumspect line, warning his colleagues that a retreat into uncompromising attitudes would result in 'a period when we govern Ulster by police power alone, against a background of mounting disorder'.[13]

In a government-commissioned report published the following year, Lord Cameron claimed that 'left-wing extremists' had infiltrated the civil rights movement in the build-up to the Derry march, believing that their cause 'would benefit from violent conflict with the authorities'.[14] Cameron specifically excluded the Communist Party from these strictures, and even praised IRA members for their conduct as stewards on NICRA demonstrations, which left the more youthful, freewheeling militancy of the Derry Housing Action Committee as the sole remaining culprit.[15]

In making this charge, Cameron blurred the distinction between two concepts of political action that must be clearly separated: on the one hand, a desire to engage in 'violent conflict' with the state; on the other, a willingness to defy the state and its laws, even if that means exposing oneself to violence. The latter approach was the one followed by Martin Luther King and the US civil rights movement, whose tactics the campaigners in Northern Ireland sought to emulate.

The confusion became apparent when Cameron addressed the events of 5 October in detail: 'Some of the marchers were determined to defy the Minister's order. They accepted the risk that some degree of violence would occur, believing that this would achieve publicity for the civil rights cause.'[16] This assertion matches the recollections of Eamonn McCann: 'Our conscious, if unspoken, strategy was to provoke the police into over-reaction and thus spark off a mass reaction against the authorities.'[17] From Cameron's perspective, this was a thoroughly disreputable strategy. Whether or not it had been right for William Craig to ban the march from the centre of Derry – 'and in all the circumstances we are of opinion it was not' – once he had made that decision, the marchers should have accepted it without question.[18] In which case, one might add, little more would have been heard of the civil rights campaign. If the Derry marchers had not been willing to flout the law, a de facto ban on all forms of effective protest would have taken hold. As Cameron made clear in his own delicate fashion, the RUC was prepared to use the 'Derry strategy' to ban civil rights demonstrations even when local Unionists raised no objections to a march.[19]

McCann, it should be said, immediately qualified his avowal of responsibility for what had happened on Duke Street: 'We had indeed set out to make the police over-react. But we hadn't expected the animal brutality of the RUC.'[20] At any rate, the initiative quickly passed from the left-wing radicals to a group of prominent Derry nationalists. Their leading spokesman was John Hume, a St Columb's graduate like McCann, but one whose relationship with the city's Catholic establishment was much less fractious. Hume was best known for his work with the credit-union movement and had no sympathy for militant leftism.

A few days after the 5 October march, Hume and his associates set up the rival Derry Citizens' Action Committee (DCAC). They invited the left-wing activists to join its steering committee, but in a clearly subordinate role. McCann stormed out in disgust, while some of his comrades decided to go along with Hume's initiative for the time being.[21] The DCAC was much more cautious than the radicals would have liked, and began its work with a couple of symbolic protest actions. But it went on to organize a full-scale demonstration in Derry's city centre on 16 November, in defiance of another ban imposed by William Craig. This time there was a huge turnout, over 15,000 strong, and the RUC was simply overwhelmed.[22]

Undue Hazard

So far, such marches were a Derry phenomenon, and Terence O'Neill's government was in no great hurry to act. On 15 October, the Labour opposition at Stormont suggested a cross-party appeal for thirty days of calm, at the end of which O'Neill would make a statement setting out his government's policy on civil rights. The prime minister welcomed the idea of a 'cooling-off period', but was not prepared to offer the NILP anything in return: 'I have no intention of committing myself, or my colleagues, to the making of any statement in parliament within a period to be prescribed by you. Frankly, this savours somewhat of an ultimatum.'[23]

However, O'Neill did announce a reform package by the end of November, after a meeting with the British government during which Harold Wilson threatened to apply financial pressure if there was no change of course.[24] Derry's city council was to be replaced with an appointed commission. O'Neill promised to scrap multiple voting by company directors in local elections and introduce a points system for the allocation of public housing. An ombudsman would be appointed to scrutinize the workings of government, and there was to be a review of the Special Powers Act, as soon as the authorities in Stormont felt this could be done 'without undue hazard'.[25]

O'Neill also promised reform of local government, but this was to proceed at a languid pace, with deliberations to conclude by the end of 1971. There was no reference to universal suffrage, even though 'one man, one vote' had been a central plank of civil rights agitation.

Before announcing the package, O'Neill pleaded with his cabinet to accept the need for a concession on the franchise, and warned that the reforms were unlikely to satisfy either Westminster or NICRA.[26] But he allowed no glimpse of that anxiety to reach the public eye. The official statement accompanying the reform package made it clear that, as far as Stormont was concerned, there could be no justification for any further protests: 'The Government must be firm in ensuring that law will be respected and enforced. Any who now continue to disturb the peace and dislocate the life of the country will be exposed as trouble-makers, concerned not with change but with disruption.'[27]

O'Neill turned up the rhetorical heat with a televised address on 9 December, warning that Northern Ireland stood 'on the brink of chaos where neighbour could be set against neighbour'. He urged the leadership of the civil rights movement to 'call your people off the streets'.[28] This 'crossroads' speech struck an emotional chord, and the prime minister's office received countless telegrams of support. NICRA and the DCAC agreed to call a marching 'truce' for the month that followed.

O'Neill then sacked William Craig from his cabinet, after the home affairs minister delivered a speech opposing any concessions to the civil rights movement. Some historians have argued that Craig's sacking was a crucial watershed, the point at which the Unionist leader was about to grasp the nettle and commit his government to 'one man, one vote'.[29] However, such claims are speculative, as we cannot know what would have happened if the truce had endured. O'Neill might have chosen to act on franchise reform; or he might have slipped back into comfortable inertia once the pressure of street agitation was removed. In any case, there is no guarantee that universal suffrage would have been enough to satisfy the protesters. Without reform of the security apparatus and its legislative framework, NICRA might well have found it necessary to resume its campaign.

As it turned out, it was not the official leadership of the civil rights movement but a newly formed group of student activists, People's Democracy (PD), that decided to break the truce. The students announced their intention to ring in the New Year with a march from Belfast to Derry that proved to be a landmark in the history of the Troubles. Historians have rarely given the group responsible for organizing it the attention it deserves. To some extent that omission reflects the amorphous nature of People's Democracy itself, which makes it unusually difficult to analyse. Lord Cameron's report is by no means an infallible source of information about PD, but its description of the group's organizational culture was accurate:

'People's Democracy has no accepted constitution and no recorded membership. At any meeting any person attending is entitled both to speak and to vote: decisions taken at one meeting may be reviewed at the next – indeed during the currency of any given meeting.'[30] PD gradually adopted a more cohesive structure, publishing a regular newspaper from the autumn of 1969 and transforming itself into a well-drilled Leninist organization. But we must piece together any account of its thinking before that point from fragmentary evidence, and cannot speak of a People's Democracy 'line' as readily as if we were dealing with a more conventional political movement.

One of the most valuable documents of PD's early phase is an interview published in the *New Left Review*, featuring some of the group's dominant personalities, all of whom were in their twenties at the time. The way in which the young activists spoke was just as revealing as the content of anything they said: there was clearly no agreed policy, and one person contradicted the other at will. Bernadette Devlin made no bones about the group's incoherence: 'We are totally unorganized and totally without any form of discipline within ourselves. I'd say that there are hardly two of us who really agree, and it will take a lot of discussion to get ourselves organized.'[31] One could not imagine the Communist Party or the IRA presenting themselves to the outside world in this fashion.

Unlike those groups, People's Democracy did not have a long organizational history behind it. It was formed at a mass meeting of Queen's University students soon after the 5 October march in Derry, and briefly provided a home for just about anyone at the university who disliked the status quo in Northern Ireland. Many of those who attended the early meetings in Queen's were more liberal than Marxist in their thinking. But it was PD's radical element that exercised the decisive influence on its trajectory.

Foremost among those radicals was Michael Farrell, a recent Queen's graduate who now worked at a teacher-training college in Belfast. Farrell had spent time living in London, where he was active in the Irish Workers' Group alongside Eamonn McCann. Insofar as Farrell and McCann brought Trotskyist ideology back to Northern Ireland with them, it was loosely defined – more a case of rejecting the Soviet Union and its orthodoxy than of aligning themselves with any particular fraction of Trotsky's Fourth International. By the time he helped establish People's Democracy, Farrell already had several years of political experience behind him, and he soon became its most influential figure.[32] According to Farrell, the 'hard core' of People's Democracy came from a pre-existing far-left group, the Young Socialist Alliance (YSA).[33] Bernadette Devlin, who was a fledgling student activist at the time, also credited the YSA with making 'a big contribution to our political education' in the early days of PD.[34]

As a result, by the end of 1968 there were two potential seeds of the New Left youth culture that had recently left its mark on Paris, Chicago and Berlin: the Derry radicals, who conducted most of their public activity through the DHAC; and PD's hard-left element, whose centre of gravity lay in Belfast. While the young left-ists were certainly uncompromising in their militancy, they directed little of that energy against the partition of Ireland. 'The partition issue', McCann later recalled, 'had for so long been the "property" of what we regarded as contending Tory factions that the mere mention of it smacked of jingoism.'[35] Affinity with the New Left, distrust of sectarian politicians ('Orange and Green Tories'), and belief in the primacy of class – these were the main strands of PD's half-formed ideology on the eve of the New Year march.

The group's decision to break the truce was controversial, and figures such as John Hume considered the marchers to be impetu-ous hotheads, or worse.[36] But they also commanded a degree of sympathy from the older generation of activists. Paddy Devlin of the NILP later explained why he supported PD's chosen course at the time. Devlin simply could not agree with those who were pre-pared to give O'Neill's proposals a chance: 'I was uneasy that they still did not go far enough to rectify the years of unionist abuse and misrule, and I favoured keeping up the pressure that had been created to achieve the fundamental and lasting changes in society that I knew in my bones were necessary.'[37] Devlin spoke with more than two decades of hindsight, so he cannot be accused of lacking perspective on what was to follow.

The march set off on New Year's Day from Belfast's City Hall with about fifty people in attendance. Paisley's associate Ronald Bunting led a small group of counter-demonstrators, but there was no serious trouble at the start. An RUC report noted that the PD marchers included Bunting's son, Ronald Jr – a striking illustration of the group's desire to reach across traditional boundaries.[38] It did not take long for those boundaries to reassert themselves. The procession gradually increased in size over the next couple of days as it made its way along country roads accompanied by a police escort. Loyalist counter-demonstrators tried to block the route at several points, and the RUC sent the march on some lengthy detours. On 2 January, the marchers spent the night in a Catholic village near Maghera. The IRA's local unit volunteered to protect them from a night-time attack and put an armed guard on the approaches to the village.[39]

By 4 January, the participants were almost ready to celebrate their arrival in Derry. Seven miles out, they ran into an ambush at Burntollet organized by Ronald Bunting. The loyalists, many of whom were later identified as off-duty B Specials, used stones, cudgels and iron bars to attack the march. The RUC escort proved unable or unwilling to intervene. Bunting himself appeared to be taken aback by the ferocity of his supporters, and made some effort to restrain them; it was mainly through luck that nobody was killed.[40] Battered and bruised, with some in need of hospital treatment, the marchers limped their way into Derry, braving a last hail of stones as they passed by a Protestant district on the outskirts of the city centre. A huge crowd was waiting to greet them. Tempers were already running high in Derry after a rally staged the previous night by Ian Paisley in the city's Guildhall. Now, several hours of rioting broke out – provoked, according to John Hume, by the RUC. Police officers went on the rampage in the Bogside that night, breaking windows and assaulting passers-by.[41] In the days that followed, NICRA and John Hume's DCAC tersely informed O'Neill's government that the truce was over.

'A calculated martyrdom'

Lord Cameron later bemoaned the political fallout from the Belfast–Derry march, and accused its organizers of wanting to undermine 'moderate reforming forces': 'Their object was to increase tension, so that in the process a more radical programme could be realized. They saw the march as a calculated martyrdom.'[42] So many writers have endorsed this damning verdict that it constitutes a hardened orthodoxy.[43] But its empirical basis is much shakier than this consensus would suggest.

Cameron's report was one of the first attempts to codify a perspective on the civil rights campaign that became increasingly prevalent and remains so to this day. Rejecting the view of NICRA propagated by William Craig and Ian Paisley, Cameron argued that the recent unrest stemmed from well-founded grievances on the part of the Catholic minority that had to be addressed. However, the civil rights agenda had been misappropriated by reckless militants who wanted to overthrow the state by violent means. One motivation for reform was to wean the moderate majority of NICRA supporters away from their extremist fellow-travellers. As we have seen, Cameron accused the Derry radicals of seeking to provoke violence on the 5 October march, and his view of People's Democracy reflected the same concern to identify 'troublemakers'.[44]

On the other hand, Cameron was keen to avoid drawing negative conclusions about the RUC; or, if that proved impossible, to attribute its failings to incompetence rather than malice. This desire was very much in evidence when he addressed the violence at Burntollet:

> It is clear that the police were taken by surprise by the scale of the attacks on the march, that the march had heavily over-strained their available resources and that, not expecting the march to get so far, or their numbers by that time to be so great, they neglected to make adequate use of their opportunities for forward planning.[45]

In its response to Cameron, People's Democracy suggested that this section should be enough to discredit his entire report, since it gave 'two quite separate and contradictory explanations' for the RUC's failure to protect the march: 'First, they expected no real trouble, and this despite a Paisleyite meeting in the Derry Guildhall on the previous night. Second, the police expected such trouble at earlier stages that they did not expect the march to reach Burntollet.'[46] Cameron's report also dismissed allegations that the RUC had led the marchers into a trap as 'wholly unjustified … baseless and indeed ridiculous', without any further discussion.[47]

How did Cameron establish that the goal of the march organizers was to 'increase tension'? On the evening of 3 January, a large and hostile crowd of Derry Catholics had gathered outside the meeting called by Ian Paisley in the Guildhall. Eamonn McCann, as the leading spokesman for 'extremism' in the Bogside, might have been expected to take advantage of this splendid opportunity for increasing tension. But in his speech to the crowd, McCann did nothing of the sort:

> I want to see a lot of radical changes in our society, and I want to see them as soon as possible. Tonight I would achieve this if it could be done. But nothing, nothing whatsoever, can be gained by attacking or abusing the people in the Hall. Don't you see that this kind of action is precisely what the clever and unscrupulous organizers expect and hope will happen?[48]

While Cameron noted the efforts of John Hume and other DCAC members to get the crowd to disperse, he said nothing about McCann's intervention.[49] Elsewhere in the report, Cameron did acknowledge that McCann and the People's Democracy leaders had 'urged moderation and sought to dissuade demonstrators from violent action on several occasions', without allowing this to compromise his indictment.[50]

The effect of the Belfast–Derry march may have been to exacerbate communal divisions, but that does not mean its organizers had that goal in mind when they set out. The main inspiration for Michael Farrell and his comrades was the US civil rights march from Selma to Montgomery that the Student Nonviolent Coordinating

Committee (SNCC) organized in 1965. SNCC's model appeared to have particular relevance for Northern Ireland: a minority facing discrimination at the hands of regional power-holders had taken to the streets in a bid to force intervention by the federal government that would open the path to reform. Farrell studied the history of the movement in the US, taking much of his analysis from a pamphlet by the Trotskyist writer George Breitman called *How a Minority Can Change Society*. The possibility of applying the same tactics in Northern Ireland excited him. According to Bernadette Devlin, Farrell and McCann were the only people involved with a clear strategic vision at the time: 'The general plan seemed to be to draw into conflict the British and the Unionists.' She confirmed that Farrell took the SNCC march as his template 'in terms of effect, slogans and everything'.[51]

This, then, appears to have been the main reason PD decided to break the truce at the beginning of 1969: not to 'increase tension' in some aimless way, nor to realize a fantasy of instant revolutionary change, but to pressure the authorities in London into confronting the Unionist establishment. Henry Patterson has suggested that PD's activist core 'saw in the burgeoning civil rights marches the possibility of the North's own revolutionary situation'.[52] But the goal of SNCC's protest had been to quicken the pace of reform, not to overthrow the state. It may be reasonable to question the wisdom of PD's approach, but to caricature them as irresponsible fanatics who sabotaged any hope of a peaceful future in pursuit of a Marxist pipe dream is profoundly unjust.

Conor Cruise O'Brien did more than most to help establish that hostile caricature. Nevertheless, O'Brien's work *States of Ireland* can be used to develop a more fair-minded critique of People's Democracy. In one of the book's autobiographical passages, its author recalled speaking at a public meeting in Queen's during the period between the 5 October march and Burntollet, where he put forward an argument barely distinguishable from that of Michael Farrell, suggesting that London could be forced to intervene over the heads of the Unionist administration through a well-organized campaign of civil disobedience, following the US example. O'Brien then added his thoughts from a later date on the limited scope of his analogy:

> It would be perfect, *either* if Northern Ireland were an island to itself, off the shores of Great Britain, *or* if there was a sovereign black-majority state to the South of Dixie, which claimed to incorporate Dixie. In the first case, Northern Ireland would now be a fairly peaceful part of the United Kingdom. In the second case, Dixie, not long after Little Rock, would have become a theatre of guerrilla and race-war, with Federal troops being fired on by blacks, and whites preparing for the day of Federal evacuation and the final show-down.[53]

O'Brien did not claim to have grasped this vital distinction at the time when he spoke in Queen's. His audience, which most likely included some of those who went on to join the march to Derry in a few weeks' time, can be forgiven for making the same error. This was the point at which lessons from the US civil rights movement began to lose their relevance. Protests in Mississippi or South Carolina never called the existence of the state itself into question. For all practical purposes, black nationalism in the US was a form of cultural self-assertion, rather than a movement with specific territorial demands, and there was no tradition of African Americans making war on the state that could be compared with the insurrectionary heritage of Irish republicanism.

The basis for non-violent civil disobedience in Northern Ireland was always likely to prove fragile, quite apart from the absence of a leader with Martin Luther King's charismatic authority. If the state responded to civil rights agitation with violence, it was only a matter of time before someone started firing back.[54]

A House Divided

Burntollet dealt a hammer-blow to Terence O'Neill's standing among the nationalist population. The prime minister might have been able to salvage something from the wreckage if he had chosen to express himself differently in the wake of the march, with a few words of sympathy for those who were attacked on the road to Derry. While O'Neill's statement did criticize the 'disgraceful violence' of Bunting's supporters, he directed the main force of his polemic against the student marchers, condemning their protest as a 'foolhardy and irresponsible undertaking' that should have been greeted with 'silent contempt'.

The Unionist leader suggested two steps that might be taken by his government in response: wider deployment of the B Specials, who had contributed so many of the attackers at Burntollet, and the introduction of new public order legislation to 'control those elements which are seeking to hold the entire community to ransom'. Both measures would have delighted Ronald Bunting. O'Neill's concluding words made his emphasis clear: 'We have heard sufficient for now about civil rights: let us hear a little about civic responsibility.'[55]

On 6 January, O'Neill's cabinet listened to a presentation from the RUC's top brass, who explained that their officers had withdrawn temporarily from Derry's Catholic neighbourhoods: 'Considerable strength, possibly even involving the use of firearms, would be required to re-enter the area in the current atmosphere.'[56] Ministers agreed that this situation could only be tolerated for a short period of time, and issued a press statement strongly defending the adequacy of O'Neill's five-point reform package, which left 'no justification whatsoever' for continued protests.[57]

However, O'Neill returned to the cabinet nine days later with a memo that dismissed the package as 'proposals which most of us knew in our hearts would not really meet the situation'. He now called for a royal inquiry into the recent disturbances, which might bring to light 'the complexities of the situation, and not least the involvement in Civil Rights of some extremely sinister elements'. Carrying on with the present course was not an option, as the government's 'loss of prestige, authority and standing' since the Derry march had been 'incalculable'.[58] Weeks later, O'Neill decided to call a snap general election as a referendum on his leadership.

People's Democracy saw the February poll as another opportunity to put its ideas before the people of Northern Ireland, and ran a slate of candidates in eight constituencies that spanned the sectarian divide. Its manifesto combined the civil rights demands for 'one man, one vote' and repeal of the Special Powers Act with left-wing economic policies, calling for a crash public housing programme and state investment in industry to guarantee full employment. PD dismissed the question of partition as 'irrelevant in our struggle for Civil Rights'.[59] There was no standard-bearer for the group in Derry's Foyle constituency, where Eamonn McCann ran as a Labour candidate. McCann and his associates still intended to work through the NILP, and discouraged efforts to set up a PD branch in the city.[60]

Michael Farrell ran against Terence O'Neill in his strongly unionist Bannside constituency, where another challenge to the prime minister came from Ian Paisley, who demanded a clampdown on the civil rights movement. In the Unionist camp, pro- and anti-O'Neill candidates stood against each other throughout the region. The divergence in vote share seemed to be emphatic – almost two to one in O'Neill's favour. But the breakdown of parliamentary seats still left the hardliners in a strong position, while many of O'Neill's erstwhile supporters were at best lukewarm in their commitment to reform.[61] The newly elected parliament passed a public order bill that outlawed many of the tactics used in recent protests.

A series of bombings at power and water installations prompted O'Neill's ultimate departure from office in April 1969. Police attributed the bombings to the IRA at the time, but they were actually carried out by the banned Ulster Volunteer Force as part of a 'strategy of tension' to undermine O'Neill.[62] James Chichester-Clark became the new Unionist leader after narrowly defeating the right-wing candidate Brian Faulkner, and finally committed the government to universal suffrage in local elections. This step might have been greeted with jubilation by NICRA a few months earlier, yet it now proved insufficient to take the heat out of civil rights agitation.

The 1969 election marked the beginning of John Hume's political career: the DCAC leader took Derry's Foyle seat as an independent, beating off competition from Eamonn McCann. But Hume and his supporters were struggling to retain the initiative on the ground, and republicans had begun to organize local defence committees. The focus of discontent shifted from issues like the franchise to the conduct of the security forces. When rioting broke out after an abortive march in April, RUC officers crashed into a private home in the Bogside and assaulted the residents, one of whom, Samuel Devenny, later died of a heart attack. At a cabinet meeting that week, Chichester-Clark expressed the hope that Devenny's death 'would have a sobering effect generally'.[63] But the mood among Derry's Catholic population predictably hardened.

As the loyalist marching season approached, many local nationalists were determined to prevent the RUC from entering the Bogside again. In the same month, Derry's republican activists held an Easter march that attracted 5,000 people, well in excess of their usual support base, to hear the young radical Johnnie White speak alongside a veteran traditionalist, Seán Keenan.[64] NICRA and People's Democracy responded to the trouble in Derry by calling protests in other parts of Northern Ireland. Rioting broke out on the Falls Road in Belfast, and local IRA units planted incendiary devices in the city's post offices.

The Stormont election and the mounting sectarian polarization raised some fundamental questions for the People's Democracy activists. Their candidates had performed reasonably well, in view of their youth and inexperience: if McCann's vote in Foyle was included in the total, PD's slate averaged about a quarter of the vote in the seats they contested. In South Down they came close to unseating the Nationalist incumbent. The greatest triumph of the student left came two months later, in a by-election for Mid-Ulster that saw Bernadette Devlin take a seat at Westminster as a civil rights candidate.

Devlin had joined People's Democracy as a psychology student at Queen's and quickly became one of its most prominent figures, running against James Chichester-Clark in the Stormont election.

After her victory in Mid-Ulster, journalists rushed to profile a remarkably eloquent young woman who clearly had more in common with the campus protesters making headlines throughout the West than with the great majority of her fellow MPs. A British publisher commissioned Devlin to write a memoir, and campaigners in the US invited her on a speaking tour to promote the civil rights cause. Eamonn McCann accompanied Devlin on the tour, and they raised hackles among conservative Irish Americans by linking the struggle for equality in Northern Ireland with the black freedom movement that had inspired it.[65]

However, by the time PD's leading members sat down to discuss their ideas with Anthony Barnett of the *New Left Review*, days after Devlin's victory, they were starting to worry about their inability to reach beyond the nationalist population. Despite their proclamations of non-sectarian intent, there had been no meaningful support for People's Democracy candidates from Protestant workers. Eamonn McCann railed against the sectarian attitudes that he saw among the Catholic working class: 'Everyone applauds loudly when one says in a speech that we are not sectarian, we are fighting for the rights of all Irish workers, but really that's because they see this as the new way of getting at the Protestants.' Michael Farrell disputed McCann's analysis, suggesting that it had been 'very much conditioned by Derry': things were different, he believed, in other parts of Northern Ireland.[66] Circumstances in McCann's home town were certainly quite unlike those in Belfast, where Farrell was based: close to the border, with an overwhelming Catholic majority, its inhabitants could afford to indulge in communal triumphalism to a much greater extent. But there could be no denying the failure of the civil rights movement to displace traditional sectarian identities.

As Northern Ireland slid towards conflict in the summer of 1969, McCann drafted a leaflet on behalf of Derry's Labour group, bemoaning the return of old political habits: 'Once upon a time we all talked about the non-sectarian nature of the Civil Rights movement. Now we are planning to seal off the Catholic area of Derry on the Twelfth of August. We are accepting, deepening and physically drawing the line between Catholic and Protestant working-class people.'[67]

Under any circumstances, the odds would have been heavily stacked against the class-based approach favoured by McCann and his comrades. But any window of opportunity that might have existed was rapidly closing. August 1969 marked the real turning point, the moment that brought two new forces into the political equation: the British Army and the Provisional IRA.

As the Apprentice Boys prepared to march in Derry on 12 August, Harold Wilson's home secretary James Callaghan warned his colleagues that the RUC might not be able to cope. The Irish foreign minister, Patrick Hillery, urged the British government to impose a ban on the parade, but Callaghan chose to leave the decision with Stormont.[68] In anticipation of trouble during the marching season, local republicans had set up the Derry Citizens' Defence Association (DCDA), a coalition that also included some of the city's Labour radicals. They asked the Apprentice Boys to call off their parade, but the loyalists were determined to go ahead. The DCDA then opted not to make the 'heroic effort', in the words of Niall Ó Dochartaigh, that would have been required to prevent clashes with the police, and began preparing for a confrontation. Derry's supply of milk bottles went missing overnight.[69]

When local youths threw stones at the marchers, RUC officers charged into the Bogside, to be met with a hail of petrol bombs from the top of Rossville Flats. The DCDA threw up barricades and put out a call for protests to take the heat off Derry. Clashes in Belfast between nationalists and the RUC led to the deployment of armoured cars fitted with heavy machine guns in a densely populated area.

Many people in Belfast's Protestant ghettoes feared that a republican insurrection was imminent, and rioting now erupted along the main communal fault lines. By the time Wilson sent in British troops at Chichester-Clark's request, ten people were dead and almost 2,000 families – 80 per cent of them Catholic – had been evicted from their homes. The refusal of the authorities in London and Belfast to ban the Apprentice Boys parade had ended in a predictable disaster. The left-wing radicals who have been accused of taking Northern Ireland past the point of no return were in no position to influence decision-making at the highest levels when it really mattered. Now, the eruption of sectarian conflict would extinguish their hopes for a new age in the politics of Northern Ireland.

4

Law and Disorder

Out of the Ashes

In December 1969, IRA members gathered in secret for an Army Convention, the movement's highest decision-making body. The ostensible purpose of the meeting was to discuss a motion calling for republicans to take their seats in Stormont, Westminster and Dublin's Leinster House.[1] But the summer's dramatic events cast a heavy shadow over the debate. After leading a rearguard action against the new policy, Seán Mac Stíofáin and Ruairí Ó Brádaigh broke away to form a rival organization, accusing the IRA leadership of rigging the vote and betraying fundamental principles.

The new group called itself the Provisional Army Council and laid exclusive claim to the republican tradition. By the time that claim was fully established, the movement led by Mac Stíofáin and Ó Brádaigh had become known as the Provisionals, or 'Provos' for short. Cathal Goulding's faction went down in history as the Officials.

For many traditional republicans, the dropping of abstention was reason enough for a split with Goulding.[2] However, the Provisionals also accused the Official IRA of neglecting its duty to protect northern Catholics from attack. In the immediate wake of the violence in Belfast, this argument carried a tremendous emotional charge and supplied the Provos with their foundation myth.

Ruairí Ó Brádaigh claimed that Goulding had opposed the defence of nationalist areas because it conflicted with the movement's desire to promote working-class unity across the sectarian divide.[3] However, there is little evidence that the republican leadership had any principled objection to the defence of Catholic neighbourhoods. According to Gerry Adams, the two Belfast IRA commanders who were closest to Goulding, Billy McMillen and Jim Sullivan, moved quickly to organize 'defensive operations for nationalist areas' as best they could when the violence erupted in August 1969.[4]

The truth was more complicated than Provisional rhetoric suggested. Military operations of any kind required weapons. The IRA had not been making any substantial preparations for a new offensive campaign, and in any case it did not have the cash needed to purchase arms. By Goulding's account, traditional sources of funding in Irish-America had dried up after Operation Harvest, because supporters would only contribute if the IRA was visibly engaged in military action.[5]

Billy McMillen reported that the Belfast Brigade had already come under pressure to use its weapons earlier in the year: 'This we were reluctant to do as we realized that the meagre armaments at our disposal were hopelessly inadequate to meet the requirements of the situation.'[6] By one estimate, the IRA was able to put together a grand total of ninety-six weapons to be sent north after the August violence, from pistols and shotguns to automatic rifles.[7]

McMillen gave a second reason for the IRA's reluctance to bring out its guns in the early summer: 'The use of firearms by us would only serve to justify the use of greater force against the people by the forces of the Establishment and increase the danger of sectarian pogroms.'[8] This consideration also weighed upon the republican leadership. The use of live ammunition by IRA Volunteers might simply have precipitated greater violence, making things worse for the people republicans were hoping to defend.

Goulding believed that this had been the case in Derry, where the RUC relied on CS gas and water cannon against the stones and petrol bombs of the Bogsiders. If the IRA had brought guns into the equation, the police would have responded in kind, with disastrous results.[9] In Belfast, he argued, the RUC's behaviour had left republicans with no choice: 'The *only* defence was an armed defence.'[10] However, Gerry Adams recalled opposing the use of weapons there when McMillen summoned him to an emergency meeting, on much the same grounds that Goulding cited for Derry: 'Any attempt to militarize the situation, to bring the IRA into it and to engage the RUC on their own terms would take it out of the hands of the people and bring the entire situation down to a gunfight, which the RUC would surely win. Anyway the discussion was to some degree academic, since the Belfast IRA had hardly any weapons.'[11]

There was another factor that contributed to the IRA's limited response in August. Cathal Goulding, Seán Garland and Roy Johnston were all Dubliners, while Tomás Mac Giolla had made his home there and Seamus Costello's Wicklow base was a short distance from the southern capital. It was hardly surprising that Dublin often loomed larger than Belfast in the thinking of Goulding's leadership team. One symptom of that was their insistence on pressing ahead with the debate over abstention immediately after the crisis in the North. It was tactically unwise to conduct the vote at such a fraught moment, but leading southern activists like Costello were impatient for the policy to be changed as soon as possible.

Seán Mac Stíofáin made great play of the fact that Goulding could not be located for some time when the violence erupted in Belfast, because he was helping a British TV crew film a documentary about the IRA.[12] That would hardly have been the case if Goulding had anticipated what was going to happen, which suggests a good deal of naivety on his part about the danger of sectarian conflict. Mac Stíofáin naturally gave himself the best lines in his account of these exchanges, but his own priority appears not to have been the defence of Catholic areas as such. Right from the start, the Provisional leader wanted to exploit the crisis triggered by the civil rights protests to launch an offensive campaign against British rule.[13]

Whether or not the accusations levelled at Cathal Goulding were justified, they certainly helped the Provos to carve out a foothold in

Belfast, which would be vital for any fresh insurgency. A group of northern veterans, most of whom had drifted away from Goulding's movement in the preceding years, joined the Provisional IRA as soon as it was founded. One of those veterans, Billy McKee, took charge of the Belfast Brigade. McKee won over some of the city's younger activists, including Martin Meehan in Ardoyne and Ballymurphy's Gerry Adams, who hesitated for a while before lining up with the Provos. The defection of Adams came as a bitter disappointment to Billy McMillen, who saw him as one of the brightest talents in the movement.[14]

While the question of armed struggle was fundamental to the split between Official and Provisional IRAs, it was not a straight-forward division between 'soldiers' and 'politicians'. A number of leading Officials saw no contradiction between political engagement and the use of force. Seamus Costello and Belfast's Joe McCann were two prime examples. Some of those who joined the Provos had a similar attitude. Looking back on the period, Gerry Adams spoke with palpable enthusiasm about his own experience of agitational work in the late 1960s alongside Belfast republicans such as McCann.[15] Adams opted for the new movement, not because he rejected 'politics' as such, but because he believed there would have to be a military struggle against British rule and saw it as a better bet from that perspective.[16]

The adherence of men like Adams, who believed that armed struggle should be combined with political action, later proved to be of great importance for the evolution of the Provisionals. But in the short term, many Provos were suspicious of such arguments, which they associated with their estranged comrades in the Official IRA.[17] Seán Mac Stíofáin expressed this militarist outlook with characteristic bluntness: 'The Officials say unless you have mass involvement of the people you haven't got a revolution. We say, the armed struggle comes first and then you politicize.'[18]

The new Provisional mouthpiece, An Phoblacht, claimed that 'Red infiltrators' had forced out 'traditional and militant republicans' before proceeding to brainwash the movement's young supporters with their doctrine.[19] As evidence of this conspiracy, the

Provos pointed to a proposal to establish a National Liberation Front (NLF) in alliance with the Communist Party. Mac Stíofáin described the NLF concept as one of the main factors contributing to the split.[20]

Much of the hostile commentary focused on Roy Johnston, a convenient lightning rod for criticism since Goulding had appointed him as the IRA's director of education despite his lack of a military record. Johnston had indeed been a member of the communist Irish Workers' Party before he joined the republican movement, and his ideas owed much to the historian Desmond Greaves – not only a communist, but a British one to boot.[21] However, the lurid claims made by *An Phoblacht* wildly overstated the case.

If Johnston had wanted to guide republicans further to the left, he was pushing at an open door. Goulding and his comrades were already moving in that direction by the mid 1960s, and they had a strong indigenous heritage to draw upon, from James Connolly to the Republican Congress. Moreover, there was a perfectly rational basis for the alliance proposal. Small as their organization was, the Irish communists still had more experience of trade union work than republicans, and their modest but tangible support base among Belfast's Protestant working class was not something that the IRA could boast.

Indeed, far from using their 'infiltrators' to impose the NLF on republicans, the communists turned out to be the ones who were hesitant about a formalized relationship, fearing it might jeopardize their standing among Protestant workers.[22] In any case, the version of left-wing politics favoured by the Officials at the time did not stem from Soviet orthodoxy. Tomás Mac Giolla argued for a non-aligned policy in world affairs – 'we condemn equally American interference in Vietnam and Russian interference in Czechoslovakia' – and stressed that the system his movement wanted to build 'will not be totalitarian, will not be bureaucratic in any way'.[23]

Facing a barrage of criticism, the Officials gave as good as they got. Refusing to dignify their rivals with the name 'IRA', they denounced the 'Provisional Alliance' as a tool of right-wing politicians in the South, and published a detailed summary of contacts between the IRA and the Irish government in support of this charge.[24] According to this account, Fianna Fáil representatives had approached the republican movement and offered to supply money and weapons for the defence of Catholics in the North. This offer came with political conditions attached: the IRA would have to cease its agitation south of the border and form a separate northern command. Fianna Fáil's intervention had, the Officials insisted, been crucial in paving the way for the split.[25]

The controversy had a sensational impact on politics in the South: the Fianna Fáil Taoiseach Jack Lynch sacked two members of his cabinet, Charles Haughey and Neil Blaney, who then stood trial for conspiracy to import weapons in 1970, only to be acquitted by the jury. There is no doubt that people acting on behalf of the Irish government made promises of money to IRA leaders. The only question is how far knowledge of the scheme reached up the chain of command, and to what extent Lynch himself was implicated.[26] But that doesn't mean an initiative from this quarter supplied the motivation for a split. Mac Stíofáin and his allies already wanted to break with Goulding over abstention. The August violence gave the dissidents a rallying cry and the chance to win over republicans in Belfast. Their new movement had strong roots in the austere republican orthodoxy that had taken shape after the defeats of the 1920s. It was the interaction between that orthodoxy and conditions in the northern Catholic ghettoes that created the Provos, not the machinations of Fianna Fáil.

Part of the Problem

It was some time before the Provisionals began to make their mark. Their leadership team always intended to launch an offensive against British rule in the North, but they were in no position to do so by the time the split became public knowledge at Sinn Féin's Ard Fheis (party conference) in January 1970. According to Martin Meehan, Billy McKee told him to prepare for the long haul when he joined the new organization: 'People have to be trained. People have to be motivated. People have to be equipped. All this won't just happen overnight.'[27] Most importantly, there would have to be a dramatic shift in the mood of the Catholic ghettoes if British soldiers were to be seen as legitimate targets for the IRA.

That shift came sooner than most people could have imagined when Harold Wilson decided to send in troops. In the meantime, however, the transformation of the political environment after the August disturbances seemed to offer the civil rights movement fresh opportunities to press for reform. After all, one of their main goals had been to force Westminster to intervene over the heads of the local government. The British political elite was now plainly involved in the affairs of Northern Ireland – not under circumstances that NICRA would have wished for, but involved nonetheless. The movement was now in a position to demand change from those at the summit of the British state, by-passing its Unionist foothills altogether.

This was not lost on the Officials. As the new decade began, they called for renewed agitation in support of the civil rights programme: 'Demand it, not from Stormont, but from the British Government and Parliament which is wholly responsible for the area.' However, they rejected the idea of direct rule from Westminster, claiming that the British government wanted to regain control over the entire island through an 'Anglo-Irish Federation' that would 'tie the whole country more closely to Britain than ever'. The Officials summed up their reformist platform with the demand for a legally entrenched Bill of Rights that could not be repealed by any local administration. This would make it possible to 'democratize Stormont, overrule the right-wing Unionists, [and] develop a more Irish-oriented frame-work in the Six Counties within which some of those one million Protestants can be won in time to stand for a united Ireland'.[28]

The end of British rule thus remained a long-term aspiration, not an immediate demand. NICRA endorsed this approach at its AGM in February 1970. In a report on the civil rights gather-ing, the *United Irishman* noted the emphasis on 'forms of protest which would be effective and yet minimize the danger of sectarian tension'. Street marches were thus 'likely to be a less common tactic than before'.[29] The Officials entered into a close alliance with the Communist Party, which also supported the Bill of Rights slogan.[30] Over the next two years, the Officials and their Communist allies had the strongest voice in NICRA's leadership, using it to advance a shared reformist perspective.[31]

The Provos now offered a home for those who considered it futile to seek reform while Northern Ireland was still part of the UK. But NICRA also faced competition on the opposite flank from a new political force, the Social Democratic and Labour Party (SDLP). The SDLP brought together a group of MPs from Stormont and Westminster who could loosely be described as moderate nationalists. Gerry Fitt was the new party's leader, with John Hume as his deputy. Some of the SDLP's founders had carved out a political foothold before NICRA took to the streets, while others rode the civil rights wave into Stormont at the beginning of 1969. Although they had taken part in many of NICRA's marches over the previous two years, the SDLP leadership now wanted to concentrate on parliamentary politics and establish themselves as the main nationalist interlocutor for the British government.[32]

Whatever strategy NICRA or the SDLP decided upon, all future developments in Northern Irish politics hinged on the choices being made in London. When Harold Wilson ordered the deployment of troops in August 1969, he decided not to revoke Stormont's authority. Shortly before the Apprentice Boys march in Derry, James Callaghan had warned the Unionist leader Chichester-Clark that Westminster would play a bigger role in local affairs if he was forced to send in the British Army.[33] However, after the deployment of troops, Callaghan told his cabinet colleagues that their policy should be to work through the Northern Irish government for as long as possible and avoid assuming direct responsibility.[34]

The logic that flowed from Callaghan's choice was very simple. Any conceivable Stormont prime minister would have to come from the Unionist Party, and if they wished to avoid Terence O'Neill's fate, would have to muster sufficient backing from the party's MPs. Chichester-Clark was already under pressure from his hard-line opponents, inside and outside the cabinet.[35] Ian Paisley had now formed a group of his own, the Protestant Unionist Party – soon rebranded as the Democratic Unionist Party (DUP). The only way for the prime minister to satisfy his critics would be through the imposition of tough security policies, directed exclusively against nationalists.

The Army's General Officer Commanding, Ian Freeland, showed that he understood the sectarian character of such policies perfectly well in remarks for a staff conference in October 1969. Freeland noted that 'many people, mainly Northern Ireland Protestants' wanted to know why the Army didn't 'restore Law and Order' when it was brought in. To Freeland, the real meaning of such questions was clear: 'Why didn't the Army counter the resistance of the Roman Catholics behind their barricades by force of arms and reduce this minority to their original state of second-class citizenship?'[36]

According to the Army's official history of the conflict, junior officers posted to the region were 'well aware of the discrimination and deprivation, and asked themselves at the time why the Government did not do anything about it'. But there was no chance of any 'substantive action' from the power-holders in Belfast: 'Stormont was part of the problem and could have been so recognized at the time.'[37]

It took a while for the logic of the British government's position to work itself out. When troops first arrived, most people believed that their mission was to protect nationalist areas from attack – including the soldiers themselves.[38] The well-worn anecdotes about British soldiers receiving endless cups of tea in Catholic neighbourhoods all date from this period. A minority of shrewd observers recognized that the Army's real mandate was to support the 'civil power', which remained wholly Unionist in character.[39] When James Callaghan visited the Bogside at the end of August, local nationalists applauded his promises of reform. The radicals who were still distrustful of British intentions could not make their voices heard.[40] The barricades that had marked out the territory of 'Free Derry' were dismantled, and soldiers began to carry out routine patrols.[41]

Callaghan's second visit in October 1969 marked the high point of nationalist goodwill towards his government. Under pressure from London, Chichester-Clark had appointed a new minister for community relations and created the post of complaints commissioner to hear allegations of unfair treatment by local councils. A new central authority was to control the allocation of public housing. However, as long as the 'Orange State' and its machinery of government remained intact, such reforms would gradually be drained of their substance in the passage from blueprint to reality.[42]

By the spring of 1970, relations between Catholics and the Army were already beginning to fray. The use of colonial-style policing methods in Derry, which imposed restrictions on whole communities rather than individual suspects, put an end to the honeymoon period.[43] An Irish civil servant, Eamonn Gallagher, visited the city at the end of March to observe the Officials' Easter parade. He found that the throwing of stones at the Army was 'becoming almost a routine occurrence', and that such activity met with 'a considerable degree of tolerance from residents of the Bogside when feeling runs high'.[44]

It wasn't just the methodology that the Army had imported from its far-flung colonial wars. Two of its units in Belfast and Derry absent-mindedly held up crowd-control banners taken from a recent campaign in Aden. The text ordering rioters to disperse was in Arabic rather than English.[45]

In April there were violent clashes between soldiers and teenage rioters in Ballymurphy, sparked off by one of the year's first Orange marches. The Official IRA commander Jim Sullivan tried to contain the violence, but to little avail.[46] When Chichester-Clark met with the Army commander Ian Freeland a few days later, he blamed his party's loss of two recent by-elections on 'a lack of faith in the Government's ability to maintain law and order', and demanded 'firm counter-measures' if there was any repeat of what happened in Ballymurphy.[47]

The Westminster general election of June 1970 guaranteed there would be no change in British policy. James Callaghan had been toying with the idea of imposing direct rule if his party remained in office, but the unexpected Conservative victory put paid to that, and Stormont remained in place.[48] Many Unionists hailed Edward Heath's accession to power, expecting a more sympathetic hearing from the new government.

Matinee Performances

In a repeat of the previous year's pattern, it was the summer marching season that brought matters to a head. Stormont had established a Joint Security Committee to coordinate between the Northern Irish government, the Army and the police. The RUC urged Chichester-Clark to ban the Orange marches in Belfast. The prime minister insisted that his party would destroy him if he did. Speaking on behalf of the Army, Freeland recommended following the path of least resistance: 'It is easier to push them through the [nationalist] Ardoyne than to control the [loyalist] Shankill.'[49]

By the time the June marches commenced, the Provisionals were ready to make their public debut, and they seized the opportunity to present themselves as defenders of the Catholic ghettoes. When sectarian rioting broke out in north Belfast, Provo bullets killed three loyalists. But the main confrontation was in the Short Strand, an isolated nationalist enclave in east Belfast, where a group of Provisionals led by Billy McKee took up position in the grounds of St Matthew's Church. The 'Battle of St Matthew's' entered Provo mythology as proof that their Volunteers could stop any repetition of what had happened the previous August.[50] Across Belfast, the weekend of 27–28 June resulted in six deaths and half a million pounds of damage to property.

Worse was to come. In the wake of the violence, the Joint Security Committee decided that the Army would respond to the next outbreak of trouble with a show of force. At the same time, Chichester-Clark's government approved legislation to impose mandatory six-month jail sentences for all those convicted of 'riotous behaviour', 'disorderly behaviour' or 'behaviour likely to cause a breach of the peace'.[51]

Shortly before the latest disturbances in Belfast, Bernadette Devlin lost her appeal against a prison sentence for her role in the 'Battle of the Bogside'. When word of Devlin's arrest filtered through to a meeting in Derry where she had been due to speak, a full-scale riot erupted.[52] Eamonn McCann described the motivation of the rioters:

> The 'defence of the area' in August 1969 had already passed into local folklore. It was a noble episode in which we had all participated when, after decades of second-class citizenship, we had finally risen and asserted in a manner which made the world take notice that we were not going to stand for it any more. The jailing of Miss Devlin was a challenge to the area to stand by that estimation of its own action.[53]

If the commanders of the British Army had grasped the nature of that sentiment, as widespread in Belfast as it was in Derry, they might have hesitated before launching a search for arms on the Lower Falls Road at the beginning of July.

The Lower Falls was a stronghold of the Officials, and it was their weapons that soldiers took from a house in the area on the afternoon of 3 July. In its propaganda since the split, the Official IRA had projected two very different faces to the outside world. Alongside the reformist civil rights platform, readers of the *United Irishman* could find a strong case being made for traditional methods: 'Only an armed, determined people will be listened to with respect. The war against Britain has never been halted and never will be halted as long as Britain claims a right to legislate for Ireland.'[54] The movement's Easter message spoke of the 'necessary and inevitable confrontation in military struggle with the forces of British imperialism', and issued a challenge to its detractors: 'Let those who have been so quick with their criticism now help the IRA to equip itself with modern weapons.'[55]

Having endured taunts from their rivals and seen the Provos win plaudits for their action in the Short Strand, the Officials now had to decide on their response to the Army's challenge. A crowd of local nationalists confronted the soldiers and began throwing stones. When Ian Freeland heard about this limited skirmish, he ordered the show of force that the security committee had mandated, and a full-scale invasion of the area began.[56]

The Officials decided to take the Army on. Their local commander Jim Sullivan ordered his men to confront the soldiers with every weapon that came to hand.[57] By nightfall, Freeland had imposed a curfew of doubtful legality on the entire district. It lasted for two days, during which the Army saturated the Falls with CS gas, fired almost 1,500 rounds of live ammunition and killed four civilians without losing a single man.[58] But their standing among nationalists suffered incalculable damage.

When the Army brought two Unionist cabinet ministers on a provocative tour of the area in Land Rovers, the fiasco was complete. The SDLP's Paddy Devlin, who observed these developments with horror, later described the impact of the curfew on nationalist opinion: 'Overnight the population turned from neutral or even sympathetic support for the military to outright hatred of everything related to the security forces.'[59] The Army's own history of the conflict picked out two examples of 'poor military decision-making' in the whole of the Troubles that had 'serious operational and even strategic consequences': the first was the Falls curfew, the second was the Bloody Sunday massacre in Derry.[60]

The Officials could now claim to have led the biggest confrontation between republicans and British forces for half a century, with the Provos nowhere to be seen. They were quick to make use of this in their propaganda. Malachy McGurran, one of the leading northern Officials, baited the Provos at Bodenstown the following year for their absence from the 'Battle of the Falls'.[61] Having taken so much abuse from the Provisionals since the split, the Officials were naturally keen to pay them back in their own coin. Recruitment to the Official IRA soared.[62] But the Falls Road curfew, and the broader political context of which it was a symptom, held as much danger as promise for the Officials. Unlike the Provisionals, they were not planning to launch a full-scale war against British rule in the North. But they could not simply cash in their chips after winning the first round: once they had started to compete with their rivals as a force that could take on British soldiers, they would have to match them every time the stakes got higher, or else fold. This proved to be a game for which the Provos were much better equipped.

On 17 July, James Chichester-Clark met with Edward Heath and his home secretary, Reginald Maudling. Maudling asked whether 'firmer action on the law-and-order front' could be combined with a gesture of some sort to the nationalist minority. Chichester-Clark insisted that a recent bill against incitement to religious hatred had 'just about exhausted legislative remedies' on that front.[63] Northern Ireland now entered a transitional phase, bridging the demonstrations of 1968–69 and the onset of direct hostilities between republicans and the British Army in the spring of 1971.

Again, Ballymurphy was in the vanguard. During the final months of 1970, there was intense rioting in the area as its teenagers confronted the Army, pelting soldiers with stones, bottles and nail bombs while dodging rubber bullets and gas canisters.[64] The use of CS by British forces cemented local hostility to their presence: the rioters mostly belonged to a narrow age group, but the gas clouds which hung over Ballymurphy's estates affected everyone. Brendan Hughes, who became one of the most important Provisional leaders in Belfast, recalled being sent to the district by Billy McKee on a mission to attack British soldiers. The local commander Gerry Adams warned Hughes and his men not to interfere with their enemy while he was making a mistake: 'He wanted to keep the rioting going. He didn't want any gunfire.'[65] That strategic patience helped transform Ballymurphy into a solid base for Adams and his comrades when the street clashes had completed their radicalizing effect.

According to Eamonn McCann, similar confrontations in Derry found their raw material among a layer of unemployed youths who had been 'briefly elevated into folk-hero status in the heady days of August, praised and patronized by local leaders for their expertise with the stone and the petrol bomb', before finding themselves 'dragged back down into the anonymous depression which had hitherto been their constant condition'.[66] After the Falls curfew, their weekly clashes with British troops on the edge of the Bogside became a regular routine: the 'Saturday matinee', in local parlance. Army intelligence identified McCann as the only prominent figure with any influence over the rioters, and the Derry Labour Party even set up a short-lived 'Young Hooligans Association' in the hope of directing them towards more constructive political tasks.[67] But such efforts were largely unavailing.

McCann noted that sympathy for the rioters was far from unanimous among older residents of the Bogside.[68] However, the Criminal Justice Act that Stormont had passed in a hurry the previous year proved to be the legislative equivalent of CS gas, striking at random and nurturing communal solidarity against the state. By the end of the year, the authorities had charged 269 people with offences carrying mandatory sentences; 109 of these charges went to court, with a conviction and six-month jail term handed down in every case.[69] British troops further stoked the fires of nationalist anger by arresting alleged 'hooligans' several days after a riot had taken place. The *Derry Journal* highlighted the case of one teenager who was identified as a rioter by two Army witnesses, when his boss, his timecard and his fellow workers all placed him on the night shift at a local factory.[70]

Sixty-Niners

For the Provisionals, everything was falling into place. There was a steady flow of recruits into their ranks, and the authorities could be relied upon to keep hostility between nationalists and the Army simmering. The vast majority of those new recruits were in their late teens or early twenties, and they came overwhelmingly from the Catholic working class.[71] Republican militants also tended to be male, although there were some high-profile female Volunteers at the time, such as Rita O'Hare and the Price sisters, Dolours and Marion.

One study identified three main pathways into 'active service'. Some had already joined the IRA before 1969, and opted for the Provos after the split; people in this category usually came from well-established republican families. Others had been active with groups like NICRA or People's Democracy, before deciding to join the IRA in response to political events. Finally, there was the largest group of recruits, who signed up with a clean organizational slate, known to their comrades as 'sixty-niners'.[72]

Gerry Adams, one of the most influential Provos in Belfast, straddled the first two categories: his father, Gerry Sr, was an IRA veteran from the 40s, but Adams had also taken part in NICRA protests and met with PD activists like Michael Farrell before the violence of 1969.[73] That hybrid formation gave him a clear advantage. While his family background made it easier for Adams to work with older IRA leaders, he was still young enough to establish a rapport with the new generation of republicans.

As a child, Adams had passed the selective eleven-plus exam and attended a grammar school in Belfast, where he encountered 'an entirely different crowd of boys from the ones I had previously associated with', whose parents belonged to the Catholic middle class.[74] His later comments on the experience suggest an underlying bitterness towards the Catholic establishment: 'We were being groomed. Certain people finished that grooming, and became bishops, parish priests, leaders of the SDLP – and other "responsible" positions.' According to Adams, the Church's hostility towards the Provos owed a great deal to the class background shared by most of his comrades, who hadn't received the appropriate training for 'positions of leadership' in the nationalist community.[75]

One figure Adams clearly had in mind when making that remark was his ally Martin McGuinness. McGuinness, the most senior Provisional in Derry by the age of twenty-one, exemplified the third category of recruit, those with no experience of political activity before the conflict began. Unlike Adams, he had failed the eleven-plus exam and seemed destined for a life of unskilled manual labour before he joined the IRA. His leadership qualities soon became obvious to his peers.[76] Michael Oatley, an MI6 officer who negotiated with McGuinness on behalf of the British government, compared his instinctive military bearing to that of 'a middle-ranking Army officer in one of the tougher regiments like the Paras or the SAS' – a double-edged compliment for a son of the Bogside, as Oatley must have been aware.[77]

An interview with McGuinness that appeared in 1972 gave a sense of the life experiences that drove so many young men to join the IRA at the time. The Provo leader explained that, in spite of his republican duties, he sometimes liked to fall in with a group of rioters throwing stones at the British Army: 'It's a way of being with my mates, the ones who have not joined the movement, and I feel just ordinary again.'[78]

The 'sixty-niners' soon rose to prominence, but for now, it was a much older group of republican activists that held the reins. The Officials derided those men as apolitical militarists with a deeply conservative mentality ('the Rosary Beads Brigade'). Some Provo commanders like Billy McKee certainly fit that stereotype, and the movement's early rhetoric drew heavily on McCarthyite tropes. Statements from the Provisional leadership denounced the Official IRA as 'Red Guards' who were propagating an 'alien social philosophy'.[79] The Provos still argued for a certain kind of 'socialism', but distinguished it sharply from the Marxism of the Officials, 'repugnant to the great mass of ordinary Irish people'.[80] Ruairí Ó Brádaigh, who now led the movement's political wing, was the main architect of its programme, Éire Nua (New Ireland). Sinn Féin's 'democratic socialist republic' would have a federal structure with four regional parliaments. The banks and major industries were to be taken into state hands, and an upper limit placed on the ownership of land, although private enterprise would still have a place in the economy.[81]

It would be a mistake to read too much into the finer details of these blueprints. According to one Provo activist, Kieran Conway, 'the vast majority of IRA members were so taken up with "military" matters and "politics" was so reviled – not least on account of where it had taken the previous leadership – that those with any interest were simply let run with it.'[82] A consensus on the need for armed struggle against British rule could bring together conservative Catholics such as McKee with radicals like Conway and Brian Keenan, who held quasi-Marxist views.[83]

Many Provos were simply agnostic about such questions, believing they could be postponed until a later stage. Martin McGuinness knew that he wanted 'a united Ireland where everyone has a good job and enough to live on', but had his doubts about whether socialism could be made to work: 'Do you not think now that people are just too greedy? Somebody always wants to make a million. Anyway, before you can try, you have to get this country united.'[84]

It was only a matter of time before the Provos were ready to take the offensive. In February 1971, after more clashes in Belfast, a Provisional sniper killed the first British soldier to die on Irish soil in half a century. James Chichester-Clark responded with a portentous declaration that 'Northern Ireland is at war with the Irish Republican Army Provisionals'.[85] The following month he tendered his resignation after Edward Heath refused to support a package of hard-line security measures.

Earlier that year, Chichester-Clark had delivered a speech that combined ideological myopia with real insight into the new republican challenge:

> Between 1956 and 1962 the IRA were seeking to achieve by force alone ends which force could never achieve, because in a straight contest of firepower and discipline the forces of the Crown were bound to prevail. But now we face a two-pronged campaign, military *and* political. It hoped to use not just, as before, the bomb and the gun, but also the resentments, fears and aspirations of whole masses of people.[86]

Chichester-Clark's error was to assume the existence of an overarching strategic plan behind the disorder. However, he correctly identified 'the growing militancy of people who were not members of subversive organizations' as the most important problem facing the authorities.[87] The new Unionist leader Brian Faulkner paid little heed to his predecessor's message and began urging Edward Heath to allow internment of suspects without trial. In order to precipitate that decisive trial of strength, the Provos just had to maintain the pressure. Their bombing campaign reinforced the sense that

Northern Ireland was becoming ungovernable. In the months leading up to internment day in August 1971, there were an average of two bomb explosions a day, leaving over 100 civilians injured.[88]

The Official IRA's Easter message pledged that its members would 'assist the people with all necessary measures in defence of their homes and their area against jackboot aggression'.[89] In the months since the 'Battle of the Falls', the Officials had been strengthening their armouries and training new recruits. However, the Provisionals had clearly outpaced them in Belfast, with the exception of a few areas like the Markets and the Lower Falls.[90] In Derry, the competition between the two groups was more evenly balanced, and the Officials' Easter parade in 1971 was significantly larger. Under the leadership of Johnnie White, the Officials managed to enlist some of Derry's young rioters, including a teenage Martin McGuinness, who was impatient for action and soon defected to the Provisionals.[91] Partly in the hope of stemming further defections, the OIRA leadership now gave their units permission to launch attacks on the Army. A British security assessment from April 1971 suggested that they had little choice in the matter: 'If they do not maintain a manifest level of terrorist action much of their "military" membership will either desert to the Provisionals or initiate violence at random.'[92]

If the reformist civil rights strategy of the Officials was now facing collapse, conditions were even less promising for the approach favoured by People's Democracy. Its supporters had withdrawn from NICRA at the start of 1970, declaring their intention to campaign around economic issues in the hope of uniting workers across the sectarian divide. Now reduced to a hard core of a few dozen radicals, PD still involved itself in a whole range of campaigns, from bus fares in Belfast to fishing rights on Lough Neagh. Moving beyond its origins as a campus-based organization, the group sought to translate its non-sectarian rhetoric into reality by leafleting outside the shipyards of east Belfast and on the Shankill Road.[93] But the physical space for such activity was rapidly shrinking in the face of communal polarization, as it simply became too dangerous to enter Protestant areas.[94]

On the eve of internment, People's Democracy had been beaten back into the Catholic ghettoes to await Faulkner's next move along with the other anti-Unionist forces. As the moment approached, its leader Michael Farrell warned that any gains made by the civil rights struggle would be 'lost for good' if Britain decided on a policy of coercion: 'The only thing that will stop the military juggernaut will be a mass movement which can once again bring thousands of people into the streets.'[95] While internment would lead to a dramatic escalation of violence, amid scenes unknown in Western Europe since the war, it also inspired fresh attempts to build mass opposition to the Unionist system. The watchword of the earlier period had been civil rights. Now, it would be civil resistance.

5

The Year of Civil Resistance

Looming Realities

Operation Demetrius began in the early hours of 4 August 1971. Throughout Northern Ireland, soldiers fanned out to arrest suspects, kicking down doors and dragging their targets away. They made over 300 arrests in the first wave, with many more to come over the following months. The authorities set up a camp to house the detainees at Long Kesh, where they were kept in prefabricated huts, surrounded by observation towers and barbed wire – a symbolic own goal for the British Army, as it reminded many people of the German POW camps from movies like *The Great Escape*.

The descriptions of brutal interrogation methods that began filtering out were much more damaging.[1] Detainees reported abuse of various kinds, from beatings to sleep deprivation. Soldiers had thrown some blindfolded men from helicopters that were hovering a few feet above the ground, after telling them they were about to plunge to their deaths. The authorities singled out a group of fourteen prisoners, dubbed the 'Hooded Men', for especially brutal treatment, using techniques that had been fine-tuned in colonial wars.[2]

The most immediate result of internment was a dramatic upsurge in violence across the region. In the first seven months of 1971, there had been thirty-four deaths. Now, seventeen people lost their lives within two days, with 140 to follow by the end of the year. In Ballymurphy, the Army killed ten civilians over the space of thirty-six hours.[3] The chaos transformed large parts of Belfast and Derry into battle-zones, with Provos and Officials temporarily forgetting their political differences to fight side by side. Recruitment to both groups skyrocketed.[4]

In contrast to its handling of the two IRAs, Faulkner's government chose not to arrest any loyalist paramilitaries in August, claiming that the banned Ulster Volunteer Force was not a significant threat.[5] In November 1971, the UVF bombed a Catholic pub in Belfast, killing fifteen civilians. The security forces falsely presented the bombing as an IRA 'own goal', making the refusal to intern loyalists easier to justify.[6] By then, a new group called the Ulster Defence Association (UDA) had taken its place alongside the UVF. It soon claimed a membership of 40,000.

A civil service briefing, drafted shortly after the arrests began, warned that the region now stood on the brink of disaster: 'Economic collapse and social chaos are not remote contingencies but are looming realities within a period which is to be measured in weeks or months rather than years.'[7] Unsurprisingly, most historians have agreed that Demetrius was a fiasco. Many attribute the failure to technical problems: lacking good intelligence, and unable to persuade Jack Lynch's government to move simultaneously against republicans in the South, the Army enraged nationalist communities by arresting the wrong people while the most important Provo leaders slipped across the border.[8] Such arguments imply that internment could perhaps have been made to work, if only the Army had possessed a more accurate picture of its enemy, and taken greater care to avoid scooping up blameless citizens in the net. But the real obstacles were political rather than technical.

As Paddy Devlin noted, the intelligence gap was not simply the result of incompetence: 'The old Catholic informers had disappeared once the Catholic community had been attacked, and the "no go" areas behind the barricades, which excluded the police, killed off any hope they had of cultivating new sources.'[9] Plotting a delicate course between his wish for good relations with Britain and widespread sympathy for northern nationalists in the South, Jack Lynch could never have assisted Faulkner by arresting known republicans (as Edward Heath grudgingly acknowledged in a message to Lynch).[10] Above all, it was the popular mood in the Catholic ghettoes that scuppered Operation Demetrius. Internment, far from stabilizing the local power structure, merely paved the way for its collapse.

Brian Faulkner had been Stormont's home affairs minister at the time of the Border Campaign, and was convinced that internment had ensured the IRA's defeat – hence his eagerness to repeat the trick. But the real problem for the IRA during Operation Harvest had been the indifference of the nationalist population. It was easy for the authorities to hook the republican fish when they were cut off from the main body of water.

However, by 1971, northern nationalists had experienced several years of intense political agitation. They had marched and rioted, built barricades and organized self-defence committees. As Eamonn McCann pointed out, the IRA of the early 70s was quite unlike its 50s predecessor:

It had grown out of the community, was physically of the community's flesh, emotionally and ideologically an element in its consciousness. As a result, when the state's forces attacked the IRA, a sizeable part of the Catholic community felt itself attacked too. The fact that many of those lifted in the internment swoop were the wrong people may not have been as important as is commonly imagined.[11]

This dramatic shift in popular consciousness would have been unthinkable without the preparatory work of those republicans and left-wing radicals who had given the civil rights movement its militant, confrontational edge. Many of those involved in such activity paid a high price for their efforts, as it made them prime candidates for the Army's arrest sheets. Official IRA members were usually active in the Republican Clubs, as the movement's political wing was known in the North, selling the *United Irishman* in defiance of a government ban and engaging in other activities that made it easy to identify them as republican militants. By October, more than a hundred Officials were behind bars, while many others had to flee south or go on the run.[12] The first wave of arrests also targeted People's Democracy members such as Michael Farrell. The Insight reporters of the *Sunday Times* described them as belonging to a 'special group' that had been arrested 'simply because they were active politicians who, in the wake of internment, could cause a fuss'.[13]

On the first day of internment, an emergency bulletin from NICRA's Belfast branch called for 'total withdrawal by non-Unionists from every governmental structure, rent and rates strikes by the people, barricades for defence where necessary and total non-cooperation with a regime which has been stigmatized by the British establishment itself'.[14] Nationalists quickly turned this blueprint into reality. The SDLP had already withdrawn from Stormont in July after the killing of two young nationalists by the Army in Derry, and there was no question of that boycott now being reversed. An unprecedented campaign of mass civil disobedience added to the pressure on Faulkner's government. A rent-and-rates strike by council tenants won solid backing among working-class nationalists. By the end of September, there were 26,000 households on strike, representing one-fifth of the 135,000 local authority tenants. Participation rates were particularly high in certain areas, such as Strabane (87 per cent of tenants) and Belfast's Divis estate (almost 100 per cent).[15]

A coalition of republicans and left-wing activists in Derry that called itself the Socialist Resistance Group issued the call for a strike in the city.[16] Their proposal simply gave organized expression to the mood among nationalists, as Eamonn McCann acknowledged: 'If the Plymouth Brethren had parked a soap-box at the bottom of Wellington Street and called for a rent strike they would have got it. The people were avid for action and it just so happened that we were first in the field suggesting what action they should take.'[17]

Faulkner's government claimed that republicans had coerced tenants into withholding payments, but in private his civil servants recognized 'the great mass of sincere and immediate support from the rank and file' that lay behind it: 'The relative success of the campaign from the beginning is probably due less to any organization behind it, which can only have been minimal, than to the conviction of individual participants that their cause was just.'[18] They began drawing up legislation that would allow the authorities to deduct rent arrears from government benefits.

In tandem with the strike, nationalist anger expressed itself in the form of 'no-go areas' in Derry and Belfast where it was no longer safe for British troops to enter. Local people re-established the barricades that had been gradually dismantled after August 1969 and turned them into impressive fortifications. A report in PD's newspaper at the beginning of 1972 described the ones in Derry as 'not just token barricades but substantial structures which frequently consist of steel girders or concrete blocks sunk into the ground', with just two entry points left for the Army into Creggan and the Bogside.[19]

Republican guerrillas may have posed the greatest threat to British soldiers who tried to breach the no-go zones, but their efforts alone would not have been enough to deter a full-scale invasion by the Army. It was the opposition they faced from the nationalist population as a whole that kept the troops out. A confidential briefing at the end of 1971 described the challenge facing the authorities in Derry: 'At present neither the RUC nor the military have control of the Bogside and Creggan areas, law and order are not being effectively maintained and the Security Forces now face an entirely hostile Catholic community numbering 33,000 in these two areas alone.'[20] The *United Irishman* spoke in exultant terms of 'mass total participation' by nationalists in the civil resistance campaign, which had 'brought the struggle of the people to a new height'.[21] For the Joint Intelligence Committee at Westminster, that campaign was 'perhaps the most threatening feature of the present situation in Northern Ireland'.[22]

'Smash Stormont!'

The British government continued to back Stormont in spite of all the turmoil. When Jack Lynch spoke to Edward Heath soon after Operation Demetrius began, he warned Heath that its effect had been to give the IRA a tremendous boost: 'Urban guerrilla warfare can only work if there is cooperation from the people. This cooperation certainly exists because the minority are looking to the Provisionals for protection.'[23] Lynch returned to Chequers a few weeks later for a meeting with Heath and Brian Faulkner. He argued that sweeping political reforms would now be required to isolate the Provos and shore up the SDLP, with a share in government for the minority 'provided as a right and not by grace and favour'. But Faulkner insisted there could be no question of allowing Nationalist politicians to enter the cabinet.[24] Soon afterwards, the Irish civil servant Eamonn Gallagher paid a visit to the North and found that 'moderate leaders' on the nationalist side were close to despair: 'Even the most pacific of them have now begun to say that they have a vested interest in the continuance of violence for as long as Stormont exists.'[25]

In January 1972, Faulkner drafted a memo that presented Operation Demetrius as a clear-cut success, but still had to acknowledge some unpleasant facts: 'Insofar as internment has not yet succeeded, this is due in no small measure to the fact that there are many people outside the IRA who do not want it to work.' The Unionist leader railed against unnamed individuals who did not want to see the IRA defeated outright 'until some at least of the organization's aims have been achieved'.[26] If Faulkner considered the fall of Stormont to be one of those aims, that complaint now applied to much of the nationalist population.

Naturally, the Provos were delighted to see nationalists turning their back on the state, and their Volunteers took full advantage of the no-go areas to evade the British Army. But it was their rivals who tried to give some political direction to the civil resistance campaign. The Officials continued to work with their Communist allies on the NICRA executive, despite tensions over the question of armed struggle.[27] They saw NICRA as the main vehicle for a new wave of protest that would combine the original platform of the civil rights movement with demands that sprang from the security crisis itself: the end of internment and an amnesty for political prisoners; cancellation of debts for those participating in the rent-and-rates strike; and withdrawal of British troops to barracks, pending their ultimate departure.

During the 1980s, opponents accused Sinn Féin politicians like Gerry Adams and Martin McGuinness of representing the party in public while directing the IRA's military campaign from behind closed doors. However, at this point in their history, most Provisionals concentrated on guerrilla warfare to the exclusion of any other tactic. Ruairí Ó Brádaigh did float the idea of running candidates on an abstentionist platform at Sinn Féin's Ard Fheis in 1971, but nothing came of that proposal at the time.[28]

As a result, it was the Officials who sought to bridge the gap between armed struggle and political agitation. Malachy McGurran combined his duties as head of the OIRA's northern command with a public role as chair of the Republican Clubs. Soon after internment day, McGurran addressed a rally of 10,000 people in Belfast's Casement Park, calling for resistance to the British Army.[29] The Clubs were still illegal, and leaders such as McGurran and Billy McMillen had to spend much of their time dodging the security forces, who knew all about their military functions.

Maintaining the movement's political focus was no easy task. The *Starry Plough*, mouthpiece of the Derry Officials, later remarked on the double-edged character of the recruitment surge after 9 August: 'Almost all of them wanted to "have a go" at the British Army. One quite obvious and glaring problem which faced all of us was how best we could deploy our newly acquired vast membership and at the same time advance our political and socialist ideas.'[30]

Outside observers could be forgiven for losing sight of the distinction between Official and Provisional IRAs, as the two factions appeared to be competing to strike the hardest blows against the British Army; yet clear differences remained. While the Official IRA's New Year's statement for 1972 praised its Volunteers as 'the army of the people' and boasted of 'the many casualties which they have inflicted on the forces of imperialism', it went on to insist that 'armed struggle on its own, or as an end in itself, is doomed to failure'.[31] The Provisionals had no such qualms, as their Ardoyne commander Martin Meehan later recalled: 'We actually believed we could throw the British Army into the sea. It was raw determination, a gut feeling that if we kept up the pressure, we could do it.'[32]

The two groups also diverged in their analysis of the unionist community. The Officials believed that Protestant attitudes were 'one of the major obstacles to the achievement of a socialist republic, and to the creation of a genuinely independent united Irish nation'.[33] Until those attitudes shifted, the focus should be on replacing the 'discredited and gerrymandered' Stormont system with a new regional government based on NICRA's reform programme.[34] They still refused to argue for direct rule from London, insisting it would be the first step towards a new Act of Union. The sound and fury of the conflict often drowned out such arguments, and many recent OIRA recruits doubtless overlooked them entirely. But they proved crucial for the subsequent trajectory of the movement.

The Provos, on the other hand, saw no reason to worry about the reaction from unionists if Britain decided to leave without their consent. Ruairí Ó Brádaigh conceded that a peace-keeping force might be necessary during the transition, but felt that the majority of Protestants would 'come to terms to make the best of it'.[35] Seán Mac Stíofáin, whose mode of expression was always much cruder than Ó Brádaigh's, inadvertently revealed some of the fault lines that ran through the Provisional mindset. He dismissed the idea of a Protestant backlash as something that would 'come and go and that would be that'. In the event of a showdown, the IRA was sure to come out on top: 'I can't see these people preparing themselves for a protracted guerrilla war. It's just not in them.' However, Mac Stíofáin did anticipate 'an exodus of the more bigoted elements' in the event of British withdrawal: 'There would be no place for those who say they want their British heritage. They've got to accept their Irish heritage, and the Irish way of life, no matter who they are, otherwise there would be no place for them.'[36]

The Provisional chief of staff was formally committed to an ideology that defined Ulster Protestants as fellow Irishmen. But his comments hinted at a darker view of the unionist population as foreign settlers – 'planters', in the local idiom – who would have to choose between assimilation and flight when Britain was forced to pull out. In areas like rural Tyrone, which were to produce some of the most active Provisional units, such attitudes ran deep.

People's Democracy echoed the Officials with a call for mass opposition to Unionist rule. The group developed a more supportive view of armed struggle as the crisis intensified. In the early months of 1971, it had described the Provo campaign as 'futile and doomed to failure'; by the start of the following year PD was arguing that republican guerrillas 'must be encouraged and not stabbed in the back'.[37] But its members related to that campaign from the outside, and channelled most of their energy into building support for civil resistance.

Before the arrival of British troops, Michael Farrell had asked whether it might be possible for left-wing radicals to advance their goals by 'posing the question of dual power in areas where the Catholic population is concentrated and militant – by getting the local Catholic population to take over and run its own affairs, a sort of "Catholic power".'[38] Now he hailed the partial fulfilment of this vision: 'The Unionists and their imperial master are far more concerned about the Civil Resistance campaign than about the current campaign of violence. The reason is simple. If the Civil Resistance campaign was defeated they could deal with the violence very quickly. If the physical force campaign was defeated, the Civil Resistance campaign would still go on.'[39]

To guide that campaign, Farrell's group put forward a clear, emphatic slogan, 'Smash Stormont!', that was all the more effective for its ambiguity. The demand could bring together Provos who saw the demise of the local assembly as a step towards British withdrawal with SDLP supporters who would be satisfied with direct rule from London as an alternative to Unionist power.

Arguing that NICRA had become 'too closely identified with a particular political viewpoint – that of the Official Republicans and the Communist Party – to be fully representative of the current mass movement', PD moved to establish a new campaigning front, the Northern Resistance Movement (NRM).[40] The NRM attracted support from the Provisionals, and from Bernadette Devlin and her fellow Westminster MP Frank McManus, an independent republican. PD argued that many Provos were already 'seeing the need for deeper involvement in politics', and just needed encouragement to go further down that path: 'With their courage, natural militancy and working-class roots, many are natural revolutionaries. Instead of screaming abuse at these men forced into fighting a war against imperialism, socialists should be trying to involve them in political action.'[41] Gerry Adams later recalled being exposed to the group's arguments because of their involvement in the NRM: 'PD argued quite correctly for wider popular mobilizations, and it struck me that all of the potential for mobilization was ours, while PD had the theory.'[42]

As 1971 drew to a close, opponents of the Unionist government began to revive the tactic of street marches that had been the catalyst for the current unrest. The division between NICRA and the NRM meant that this attempt to bring the movement back onto the streets came from two competing sources. All the same, it is striking to note that three years after the first civil rights marches, it was the same loose coalition of forces – the Officials and the Communist Party, People's Democracy and the Derry radicals – who were pushing for a revival of mass action as an alternative to armed struggle. Ironically, the result of their efforts was to give the Provos their greatest boost to date.

Bloody Sunday

The importance of the Bloody Sunday massacre in Derry should require no emphasis. The killing of fourteen nationalist civilians by the British Army in January 1972 has received more attention than any other incident of the Troubles, and was the subject of a decade-spanning inquiry that cost several hundred million pounds.

However, for all the ink spilt on the events of that day, the wider context in which Bloody Sunday was embedded has not been given the same attention. Without examining that context, it is impossible to make political sense of what happened in Derry.

In the final weeks of 1971, Brian Faulkner suddenly had to grapple with an upsurge of protest. On Christmas Day, the NRM led an anti-internment march that reached the gates of Long Kesh. Then, on the first weekend of January 1972, NICRA organized a demonstration on the Falls Road.[43] Five thousand people heard Paddy Devlin and Austin Currie of the SDLP pledge there would be no talks with the British government until it released all the internees.[44] These protests posed an immediate challenge to Stormont's authority, as Faulkner had imposed a ban on all street processions to coincide with internment, which he extended in January.[45] But the forces behind the new wave of protest were determined to assert the legitimacy of such tactics, as Eamonn McCann later explained: 'None of the other forms of protest provided a way for the mass of working-class people to become actively involved in the fight. The rent-and-rates strike had its attractions, but it was a passive sort of activity. The armed struggle could, of its nature, involve only a few, while rioting was appropriate mainly to the energetic young.'[46]

NICRA raised the stakes higher still by organizing a march on 22 January to Magilligan, just north of Derry, where the authorities had recently opened another camp for internees. Soldiers of the Parachute Regiment prevented the marchers from reaching the camp by firing rubber bullets and striking freely with their batons. One soldier was heard remarking to his officer: 'I thought we were here to stop them, not massacre them.'[47] NICRA then announced its intention to defy the ban once more with a demonstration in Derry on 30 January. The local branch of Paisley's DUP called off its plan for a counter-protest at the last minute, claiming to have received assurances that the marchers would be stopped 'by force if necessary'.[48] NICRA urged its supporters not to give the authorities any pretext for the use of such methods.[49]

The local RUC commander, Frank Lagan, also wanted to minimize the danger of a violent confrontation. According to Brendan

Duddy, who acted as an intermediary between Lagan and the two IRAs, he received assurances from both factions that their members would not bring weapons on the march or use it as an opportunity to attack the Army. But the Army commander Robert Ford ignored Lagan's advice and decided to use the protest as the occasion for mass arrests, aiming to 'scoop up as many hooligans as possible'.[50]

Ford chose the Paras, known to be the most aggressive of all the regiments stationed in Northern Ireland, as the agent of his plan. By one reporter's estimate, 20,000 people joined the demonstration as it made its way towards the city centre.[51] When the marchers reached the Army barricade, the Paras went into action, cheered on by Ford. By the time they were finished, the soldiers had shot thirteen civilians dead; another victim later died of his wounds.

Journalists quickly established that every known fact and every available eyewitness contradicted the Army's version of events.[52] But Home Secretary Reginald Maudling still used that account as the basis for his speech in the House of Commons, claiming that the soldiers had acted in self-defence after coming under sustained fire. Bernadette Devlin, who had been present on the march, could not endure Maudling's performance and threw a punch at him. A Conservative MP spoke about Devlin as if she was an exotic anthropological specimen: 'It is only by listening to her words that one can plumb the depths of the bitterness and hatred that is rampant amongst the minority in Northern Ireland today.' But the SDLP leader Gerry Fitt gave Devlin his firm support. Facing a chorus of heckling from Tory backbenchers, Fitt lashed out at his fellow MPs: 'I realize more and more as this debate progresses that I am an Irishman, and you are Englishmen. You have no under-standing, no sympathy, and no conscience for the people who live in Londonderry.'[53]

For supporters of the Provisional IRA, Bloody Sunday sounded the death knell for the tactic of unarmed protest: from now on, force would have to be met with force. That was certainly the view of the young men and women who flocked to join the Provos after the Derry massacre.[54] But in fact the civil resistance cam-paign entered its most intense phase in the weeks that followed. On

6 February, a NICRA demonstration in Newry attracted more than 50,000 people, despite warnings that the violence in Derry might be repeated and threats of mass arrest broadcast to the marchers from a low-flying helicopter.[55]

Sympathy for northern nationalists in the South began to assume organized form for the first time, with protest committees springing up and trade unionists calling for a general strike, hastily rebranded as a day of national mourning by Jack Lynch's government. In his statement to the Dáil, Lynch demanded the withdrawal of British troops from the Catholic ghettoes, and promised to fund 'peaceful action by the minority in Northern Ireland, designed to obtain their freedom from Unionist misgovernment'.[56] Meanwhile an angry crowd burnt the British Embassy in Dublin to the ground as police stood by helpless. The no-go areas were consolidated, the rent-and-rates strike strengthened. With the SDLP still boycotting Stormont and refusing to negotiate while internment continued, Faulkner and Heath now faced a nationalist population united in rejection of their authority.

Two months after Bloody Sunday, the British ambassador in Dublin passed on a copy of the report by Lord Widgery, who had been tasked by Heath with investigating the events in Derry. The civil servant who received the ambassador drily observed that Widgery's account appeared to be 'a rather one-sided interpretation', and wondered 'how those in Derry, who were fully familiar with what had happened, would take the report'.[57] This proved to be a classic case of diplomatic understatement. The Widgery Report did almost as much to inflame nationalist fury as the massacre itself. Its author held the organizers of the march responsible for what had happened, expressed 'strong suspicion' that some of the victims had been 'firing weapons or handling bombs', and found 'no reason to suppose that the soldiers would have opened fire if they had not been fired upon first'.[58]

Widgery's conclusions are no longer considered defensible by the British authorities after the publication of Lord Saville's 2010 report and the acceptance of its findings by the Conservative prime minister, David Cameron. However, Saville's report did not resolve the dispute about political responsibility for the massacre. In the wake of Bloody Sunday, those who had been pressing for a return to the streets had no doubt the killings were the intended outcome of British policy. The goal, according to the Officials, was to abort the revival of protest before it developed unstoppable momentum: 'While they can outshoot purely military campaigns, mass action on the streets will be their downfall. This was why the British government ordered their troops to fire on a defenceless and peaceful crowd.'[59]

Saville rejected such arguments, placing the blame firmly on the soldiers and their immediate commanding officer, Derek Wilford. But his report glossed over the role played by Wilford's superior Robert Ford and his deputy Mike Jackson, who later became the Army's chief of staff.[60] If Saville had given Ford and Jackson their due share of attention, it would have been much harder for David Cameron to endorse his findings without discrediting the Army as an institution.

In any case, the question of responsibility cannot be limited to the decisions made before and during the march. Widgery's report was as much a part of the story as the shots fired three months earlier. By carefully obscuring all the evidence that members of 1 Para were guilty of unlawful killings, Britain's most eminent judge gave his stamp of approval to the battalion's conduct in Derry, indicating to nationalists that participation in a banned march could now be punished by summary execution. The Heath government fully endorsed this verdict.

Those who spoke of a carefully planned massacre designed to force protest off the streets exaggerated the degree of political forethought behind the killings. It appears much more likely that the Army's intention was to goad the IRA into a shoot-out that it expected to win.[61] But they were right to insist that Bloody Sunday was no accidental misfortune. Westminster's policy of upholding Unionist rule was bound to provoke a test of strength between the Army and the nationalist population. Once NICRA and the NRM started to revive street demonstrations as the cutting-edge of resistance to the 'Orange State', British soldiers had to shoulder the burden of confronting them. Robert Ford's decision to use the march in Derry as cover for his reckless plan then turned the risk of disaster into a near-certainty. Instead of breaking the IRA, Ford gave it an impetus and popular legitimacy that would have been unimaginable a year earlier.

In March 1972, as Stormont descended into a terminal crisis, a court in Belfast gave the PD activists Michael Farrell and Kevin Boyle six months in jail for their role in organizing the marches that preceded Bloody Sunday. According to a report in PD's *Unfree Citizen*, the courtroom was packed with soldiers who 'amused themselves by clicking and unclicking the safety catches of their rifles in the crowded room'.[62] Farrell spoke from the dock, surrounded by his NRM allies, Kevin Agnew and Gerry O'Hare of the Provisionals, and the Westminster MPs Bernadette Devlin and Frank McManus. After objecting to the presence of the soldiers, which, he suggested, made the court resemble a scene from the dictatorships of southern Europe, the People's Democracy leader went on to deliver a passionate defence of the entire civil resistance campaign:

> Some evidence is being offered that I have committed certain actions but I want to challenge the whole basis of the legal set-up here which decides what is legal or illegal. I am not guilty of any offence, because it appears to me that the system of law and justice in this state has broken down and collapsed. On the 9th August 1971, the door of my house was broken in and armed soldiers burst in and took me away at gunpoint. Later that day I was assaulted, beaten up and maltreated at Girdwood Park military barracks and then lodged in Crumlin Road jail. I was held there for five weeks and then released. At no time was I given any explanation for this treatment. It was later shown that it was all quite illegal even under the terms of the Special Powers Act. Yet I have no redress and there are some 700 or 800 others like me, still being held.

Farrell ended his speech with a rhetorical flourish: 'The law in any society is based on a contract between the State and the citizen.

When the State oversteps this authority, when it tramples on the rights of citizens, when it shoots down people in cold blood, then that contract is dissolved.'[63]

The End of Civil Resistance

By the time Farrell and his comrades brought an appeal against their convictions, the regime that had prosecuted them was no more. The turbulent aftermath of Bloody Sunday dealt the final blow to Stormont and obliged the Heath government to change direction. When Faulkner refused to hand over security powers to Westminster, Heath imposed direct rule on 24 March, ending half a century of Unionist Party rule. British civil servants began putting out feelers for a new political initiative that might bring the SDLP and the Irish government back onside and isolate the republican guerrillas. As Faulkner and William Craig addressed a rally of supporters outside their suspended parliament, those who had raised the slogan 'Smash Stormont!' had to ask themselves: what now?

A few months earlier, a prescient article in PD's newspaper had suggested that, while the Provos were determined to keep fighting until Irish unity was achieved, 'in practice much of the Catholic support would evaporate – and probably many of the Volunteers would be satisfied – if the internees were released, Stormont smashed and the British Army removed.'[64] One of these conditions had now been fulfilled, and the mood among nationalists was predictably triumphant. Divisions within the nationalist community that had been papered over since internment – between radicals and conservatives, militarists and those who favoured civil resistance – now reasserted themselves.

For a time, it looked as if the Officials would continue to wage war on the British Army. In the weeks following Bloody Sunday, they planted a bomb at the headquarters of the Parachute Regiment in Aldershot, killing a number of civilian workers, and tried to assassinate the Unionist home affairs minister, John Taylor. When British soldiers gunned down the Official IRA's most charismatic figurehead, Joe McCann, in April 1972, Cathal Goulding promised revenge at McCann's funeral in Belfast: 'Those who are responsible for the terrorism that is Britain's age-old reaction to Irish demands will be the victims of that terrorism, paying richly in their own red blood for their crimes.'[65] But Goulding also declared that the Officials would 'fight them on our terms, not on theirs'. The OIRA's chief of staff was already contemplating a ceasefire at the time of McCann's death, although most of his audience probably missed the hint.

That move came in May 1972, with a message from the Official IRA that described 'a growing awareness by the leadership of the Republican Movement that we had been drawn into a war that was not of our choosing'.[66] The immediate cue for the ceasefire was a controversy that engulfed one of the movement's strongest northern units in early May. After the Army shot dead a teenage boy, the Derry Officials responded by killing a young British soldier from a regiment deployed in West Germany who was home on leave in the Bogside. The death of William Best provoked a hostile reaction from many Derry nationalists who saw him as one of their own, greatly encouraged by the Catholic Church. The *Starry Plough* hit back with a firm anti-clerical line: 'One of the curses of this area for ages past has been the identification of religion with politics. We are not part of that set-up, we are fighting to destroy it. We are out for a socialist Ireland in which, among other things, religion will be a thing for a man's private conscience.'[67]

When the Official IRA leadership in Dublin announced the ceasefire three weeks later, they denied having been influenced by the turmoil in Derry, and were widely disbelieved. In fact, the Ranger Best affair merely supplied the opportunity for a move that had much deeper political roots. But the use of this pretext stored up trouble for the leadership with their Derry unit, whose members felt they had been the targets of a spurious 'peace campaign', orchestrated by a Church that was highly selective in its moral indignation.[68]

A confidential briefing prepared for Edward Heath in the summer of 1972 gave a shrewd assessment of the OIRA ceasefire, noting that Cathal Goulding's movement had 'always been more willing than the Provisionals to envisage the possibility of working through the institutions of Northern Ireland – as an intermediate measure – and to cooperate so far as they have been able with the Protestant working class'. The Officials had felt obliged to match the violence of the Provos in order to keep their own members on board and maintain their position in the Catholic ghettoes, but their desire to avoid sectarian conflict was perfectly genuine: 'Secret sources have confirmed their feelings in this regard.'[69]

OIRA commanders often sold the ceasefire to rank-and-file members as a tactical expedient that left plenty of room for manoeuvre. Two years later, the *United Irishman* could still carry a report that the Army had shot two OIRA Volunteers dead while they were planting a landmine 'as retaliation for the intimidation and harassment of the working-class people of Newry', prompting a revenge attack that killed one soldier.[70] But May 1972 marked a clear turning point in the history of the Officials, after which they gradually wound down their armed wing and gave priority to political action.

The OIRA ceasefire made it easier for the Provisionals to call a truce of their own. When the British government imposed direct rule, Ruairí Ó Brádaigh warned against a 'truce hysteria' that would stampede the IRA into a premature halt: 'Let there be no settlement short of the mark. If we do, we are sentencing the next generation to death and destruction.' Seán Mac Stíofáin was much blunter: 'Concessions be damned, we want freedom!'[71] But the Provos still came out with their own set of peace proposals and indicated a willingness to talk. An MI6 officer, Frank Steele, held preliminary discussions with two Provo commanders, Dáithí Ó Conaill and Gerry Adams, which paved the way for a ceasefire in June. The briefing given to Steele described Adams as one of the most senior IRA men in Belfast. Expecting to meet an 'arrogant, streetwise young thug', Steele instead found Adams to be 'a very personable, intelligent, articulate and self-disciplined man', who 'obviously had a terrific future ahead of him'.[72]

As soon as the truce began, Heath's secretary of state for

Northern Ireland, William Whitelaw, invited the Provisional leadership for secret talks on the region's future. Mac Stíofáin headed a delegation that included several younger militants such as Adams, Martin McGuinness and Ivor Bell, who had to be talked out of wearing his combat fatigues for the occasion.[73] The Provos insisted that Britain should declare its intention to withdraw all troops by the end of 1974, and allow the island's future to be determined by an all-Ireland poll. Along with this maximum programme, the movement's political wing also put forward a more limited set of demands that bore some resemblance to NICRA's platform: release of internees; repeal of the Special Powers Act; PR for all elections; a lifting of the ban on Provisional Sinn Féin, and the scrapping of all oaths of allegiance to the British Crown.[74]

British officials who took part in these abortive negotiations later accused the Provisional leaders of adopting a completely unrealistic attitude.[75] According to one participant from the British side, Seán Mac Stíofáin conducted himself 'like Montgomery at Lüneberg Heath telling the German generals what they should and shouldn't do if they wanted peace'.[76] This description of Mac Stíofáin's outlook appears close to the truth, judging by his own recollections of Provo super-confidence after the fall of Stormont, as well as the account of the talks that Gerry Adams later supplied. According to Adams, when the Provisional delegation broke off to discuss what their British counterparts had said, Mac Stíofáin exclaimed, 'Jesus, we have it!'[77]

If so, the Provisional chief of staff had a greatly exaggerated sense of what could be achieved at the time. Sinn Féin's short-term programme probably represented the outer limit of what the British government would have been willing to concede. Having failed to achieve their maximum goals, the Provos had little alternative but to return to war, since the movement had no political wing that could advance their agenda in the absence of a military campaign. A stand-off provoked by loyalist paramilitaries in Belfast was the immediate trigger for the resumption of hostilities, but there would most likely have been another incident to scupper the ceasefire if the loyalists had not intervened.

The Provisionals were now keen to make full use of a weapon that they had stumbled upon almost by accident: the car bomb. As Mike Davis points out in his history of the 'poor man's air force', the conflict in Northern Ireland became a grisly milestone: the first time that urban guerrillas combined homemade bombs with motor vehicles to ravage a modern city.[78] The military potential of this innovation exhilarated Mac Stíofáin and his comrades, who geared up for a final push that would eject Britain from Irish soil once and for all.[79]

However, they had not reflected on another aspect of the new weapon noted by Davis: 'Like even the "smartest" of aerial bombs, car bombs are inherently indiscriminate: "collateral damage" is virtually inevitable. If the logic of an attack is to slaughter civilians and sow panic in the widest circles, to operate a "strategy of tension" or just demoralize a society, car bombs are ideal. But they are equally effective at destroying the moral credibility of a cause and alienating its mass base of support.'[80]

On the afternoon of 21 July 1972, twenty-one bombs went off in Belfast's city centre, killing seven civilians and two soldiers and leaving more than 130 people wounded. Although the IRA had phoned in warnings, there were too many devices for the security forces to cope with at once. Gruesome scenes of human flesh and body parts being shovelled into plastic bags featured on the national news.

'Bloody Friday' was a propaganda disaster for the Provos, and provided William Whitelaw and the Army with the opportunity they had been waiting for. Ten days later, Operation Motorman swept aside the no-go areas in Belfast and Derry. The Army started to impose a new military architecture of barracks and observation towers on the Catholic ghettoes, destined to overshadow the urban landscape for the next two decades.[81]

The Derry Officials urged their republican rivals to end the dalliance with car bombs: 'Bombing is an elitist tactic. It does not involve the people. This is true, of course, of all military activity, of the armed defence of the area or of offensive guerrilla activities such as we, as well as the Provisionals, engaged in until recently. But it is uniquely true of urban bombing which demands a tiny group, or perhaps a single person acting clandestinely.' Such methods were no substitute for a political organization 'confident of its own strength, conscious of its own involvement in real politics and clear about its objectives. You cannot bomb an organization like that into existence. You have to build it, and there are no short-cuts.'[82]

But the exhortation fell on deaf ears. Car bombs had a long future ahead of them in Northern Ireland. The Provisionals went on to devise ever-more sophisticated versions and take their war to the heart of Britain's elite, claiming hundreds of civilian lives along the way. They would also belatedly accept the need for a political struggle to be waged alongside their military campaign. But civil resistance never reached the heights it had known between Demetrius and Motorman again.

6

Roads Not Taken

The Gun and the Typewriter

In its history of the conflict, the British Army identified the summer of 1972 as a crucial turning point: the moment when republican guerrillas shifted from 'insurgency' to 'terrorism' in their methods.[1] Operation Motorman had eliminated the no-go areas for good, and the casualty figures for 1972 – almost 500 deaths, including 130 British soldiers – were never to be repeated. However, the Provos had no intention of accepting defeat. Arrests on both sides of the border took a number of leading IRA commanders out of circulation, but those still at liberty now drew up plans to extend their bombing campaign to Britain.[2]

Sinn Féin remained the poor cousin of the movement's military wing, with no real life of its own, but the IRA leadership saw little cause for concern. The movement's Army Council turned down another proposal from Ruairí Ó Brádaigh to contest elections in the North if legal barriers could be overcome: partly on grounds of principle, partly for fear of being trounced by the SDLP.[3] A year after Motorman, Ó Brádaigh assured supporters that in any case, salvation was at hand: 'We are in sight of the British declaration of intent to withdraw.'[4]

The outlook of their republican rivals could hardly have been more different. In July 1972, Tomás Mac Giolla delivered a speech

in Tyrone that set out the thinking behind the Official IRA's ceasefire, putting forward two main arguments against Provo militarism.
First of all, it was bound to alienate the unionist population, whose
opposition to a united Ireland meant partition would have to
remain in place for the time being: 'Understanding the justified and
unjustified fears of the Protestant working class we have correctly
decided that a form of government will exist in the Six Counties,
but it must be a government based on the democratic demands of
the Civil Rights Association.'[5] Mac Giolla was also concerned about
the effect of a narrow military campaign on nationalist opinion.
When the moment of exhaustion arrived – as it inevitably would
– 'without political guidance, without a leadership that articulates
their demands, the people will blindly opt for peace at any price.
And their paper hero will become a paper monster overnight, isolated and remote.'[6]

Having rejected the military road, the Official republicans had
to find another way to advance their agenda. They had set great
store by NICRA as a campaigning group that could spearhead the
struggle for reform in Northern Ireland. But the civil rights body
was now a greatly diminished force, lacking the broad support it
had formerly enjoyed. The Officials also cherished hopes that the
trade union movement could be used for their purposes, as it was
'the only mass organization capable of achieving success without
irreparably dividing our people'.[7]

However, communal divisions stood obstinately in the way of
that prospect. A briefing prepared for Edward Heath in March
1972 set out the essence of the problem. Heath had seen a news
report claiming that the Official IRA was 'working on schemes
to promote industrial action in Northern Ireland along lines followed in the recent miners' strike', which he considered 'very
important'. Civil servants assured the prime minister that there
was no need to be concerned: 'Protestant workers would regard
picketing in support of an IRA-inspired strike as a challenge and
would accordingly be more determined to work.' There might be
some areas with a predominantly Catholic workforce, such as
Belfast's deep-sea port, where industrial action was more likely to

succeed. Even there, it should prove easier to contain than a strike in Britain.[8]

If NICRA was in decline and the trade unions ill-equipped to perform the role assigned to them by the Officials, there was still another vehicle for the movement's ambitions. Its political wing, the Republican Clubs, had their first real outing in the council elections of 1973, pledging not to take their seats until internment ended. Ten candidates were successful, with support coming almost entirely from nationalist voters.[9] The *United Irishman* hailed the result as 'ample evidence that there is clear support for the Movement's national and social policies throughout the Six Counties', but complained that enthusiasm in the ranks was limited: 'Some areas played little or no part in the campaign although the decision to contest was arrived at nationally. This displays a total misunderstanding of the opportunity the elections provided to publicize Republican policy, and is dangerously close to elitism.'[10]

In truth, while the election results offered a base that could be built upon, it was hardly an electrifying performance. The Clubs were certainly in no position to challenge the SDLP, by now a well-established party with several high-profile representatives, some of whom had a leftish tinge to their politics. The Officials had a long slog ahead if they expected to become a serious political force.

Seamus Costello now formed an alliance with Seán Garland to try and overturn the movement's reformist strategy. Both men were staunchly committed to the idea of a left-wing, politicized republicanism, but feared that the emphasis on civil rights was becoming a distraction from the struggle against British rule. The arguments of Gerry Foley, an Irish-American Trotskyist who had befriended several leading Officials, influenced their critique of the established line. Foley welcomed the OIRA ceasefire, arguing that a military campaign would serve only to divide and isolate the nationalist population, but dismissed the idea of gradual democratic reform as a utopian folly.[11] A document circulated by Garland and Costello at the end of 1972 argued for a change of focus, and met with approval from both wings of the movement.[12] The main resolution from that year's party conference demanded that the British government 'commit themselves to a total withdrawal of their military and political control from the Six Counties at an early specified date'.[13]

When William Whitelaw published a white paper on the future of Northern Ireland in March 1973, the Officials insisted that 'any solution which advocates the continuation of a Six or Nine County Ulster state, whether it has constitutional links with Britain or not, must be rejected.'[14] This baldly contradicted what Tomás Mac Giolla had said at Carrickmore a few months earlier. Mac Giolla and Garland brought the movement's new policy with them to the World Congress of Peace Forces held in Moscow that November.[15] According to Gerry Foley, Garland returned from the conference believing that Soviet aid could give the Officials a vital boost, having been 'most influenced by discussions he had with representatives of guerrilla movements in Africa'.[16] In the following years, Soviet-style Marxism gradually supplanted the eclectic left-wing ideology of the early 70s, to the dismay of those Officials who wanted a more independent line.

For its part, People's Democracy could only hope to make an impression on the political scene by linking up with other forces. The Northern Resistance Movement was defunct by the end of 1972, but PD kept on trying to draw the Provos into broad alliances that could revive the campaign of civil resistance. The group had decided that the priority for socialists was to destroy the 'Orange State' and drive Britain from the island for good. It abandoned talk of uniting the working class across sectarian boundaries, believing that partition would have to be ended before such unity could materialize. Since the Provisional IRA was the main force challenging British rule, its campaign should be supported wholeheartedly: 'There can be no progress made until the age-old problem of the domination and exploitation of Ireland by British imperialism is settled. We therefore support the war of resistance against British control in the North and have agitated and will continue to agitate to back up that war.'[17]

PD still insisted that armed struggle would have to be accompanied by political action. An opportunity to promote that vision arose in the summer of 1973, when the courts imprisoned Michael Farrell and his comrade Tony Canavan for organizing an illegal march in Belfast.[18] Farrell and Canavan began a hunger strike to demand special-category status after their transfer to Crumlin Road jail. The fast galvanized the formation of a new alliance, the Political Hostages Release Committee (PHRC), which attracted support from both republican factions.

A campaign of protest culminated in the release of the two men after thirty-four days without food. The Provisional mouthpiece *Republican News* praised Farrell as a 'fearless opponent of the Unionist regime and British interference in Irish affairs', and suggested that further victories could be won by combining 'mass popular action with the military campaign'.[19] Gerry Adams later identified the PHRC as 'the principal anti-Unionist political success in 1973'.[20]

However, the unity it had forged proved to be ephemeral. A rally hosted by NICRA in West Belfast to mark the second anniversary of internment ended in a messy dispute over speaking rights.[21] The Republican Clubs and the Communist Party pulled out of the PHRC soon after this very public row, which underlined the fragmentation of political forces since the high point of civil resistance. A few months later, the Provos finished off the alliance by announcing their own departure, adding some choice words about People's Democracy for good measure: 'Sinn Féin will not allow itself to be used to support the meandering politics of PD nor will it allow pseudo-revolutionaries to bathe in the glory of Ireland's recent dead.'[22] *Republican News* combined faint praise for PD, whose members had 'played their part in organizing the people against jackboot policies', with a blunt statement of essentials: 'When the People's Democracy decide to couple use of the typewriter with use of the gun, as Connolly did, then they can jettison the label of armchair revolutionaries.'[23]

Not everyone was so dismissive. Kieran Conway, the IRA's director of intelligence in the mid 70s, recalled a conversation with its chief of staff Seamus Twomey. Conway argued that Sinn Féin was a dud party that should be scrapped altogether, 'to make room for an organization like the Northern Resistance Movement, which included Michael Farrell and others whose politics and ability I admired'. Far from being shocked, Twomey found the suggestion 'hilarious', and promised to tell the Sinn Féin leaders what Conway thought of them.[24] One leading Provisional, Jim Gibney, later described People's Democracy as 'the recognized political leadership of what we loosely called the anti-imperialist movement', at a time when the Provos concentrated exclusively on armed struggle. According to Gibney, it was PD's role that inspired republicans to start cultivating their own team of political spokesmen.[25] But this change of focus still lay some years in the future.

Ulster Will Fight

The main political action during this period was taking place elsewhere. When the SDLP leadership met William Whitelaw in December 1972, they pressed for joint sovereignty between London and Dublin and the formation of a new police force acceptable to nationalists.[26] But the party soon accepted Whitelaw's much less ambitious blueprint for the restoration of devolved government in Northern Ireland. There would be elections for a new regional assembly, held under proportional representation, with the aim of setting up a power-sharing government as soon as possible. Brian Faulkner's Ulster Unionist Party also decided to embrace this political framework, as did the bi-confessional Alliance. Elections in June 1973 delivered a working majority for those who were prepared to cooperate with Whitelaw's scheme, although Faulkner had to face a substantial rejectionist bloc on the Unionist side composed of UUP dissidents, Ian Paisley's Democratic Unionist Party, and a new movement led by William Craig called Vanguard.

Craig came to the fore as the champion of the Unionist Right after Stormont's fall. While Ian Paisley flirted with the idea of full integration between Northern Ireland and Britain, Vanguard put the question of Ulster independence on the table. A paper drafted for Craig by a Canadian academic demanded that the region be given its full share of the UK's national assets, 'right down to a sector of British territory in the Antarctic'.[27] In March 1972, a rally staged by Vanguard in Belfast drew a crowd of 60,000 people, including a phalanx of uniformed paramilitaries. Craig told his audience to 'build up dossiers on the men and women who are the enemies of Northern Ireland because one day, if the politicians fail, it will be our job to liquidate the enemy'.[28] The Vanguard leader had a similar message when he addressed the right-wing Monday Club at Westminster later that year: 'I am prepared to kill and those behind me will have my full support.'[29]

Brian Faulkner derided Craig's rallies as 'comic-opera parades' that were 'part menacing, part ridiculous'.[30] But there was nothing comical about the loyalist assassination campaign spearheaded by the UVF and its larger rival, the Ulster Defence Association. From 1972 to 1976, loyalist paramilitaries killed 567 people, the vast majority of whom were Catholic civilians.[31] The UDA's front-group, the Ulster Freedom Fighters, presented such attacks as collective punishment for the actions of the IRA: 'We would appeal to the RC populace: throw these gangsters out of your midst. Until you do this, you must bear the agony.'[32] Ignoring such clear statements, RUC spokesmen persisted in referring to the sectarian killings as 'motiveless murders'.

The British authorities applied a different standard to loyalist paramilitary groups than they did to the IRA. The UDA remained a legal organization until 1992, and the Army permitted UDA members to join its locally recruited force, the Ulster Defence Regiment.[33] Facing a European court challenge, spokesmen for the Army and RUC acknowledged the discrepancy and sought to justify it, claiming that the loyalist groups were not disciplined, structured organizations like the IRA. There was ample evidence in their possession to contradict that view.[34] The permissive attitude towards the loyalist paramilitaries made it easier for them to frustrate the British government's most ambitious plan to stabilize the region.

By the end of 1973, Brian Faulkner had agreed to a deal on power-sharing with the SDLP that was sponsored by the two governments. Under the terms of the Sunningdale Agreement, as it became known, Northern Ireland would remain part of the United Kingdom for as long as a majority wished. A cross-border Council of Ireland satisfied the SDLP's call for an 'Irish dimension'. The new government would have six ministers from Brian Faulkner's party, four from the SDLP and one from the Alliance. On the security front, internment remained in place, and SDLP politicians who had previously supported the rent-and-rates strike now urged council tenants to pay their arrears and bring the campaign of civil disobedience to an end.

Unsurprisingly, the Provos rejected Sunningdale out of hand and vowed to fight on to victory. Unionist hardliners concentrated their fire on the Council of Ireland, presenting it as a Trojan horse for Irish unity: one anti-agreement poster parodied a tourist campaign with the slogan 'Dublin is just a Sunningdale away'. Supported by a narrow majority of unionists at best, Brian Faulkner needed a fair wind if he was to survive for long. But he had to face a sudden test of strength in February 1974 when Edward Heath called a snap UK general election, which brought Harold Wilson's Labour Party to power.

To compound Faulkner's difficulties, he lost control of the UUP apparatus to opponents of Sunningdale and had to establish a new party on the hoof. Anti-agreement Unionists agreed a common platform and trounced their opponents, winning all but one of Northern Ireland's eleven seats. Faulkner and his cabinet still tried to keep the show on the road, hoping that opposition to Sunningdale would recede before the next Assembly election. A loyalist umbrella group called the Ulster Workers' Council (UWC) threatened to launch a campaign of mass resistance if Faulkner did not resign. On 14 May, it called an open-ended general strike in a bid to make Northern Ireland ungovernable. The loyalist paramilitaries backed up that call by constructing barricades to block the flow of traffic. Three days later, the UVF took its war south of the border with bomb attacks in Dublin and Monaghan that claimed the lives of thirty-three civilians. After a fortnight of disruption, with the UWC leadership having effectively usurped Faulkner's prerogatives, he threw in the towel and the power-sharing experiment collapsed.

The failure of Sunningdale threw the whole political landscape into confusion. The British government wanted to restore Stormont on a more inclusive footing, but that plan now lay in tatters, with the parties willing to support it thoroughly demoralized. Unionist opponents of power-sharing had won a major victory, yet their ultimate goal – a return to straight majority rule – could only be secured with the consent of politicians at Westminster, who had every reason to reject such a quixotic enterprise. In 1975, Harold Wilson's government ordered elections for a Northern Ireland Convention that resulted in a thumping majority for the rejectionist front led by Craig, Paisley and the new Ulster Unionist chief, Harry West.

Craig tentatively suggested that the SDLP might be invited to join a coalition with Unionist parties until stability had returned. This version of power-sharing would have been voluntary, with no Council of Ireland to accompany it, but it was still too much for Craig's allies to accept and he found himself ostracized.[35] The majority report demanded a return to the old Stormont regime. To no one's great surprise, Wilson and his colleagues rejected that option and disbanded the convention. Unionism had shown that it could veto British government policy, only to find itself vetoed in turn.

The Provos shed no tears for Sunningdale, but still had to face some difficult questions of their own. By the end of 1974, the conflict in the North had lasted for twice as long as the War of Independence and claimed many more lives, yet victory remained elusive. The Birmingham pub bombings in November 1974, which killed twenty-one people, reinforced the sense of an IRA campaign that was directionless and spiralling out of control. For many years the IRA leadership denied responsibility for the bombings, although they knew that one of the organization's British-based units was to blame.[36]

The downfall of Seán Mac Stíofáin, after an abortive hunger strike in prison, removed one of the main barriers to a ceasefire on the Provisional side. When representatives of the British government suggested that they were willing to discuss 'structures of disengagement', the Provisionals seized the opportunity to declare a second truce in February 1975.[37] In hindsight, their decision looks rather naive, and the new IRA leaders who took the helm after the ceasefire broke down certainly presented it in that light. However, there was a space of rhetorical ambiguity at the time that made it seem like a gamble worth taking.[38]

For politicians in London and Belfast alike, 'disengagement' could refer to the idea of independence for Northern Ireland, rather than a thirty-two-county republic. The Provisionals believed that Unionist intransigence might provoke the British government into pulling the plug altogether after the failure of Sunningdale. This was by no means inconceivable: the Irish foreign minister, Garret FitzGerald, was so apprehensive about Harold Wilson's intentions that he asked Henry Kissinger to lobby against British withdrawal.[39]

As talk of a truce intensified in late 1974, Ruairí Ó Brádaigh tried to reach out to unionists, presenting the Éire Nua programme, with its blueprint for a federal Ireland, as a guarantee of their rights: 'There would be a nine-county Ulster in which they would have 57 per cent of the population and a two-tier system of policing.'[40] He hoped that the gap between this vision and Vanguard's idea of an independent Ulster could be bridged once Britain declared its intention to pull out. Ó Brádaigh also suggested that withdrawal could take place over a period of time: 'No one is saying they should pull out this year or next year or anything like that.'[41]

Despite the truce, or perhaps because of it, 1975 proved to be one of the bloodiest years of the entire conflict. The loyalist groups worried about the prospect of a British 'sell-out', and stepped up their assassination campaign against Catholic civilians. In 1975, for the first time since the conflict began, loyalist paramilitaries were as lethal as their republican counterparts. Many of these killings were especially gruesome, such as those carried out by the Shankill Butchers, a gang of UVF members whose exploits left the Catholics of Belfast in a state of terror. The Provos responded in kind, bombing Protestant bars and shooting civilians at random, in what was unquestionably the most sectarian phase in the movement's history.[42]

Allegations of security-force collusion with loyalist paramilitaries were common coin for nationalists at the time.[43] Official reports published in recent years have shown that those suspicions were entirely justified. One such report found 'indisputable evidence' of widespread collusion in the 1970s that 'should have rung alarm bells all the way to the top of Government'.[44] Several RUC officers eventually stood trial for their role in a sectarian attack, with ballistic evidence linking the weapons they had used to the Glennane Gang, a loyalist militia responsible for more than a hundred deaths. Lord Lowry, Northern Ireland's most senior judge, handed down suspended sentences to all but one officer, who had already been convicted of murder. Lowry described the defendants from the bench as 'misguided but above all unfortunate men' who were motivated chiefly by 'the feeling that more than ordinary police work was needed and was justified to rid the land of the pestilence which has been in existence'.[45]

As their talks with the British government dragged on without agreement, the Provos began to fear that their negotiating partners were taking them for a ride.[46] In October 1975, Ruairí Ó Brádaigh maintained his conviction that British withdrawal was 'now inevitable', but warned that the IRA would 'renew the struggle' if he turned out to be wrong.[47] Without a deal they could present as some kind of victory, Ó Brádaigh and his comrades were in danger of being supplanted by a younger generation of militants, already straining at the leash. To compound their difficulties, they now faced competition from a rival movement that was ready to continue the war.

Up for Grabs

The alliance between Seamus Costello and Seán Garland soon broke up over the question of armed struggle. Costello wanted the Official IRA to resume its campaign, but found himself isolated in the leadership: both wings of the movement expelled him in rapid succession. A crushing majority of delegates voted down the last

attempt by Costello's supporters to have him reinstated at Official
Sinn Féin's party conference in December 1974.[48] In effect, once
Costello lost the battle for influence at the summit, the game was
up. Although the Officials had abandoned guerrilla warfare as a
tactic, the culture of their movement was still rigidly hierarchical,
with power concentrated in the hands of the OIRA's Army Council.
If Costello had won the argument at that level, it might have been
his opponents who were obliged to break away. In his absence, the
Officials quickly reverted to their old reformist strategy.

Costello launched his new vehicle, the Irish Republican Socialist
Party (IRSP), at the beginning of 1975, with an ideological platform
that distinguished it from both of the existing factions. The main
point of contention between Costello and the Officials was the right
approach to adopt towards the unionist population. According to
the IRSP leader, his former comrades believed there was 'no hope
of achieving national liberation until such time as the Protestant
and Catholic working class in the North are united' – a far-fetched
prospect, in Costello's view, since 'the British presence in Ireland is
the basic cause of the divisions'.[49]

That put him on the same ground as the Provisionals – as did
his commitment, aired more discreetly, to wage war on the British
Army. But Costello saw the Provos as an essentially conservative
force: 'Many of them would accept a theoretically independent
state, with no significant change being made in the social and political structures.'[50] He was also committed to building up the IRSP as
a legal party that would contest elections and take any seats it won,
unlike Provisional Sinn Féin.

The IRSP's platform attracted support from many OIRA
Volunteers in the North who had opposed the ceasefire. Ronnie
Bunting, one of Costello's leading supporters in Belfast, came from
a middle-class, Protestant background and stood out for his unique
personal trajectory: his father Ronald had been the main organizer
of the Burntollet ambush in 1969, but Bunting Jr graduated from
People's Democracy to join the Official IRA and became an active
combatant with a reputation as a skilled marksman. In Derry, the
majority of OIRA members lined up with Costello.[51] The Ranger

Best controversy in 1972 had left a legacy of bitterness among local activists, who accused Cathal Goulding of hanging them out to dry when they were under attack. There had also been a strong Trotskyist influence among the Derry Officials, and the pro-Soviet line that the movement's leadership had started to peddle helped smooth their passage towards Costello.[52]

It wasn't merely disgruntled Officials who found Costello's blueprint attractive. People's Democracy and another far-left group, the Socialist Workers' Movement, considered joining the new party. The IRSP's most important recruit from this milieu was the former civil rights MP, Bernadette Devlin – now generally known by her married name, McAliskey. She had lost her Mid-Ulster seat at the 1974 general election, but remained a high-profile figure whose involvement gave the new party some real political heft. McAliskey argued that Costello's movement was needed to fill a space left vacant by the established groups: 'The Provos are concentrating on getting rid of the British in a military campaign without any policy on the class war. And the Officials now have no policy on the national question.'[53] At the IRSP's first public meeting in Dublin, attended by 500 people, she described the party as 'an attempt to create a revolutionary socialist alternative to 800 years of failure'.[54]

McAliskey set out her rationale for joining Costello's movement in a series of articles and interviews. She disagreed with the reformist approach of the Officials – 'you cannot democratize an artificial state which is set up in the face of democracy' – and accused them of promoting a 'false unity' with working-class Protestants on economic issues, 'at the expense of asserting the true nature of the British role in Ireland'.[55] For McAliskey, the IRSP was important because it had 'discovered the problem of twentieth-century Republicanism – the relationship of the national struggle to the class question'. No revolutionary movement could be successful unless it combined the struggles for national independence and social emancipation: 'The place for those socialists who think they have a constructive answer is inside the party.'[56] The IRSP's first policy statement declared its readiness 'in principle' to contest Northern Ireland's Convention elections in 1975. McAliskey was sure to be the main candidate, and most observers expected her to win a seat for the party in Mid-Ulster.[57]

Having come to the IRSP from outside the republican tradition, McAliskey had no place in the leadership of its military wing, the Irish National Liberation Army (INLA). In other respects it was hard to distinguish between the two organizations. Costello became the INLA's first chief of staff, with men like Ronnie Bunting and Derry's Johnnie White at his side. He wanted to keep the INLA under wraps until it had carried out several attacks on the security forces, allowing the group to make its public debut in a blaze of glory.[58] But Costello's rhetoric and reputation gave his opponents every reason to think he would be making preparations for war. As McAliskey tactfully observed: 'Given the people who are within our organization, it would be ridiculous to suggest that we see the Socialist Republic being brought about by force of moral argument.'[59]

A briefing for the Northern Ireland Office (NIO) expressed alarm about the IRSP's potential to attract support with its blend of Marxism and nationalism – 'a combination greatly more in tune with international revolutionary movements than the monoplane dogma of either the Officials or the Provisionals'. Furthermore, the extended Provo truce had created a political vacuum that Costello might be able to fill: 'The Republican protest elements are at this moment in a period of disorientation where the goals have either been met or have drifted into the distance. This considerable corpus (which of course has never been numerically tested as a distinct electorate) is basically therefore up for grabs.'[60]

The fact that the Provisionals had now called a ceasefire sharpened the hostility of the Officials to Costello's new movement, and they were determined to prevent their former comrades from launching a fresh insurgency. Billy McMillen suggested that a programme of punishment beatings was the best way to keep a lid on the IRSP; he also ordered that anyone who tried to take OIRA weapons would be killed.[61]

As soon as the Officials launched their crackdown in Belfast, the violence began spiralling out of control. OIRA members drew first blood in February 1975 by shooting an IRSP supporter, Hugh Ferguson. At Ferguson's funeral, Costello accused the Officials of 'running away from the fight' but denied that the IRSP had a military wing.[62] He repeated that denial when his supporters hit back by killing an OIRA Volunteer, Sean Fox.[63] After the deaths of Ferguson and Fox, it was open season. On 1 March, IRSP members from Belfast travelled to Dublin without seeking Costello's approval and tried to kill Seán Garland.[64] Garland lived to tell the tale, despite being shot six times, cementing his reputation as the OIRA's hard man. The IRSP's Ronnie Bunting survived another assassination attempt the following week.[65]

Terror gripped Belfast's Catholic ghettoes as attempts at mediation proved fruitless and the feud ground on. The IRSP leadership did its best to avoid coming clean about the INLA's existence. After the killing of another supporter in April, an IRSP spokesman claimed that a hitherto unknown group calling itself the 'People's Liberation Army' had offered to protect its members.[66] This attempt at subterfuge fooled nobody. Meanwhile, the party's maiden conference decided not to contest the Convention poll that was due to be held in May 1975 and called for a boycott instead.[67] On 28 April, Costello's supporters took the vendetta to a new level by gunning down the OIRA leader Billy McMillen in West Belfast. Cathal Goulding gave the oration at McMillen's funeral, which proved to be the Official IRA's last great show of strength.

The IRSP issued a statement denying responsibility and pointing the finger at British intelligence, but that cut no ice with Goulding, who denounced McMillen's killers as 'enemies of the people, allies of imperialism as surely as if they wore the uniform of the British Army'.[68] A few days later, the Official IRA tried to kill Seamus Costello after a meeting in Waterford. The IRSP leader survived, and the clashes in Belfast gradually fizzled out thereafter; but the OIRA Army Council never retracted the capital sentence it had imposed on Costello after McMillen's death.[69]

In the meantime, Costello tried to pick up the pieces following the IRSP's disastrous introduction to the political stage. Bernadette McAliskey made no attempt to conceal her frustration at the erratic behaviour of the party's unacknowledged military wing. She now posed some searching questions about the organizational culture in which Costello had been immersed since his teens. McAliskey saw a basic contradiction between working-class politics, which required 'mass organization on an open basis', and the top-down, conspira- torial nature of republicanism, 'more alien to the factory workers of Belfast and Dublin than some would have us believe the philosophy of Marx and Lenin to be'.[70] With her allies on the IRSP's national executive, she pressed for the movement's armed section to be made subordinate to its political leadership.

Costello had every intention of building up the IRSP as a serious organization in its own right, but he wanted the INLA to retain separate structures of command. The dispute came to a head at the end of 1975 when McAliskey and her supporters – including the INLA's adjutant general, Johnnie White – resigned en masse from Costello's party. The IRSP accused the defectors of failing to rec- ognize 'the vital link between the national liberation struggle and the struggle for socialism in Ireland'.[71] Costello phrased the charge ambiguously to avoid making any direct reference to the INLA. Soon afterwards, a statement in the party press claimed credit for a string of gun and bomb attacks on 'enemy personnel and installa- tions' that had resulted in three deaths.[72] The group that was to be Costello's most enduring legacy had finally made its public debut.

And Then There Was One

Just as Costello was preparing to draw back the veil on the INLA, his former comrades faced a battle for survival. Believing that the split and Billy McMillen's death had left the Officials defenceless, the Provo leadership in Belfast decided it was time to finish them off for good. On the night of 29 October, OIRA members came under attack throughout the city.[73] Over the next fortnight there were more than 100 incidents as the movements traded blows. The Officials came off worse, with seven of the eleven deaths during the feud. But they survived the onslaught and managed to score a few hits of their own. The OIRA's victims included the chairman of the Falls Taxi Association, which had strong Provo connections. After his death, taxi drivers threatened to block the Falls Road, ramping up the pressure for a truce.[74]

The violence they had initiated in Belfast was extremely damaging for the Provos. A tightly knit community, already terrorized by the loyalist assassination campaign, now had to endure another fratricidal conflict that cut across ties of friendship and family. Journalists described a mood of 'near hysteria' in West Belfast during the clashes, with 'groups of youths no longer standing at corners, a curfew more effectively in operation than ever attempted by the British Army, [and] the familiar process of intimidated families on the move'.[75] The Northern Ireland secretary Merlyn Rees seized the opportunity to announce that he was scrapping special-category status for paramilitary prisoners, who would now be dealt with as common criminals.[76]

One motivation for the Provos in starting the feud had been to give their Volunteers an outlet during a prolonged truce that was clearly going nowhere. In January 1976, the Provisional IRA formally called time on the experiment and announced that it was going back to war. The announcement came weeks after the massacre of ten Protestant civilians by gunmen in Kingsmill, claimed by the 'South Armagh Republican Action Force', but generally assumed to be the work of the Provisionals.[77] For a movement that claimed to be strictly non-sectarian, Kingsmill represented a moral nadir. There could hardly have been a less auspicious moment to start the new Provo campaign.

For the Officials, the events of 1975 proved to be a watershed. Having already lost part of their membership to the IRSP, they now embarked on a political course that put paid to any ambitions of winning support in Northern Ireland. The first stage in this mutation was a shift in their attitude towards the Provos. There had been many bitter polemics since the split, and even violent confrontations that left both factions mourning lost comrades. Throughout it all, the Officials had continued to argue that Britain's ruling class was the main enemy, however foolish and misguided their rivals might be. In 1972, when the Provisionals accused OIRA members in Belfast of betraying their comrade Martin Meehan to the Army, the Officials responded with a furious denial, putting their 'respect and esteem' for Meehan's 'soldierly qualities, courage and dedication' on record.[78] After the 'pogrom' of 1975 – as the Officials immediately dubbed it – there would be no more tributes paid to the courage and dedication of leading Provos.

Tomás Mac Giolla insisted that a clear line now had to be drawn: 'No spurious arguments should be made about Provisional fascists and sectarian bigots being part of the anti-imperialist struggle when in fact they are part of the anti-republican and anti-working-class struggle.'[79] An intense loathing developed between the two movements that made any form of cooperation inconceivable. Another lethal feud erupted in 1977 to keep that hatred simmering. There could be little doubt now who the Officials considered their main enemy to be.

This made it easier for an intellectual faction within their movement to push for a drastic ideological turn. The driving force behind this shift was Eoghan Harris, a television producer at the Irish state broadcaster who had been a supporter of Cathal Goulding since the 1960s. Harris helped organize a specialized unit known as the Industrial Department, that functioned as an in-house think tank. Goulding had a high opinion of Harris and supported his projects, although Seán Garland took a more jaundiced view.[80]

The Industrial Department took up the ideas of a tiny Marxist–Leninist group called the British and Irish Communist Organization (BICO), whose principal ideologue, Brendan Clifford, had launched a ferocious assault on the tenets of Irish nationalism.[81] BICO's so-called Orange Marxism was so accommodating to the Unionist position that it earned the praise of Enoch Powell and exercised a strong influence on William Craig's Vanguard lieutenant, David Trimble.[82] The platform crafted by Harris helped attract several young intellectuals, including the historians Paul Bew and Henry Patterson, who dismissed the struggle against British rule as a chimera and a barrier to the development of class politics.[83]

Such ideas soon began to influence the movement's public stance.

While the Officials were still formally committed to the goal of a united Ireland, their policy documents now simply called for a restored local assembly, with a Bill of Rights but no compulsory power-sharing.[84] As Bew and Patterson acknowledged, many nationalists found it hard to distinguish this blueprint from the programme of the Ulster Unionist Party.[85] There was little chance of the Republican Clubs expanding or even preserving their base among working-class nationalists with such arguments, and the movement's support in the Catholic ghettoes began to wither away. South of the border, its prospects appeared to be much brighter, and that was where the Officials directed their energies. Official Sinn Féin became Sinn Féin the Workers' Party in 1977, then simply the Workers' Party five years later. In public, the Official IRA ceased to exist; in private, it soldiered on as an unacknowledged fund-raising division that could also protect members in the North from intimidation by the Provos.[86] The Workers' Party positioned itself as a hard-left scourge of the southern political establishment and began to reap the electoral benefits. By the early 1980s, it had three seats in the Dáil.

If Seamus Costello had stuck with the Officials, he would almost certainly have become one of their first TDs. However, when he stood for the IRSP at the 1977 general election he was the lowest-placed candidate, with half of his previous vote. Two years after its launch, the IRSP had little substance as a political force on either side of the Irish border. The feud with the Officials crippled Costello's new party before it had time to cohere. After Bernadette McAliskey's departure, it never had the chance to run a candidate of her stature in the North again.[87] The INLA, on the other hand, was a far more significant threat to British interests, but the indiscipline that had been apparent during the feud still dogged the group, and Costello had to spend much of his time trying to preserve its fragile unity.[88]

In October 1977, that time abruptly ran out. An OIRA hit man took revenge for Billy McMillen's death as Costello sat in his car on Dublin's North Strand. On hearing of his death, members of Wicklow County Council decided to adjourn the monthly meeting in a show of respect for their late colleague. One of the councillors, a Fine Gael TD, paid tribute to Costello as 'a person of exceptional ability who had more than left his mark on the various bodies, both local and national, with which he involved himself'.[89] There could be no arguing with that. As the movement founded by Costello lurched from one crisis to another over the following decade, his supporters became increasingly fixated on their lost leader, dreaming of what might have been.

Costello's main contribution to the IRSP had he lived would have been his commitment to build it up as a credible force alongside the INLA, even though he rejected McAliskey's call for political control over the military wing. The journalists Derek Dunne and Gene Kerrigan found that senior officers in the Irish police force 'sincerely regretted' Costello's loss, as they 'recognized that he was fundamentally political' and feared that without his leadership, the INLA would simply become 'a minor gun-happy outfit'.[90] That was precisely what happened in the 1980s. Brendan Hughes, one of the most senior Provos in Belfast, had considered switching to the IRSP's cage in Long Kesh before Gerry Adams talked him out of it.[91] Future defectors tended to be loose cannons that the larger group wanted rid of.

Soon after Costello's death, Ronnie Bunting took over as the INLA's chief of staff. A nervous, jittery man with much to be nervous about, Bunting was a particular hate figure for loyalist paramilitaries and the RUC because of his Protestant background. Under his leadership, the INLA carried out its most successful operation in March 1979 by assassinating the Conservative politician Airey Neave in the grounds of Westminster. Bunting was granted little time to savour the triumph: in October 1980, gunmen broke into the INLA leader's home in West Belfast and shot him dead. Bunting's widow Suzanne, who survived the attack, was adamant that his killers belonged to the SAS. There was a brief tussle over the funeral arrangements between Bunting's comrades and his distraught father, Ian Paisley's one-time associate, who insisted on a low-key family service. Eight members of the IRSP joined a handful of close relatives to see Bunting laid to rest in an Anglican cemetery that contained the graves of several United Irishmen.[92] In his absence, the INLA began a downwards spiral into chaos.

For all practical purposes, the Provisionals now had the field to themselves. The Officials were on a path towards complete marginalization, and there was no reason to fear that the IRSP and its military wing would displace them as the spearhead of resistance to British rule. Smaller groups might nibble around the edges of their base, but that was as far as the challenge went. However, the Provos had little time for self-satisfaction. Their capacity to fight on now depended on their willingness to borrow ideas from vanquished rivals. The left-republican project first devised by men like Cathal Goulding and Seamus Costello acquired a fresh lease of life as a new Provisional leadership sought its way out of a seemingly terminal crisis.

7

The Broad Front

'A growing Marxist feeling'

At Bodenstown in 1977, Jimmy Drumm delivered a speech on behalf of the Provisional leadership that curtly dismissed the hopes animating their campaign for the past six years: 'A successful war of liberation cannot be fought exclusively on the backs of the oppressed in the Six Counties, nor around the physical presence of the British Army. Hatred and resentment of the Army cannot sustain the war, and the isolation of socialist republicans around the armed struggle is dangerous.' Drumm insisted on the need for 'a positive tie-in with the mass of the Irish people who have little or no idea of the suffering in the North' if British rule was to be ended: 'The forging of strong links between the Republican movement and the workers of Ireland and radical trade unionists will create an irrepressible mass movement and will ensure mass support for the continuing armed struggle in the North.'[1]

The ideas expressed in Drumm's speech came from Gerry Adams and Danny Morrison, two of the central figures in a group of younger northern Provos poised to take control of the movement. Adams set out his stall from Long Kesh in a series of articles under the pen name 'Brownie', when the Provisionals were at their lowest ebb since the Troubles began.

The timing of the IRA's return to war in 1976 could not have been worse, as the nationalist population had no real stomach for the resumption of armed struggle, even in republican strongholds. This war fatigue found an opportunity to express itself soon after the Provos resumed their campaign. British soldiers in Belfast opened fire on a car driven by an IRA member called Danny Lennon, causing him to lose control of the vehicle. Lennon was killed, along with three young children who were hit by the car. A spontaneous backlash against paramilitary violence mushroomed into the Peace People movement, whose demonstrations attracted crowds of up to 10,000.

IRA supporters attacked the Peace People as stooges of the British, and they certainly received support from long-standing republican adversaries in the media and the Catholic Church. But as People's Democracy pointed out, the protests also attracted many working-class Catholics from what had been the movement's core constituency: 'For everyone who marched, there were more who couldn't stomach the hymn-singing, anti-IRA histrionics but who sympathized with the peace campaign. And many of them were the civil rights or anti-internment marchers of other days.'[2]

It would be extremely difficult for the Provos to sustain a war in the face of such attitudes. Adams urged republicans to draw the right lessons from the demonstrations of 1976: 'The peace campaign should remind us all that people are tired and that they desire peace. It is self-defeating, stupid and counter-productive to attack these people.'[3] The armed struggle would have to continue, he insisted, but in a way that was 'controlled and disciplined': 'Republicans must ensure that our cause and our methods remain within the bounds of our consciences.'[4]

Already tainted by feuds and sectarian killings, the IRA now came under intense pressure from the security forces after the breakdown of the truce. The RUC routinely took Provo suspects to its interrogation centre at Castlereagh and coerced them into signing confessions, which non-jury Diplock courts then accepted as sufficient grounds for conviction. Such methods eventually became a source of embarrassment for politicians in London, but in the short

term they were highly effective, delivering the benefits of internment with none of the political costs.[5]

The British authorities demolished the 'cages' at Long Kesh to
make way for a new prison, the Maze, whose inmates were to
receive the same treatment as those convicted of violent offences
in the rest of the UK. Laid out in H-shaped blocks and surrounded
by a dense security cordon, this ultra-modern jail was designed to
be escape-proof. To symbolize their loss of special-category status,
newly convicted prisoners no longer had the right to civilian clothing. The first of those prisoners, Kieran Nugent, arrived in the
H-Blocks in 1976 and refused to wear the uniform supplied. With
no other garb available, Nugent wrapped himself in a blanket to
keep warm. By the year's end, there were more than forty 'blanketmen' in the Maze following his example.

The Northern Ireland Office privately acknowledged that many
republican prisoners were 'not regarded as "criminal" by the communities from which they come', and warned that this might give
rise to problems down the line:

> Their organization and immediate friends and relatives are unlikely
> to become reconciled to society as long as there remains a substan-
> tial group whom they regard as 'prisoners of war'. Any untoward
> event taking place in prison may therefore provoke limited violence
> outside the prison. Conversely the prisoners themselves, enjoy-
> ing a measure of moral support from their own communities, are
> unlikely to settle down to serve their sentences quietly.[6]

But this was a challenge that the British government expected to
handle with comparative ease. Meanwhile, the security regime
pushed the RUC and the Ulster Defence Regiment into the front-
line of the struggle against the IRA. From London's perspective,
'Ulsterization' had two obvious benefits. By granting the local
police force a leading role, it drove home the message that republican violence was the product of a criminal conspiracy by terrorist
'godfathers' with no popular support. It also reduced the number of
British soldiers being killed or injured by IRA attacks.

Republicans were ill-equipped to mount a political challenge to Britain's new offensive. People's Democracy contrasted the mood of the Catholic ghettoes at the beginning of 1976 with the heyday of civil resistance: 'The bulk of the minority population are apathetic if not hostile. Let any organization, including Sinn Féin, call a demonstration now around some political demands and how many will turn up? Hardly any except their own members and a handful of dedicated activists.'[7]

Adams and his comrades understood this all too well, and Drumm's speech at Bodenstown was their attempt at a response. PD welcomed it as 'a major development in Provisional thinking, which opens the way for intense and fruitful discussion within the anti-imperialist movement'. They had observed with keen interest a 'complex and at times confused debate going on within the Provisionals', which now emerged into public view: 'A section of the movement, particularly in Belfast, has gradually but definitely moved away from militarism and from exclusive concentration on the Northern question.'[8]

A new leadership team took shape around Adams that included young ex-prisoners such as Danny Morrison and Jim Gibney, with the northern Provo newspaper *Republican News* as its platform. In December 1977, the Irish police captured an IRA 'staff report' drafted by Adams and his associates which elaborated on their plans: 'Sinn Féin should be radicalized (under Army direction) and should agitate about social and economic issues which attack the welfare of the people. SF should be directed to infiltrate other organizations to win support for, and sympathy to, the movement.'[9] At Bodenstown in 1978, Sinn Féin's Johnny Johnson took another step down the path opened up by Jimmy Drumm the previous year: 'We promise the economically deprived, the poor and the oppressed our wholehearted support. We are not in this to exchange one set of capitalist rulers for another.'[10] An observer from the British embassy noted a 'growing Marxist feeling' among the delegates at Sinn Féin's 1978 Ard Fheis – 'some of them even addressed each other as comrade!' – and a palpable desire to strengthen the movement's political interventions.[11]

At the beginning of 1979, the Dublin-based *An Phoblacht* and *Republican News* merged with Morrison as editor, symbolizing a shift in the movement's centre of gravity. Morrison recruited several contributors from the left-wing scene, including PD's John McGuffin and the cartoonist Brian Moore ('Cormac'), and turned the paper into a lively mouthpiece for the Provos with a highly effective distribution system that by-passed commercial newsagents.[12]

Later that year, it was the turn of Gerry Adams to deliver another left-republican homily at Wolfe Tone's graveside. He pledged to oppose 'all forms and all manifestations of imperialism and capitalism', and urged his audience to build 'an economic resistance movement, linking up Republicans with other sections of the working class'.[13]

For some Provisionals, this language was all too reminiscent of their hated rivals, the Officials. The role of a British Trotskyist called Phil Shimeld, who contributed articles to *Republican News* under the pen name 'Peter Dowling', particularly angered the old guard. Ruairí Ó Brádaigh and his allies compared Shimeld to Cathal Goulding's adviser Roy Johnston and noted where that experiment had led.[14] In a bid to pre-empt such criticism, an early edition of Morrison's new paper insisted that coverage of working-class struggles 'doesn't mean we are going "sticky"'.[15] (The Officials had become known as 'Stickies' or 'Sticks' in the early 70s, after selling adhesive Easter lilies to mark the 1916 Rising.)

But there was another strand of Irish Marxism that Adams and his comrades found much more attractive. Jim Gibney in particular paid close attention to the arguments made by People's Democracy about the limits of republican militarism and the need for class politics.[16] Michael Farrell was already a well-respected figure in republican circles, and his book *The Orange State* became a touchstone for opponents of British rule when it appeared in 1976. Based on extensive historical research, Farrell's work set out the case for British withdrawal with a polemical force that no republican pamphleteer could match. The Provos hailed it as a vindication of their cause: when a second edition came out in 1980, Sinn Féin's Richard McAuley described it as 'a book not to be missed'.[17]

Eamonn McCann had always been more sceptical of republican-ism than Farrell. However, when McCann published a new version of his book *War and an Irish Town* in 1980, he dedicated the text to republican prisoners and rounded it off with an emphatic declara-tion of solidarity: 'There is no such thing as an anti-imperialist who does not support the Provos and no such thing as a socialist who is not anti-imperialist.'[18] The transformation of the Provisionals had enthused McCann, and he quoted the speech delivered by Gerry Adams at Bodenstown approvingly, but added a note of caution about the new platform: 'Given the structure and traditions of the Republican movement it would be damnably difficult to put into effect. It would mean making a fundamental break from the poli-tics of the founding father – at whose graveside he was speaking.'[19] Danny Morrison's *An Phoblacht* gave the book a friendly review, describing it as a 'welcome and stimulating' contribution to the debate: 'McCann's criticism aims to be honest, comradely and con-structive, rather than smug or divisive.'[20]

The Long War

Another intervention from Eamonn McCann was much less welcome to the new Provo leadership. Towards the end of 1979, Gerry Adams drafted a new programme to replace Éire Nua that was Marxist in everything but name. The document called for private farms to be nationalized, however small the holding might be. Many rural republicans who made a vital contribution to the movement, allowing it to use their land for arms dumps, safe houses and training camps, were horrified by the idea of replacing family plots with 'custodial ownership'. Opponents of the new line seized the opportunity to push back. On the eve of a special conference in October 1979, McCann published a story in a Dublin tabloid based on information from a well-placed source, predicting a dramatic shift to the left. A furious backlash confronted Adams, who had no choice but to deny the reports.[21]

In an attempt to defuse the row, Adams gave an interview to the magazine *Hibernia* that *An Phoblacht* reprinted, seeking to reassure the movement's conservative supporters: 'I know of no-one in Sinn Féin who is a Marxist or who would be influenced by Marxism.'[22] The same edition of the paper carried statements from both wings of the movement denying that it had embraced Marxist ideology.

Several historians of republicanism have taken these statements as proof that the left turn initiated by Adams was a sham, or at most a weapon in his battle against the old guard.[23] But the political context in which they were made suggests a more complex picture. Adams was unquestionably bending the truth with his claim that Marxism had no influence in the movement. One of his main concerns was to guard against another 'Red Scare': 'In the past this sort of ploy has succeeded and many very good Irish radicals and organizations have been swamped by a combination of government, grassroots and Church attacks.'[24]

In another interview, Danny Morrison tried to sidestep Catholic anti-communism by drawing attention to the role of priests in Latin American guerrilla movements: 'There's no reason why the revolutionary aspects of Marxism should not be taken up by Catholics.' The Provisionals stressed the indigenous roots of their socialism – 'a radical native brand taken from Tone, Lalor, Connolly and Mellows' – as a way of deflecting conservative attacks.[25]

In several important respects, the Provos were right to deny the parallels with Cathal Goulding's movement drawn by their critics. When Goulding wanted to strengthen the IRA's political thinking in the 1960s, he recruited intellectuals such as Roy Johnston and Anthony Coughlan from outside its ranks and gave them responsibility for drawing up a new programme. After Johnston and Coughlan parted company with the Officials, a new intellectual cohort, clustered around Eoghan Harris and the Industrial Department, performed much the same role in subsequent years. In contrast, the new Provo leadership kept figures like Michael Farrell and Eamonn McCann at arm's length, drawing upon their work but never adopting their ideas wholesale. In time, they went on to produce an entire layer of capable, articulate politicians from within the ranks of the IRA.

Another crucial divergence lay in their attitude towards the unionist population. Goulding's supporters stressed the need to reach out
to working-class Protestants, but the new Provisional leadership
dismissed that out of hand and even saw their own movement's Éire
Nua programme as an unacceptable sop to loyalism. Journalist Ed
Moloney suggested that the northern Provos led by Adams were
'undeniably more sectarian than their southern counterparts', and
gave the following terse summary of their outlook: 'The Northern
state is irreformable and so are most northern Protestants.'[26] One
interview with a Provisional spokesman icily referred to 'an element
who call themselves Loyalists', whose 'traditional role' had been to
help perpetuate British rule: 'These people play the role of a fifth
column in Ireland. As such, they will be eliminated.'[27]

A debate over armed struggle showed that the Provos were determined to keep their own counsel. People's Democracy turned away
from support for militarism after a split in the group's ranks at
the beginning of 1976: 'Violent actions are largely irrelevant in the
absence of a mass movement and detract from the building of such
a movement. There was a tendency in our organization and in the
left generally to avoid such criticism but elitist action without a
mass movement is an act of despair and shows contempt for the
masses.'[28] For PD, it was essential to resurrect the tactics of the early
70s if the setbacks of recent times were to be reversed. *Republican
News* dismissed this argument as the brainchild of 'a whole mish-
mash of left-wing groups and tired radical intellectuals, many of
whom were mentally defeated by the Brits five or more years ago'.
It rejected the idea that armed struggle had displaced mass action:
'In fact the development of guerrilla warfare with popular support
was the development of the struggle onto a higher level which a
group like PD failed to match up to.' Another article referred scornfully to 'attacks from the revolutionary left on the war strategy of
the oppressed Irish people'.[29] If civil resistance was going to return
to the political stage, it would have to find room alongside the
IRA campaign.

In fact, the new leadership bitterly reproached Ó Brádaigh's
old guard for alleged softness on the question of armed struggle.

They denounced the 1975 truce as a fiasco and rejected the idea of further talks with the British government unless there was an explicit commitment to withdrawal.[30] In tandem with their public embrace of class struggle and 'economic resistance', Adams and his comrades steered through a reorganization of the IRA along cellular lines that was intended to blunt London's security offensive.[31] Adams became the IRA's chief of staff after his release from prison and won the support of several important figures for the project, including Martin McGuinness, Ivor Bell and Brian Keenan.[32]

The new-model IRA was much smaller than its predecessor. One estimate put the movement's core strength at 300 or so, with another 3,000 'active sympathizers' providing assistance. By comparison, in 1972 there had been 300 Volunteers in Belfast's First Battalion alone.[33] The Provos told their supporters to prepare for a 'long war' that might last for ten, fifteen or even twenty years. As an Army Council spokesman told Ed Moloney, the IRA's objective was now to 'wear down the will' of its opponents: 'Either the British government itself comes to the conclusion that it must leave, or that conclusion will be forced on them by British public opinion.'[34]

The La Mon Hotel bombing in February 1978 threw the conflict between armed struggle and political action into sharp relief. IRA members had been planting incendiary devices as part of their bombing campaign against commercial targets. This time, the warning they supplied was totally inadequate and a fireball swept through the building, burning twelve civilians alive. The RUC distributed horrifying photographs of the corpses as part of a media campaign against the IRA.

Facing a popular backlash, republicans had little prospect of strengthening their base. Adams later said that he could feel 'two years of work going down the drain' on the night of the bombing.[35] But the Provos strongly defended the use of such methods: 'The political effects of the bombing campaign have been productive. It has created insecurity and confusion among Unionists and helped break up the loyalist monolith, brought down Stormont, made and makes the Six Counties internally ungovernable, and has made government under British direct rule difficult and often impossible.'[36]

Later that year, the ministry of defence prepared a confidential assessment of the IRA's strengths, 'Future Terrorist Trends'. To its great embarrassment, the Provos managed to obtain a copy, and it supplied them with a welcome propaganda boost. The document paid reluctant tribute to the IRA's recruitment policy: 'Our evidence of the calibre of rank-and-file terrorists does not support the view that they are merely mindless hooligans drawn from the unemployed and unemployable. PIRA now trains and uses its members with some care.' The IRA was now farther removed from the communities in which it operated, but this need not prove fatal to its campaign: 'There is seldom much support even for traditional protest marches. But by reorganizing on cellular lines PIRA has become less dependent on public support than in the past.'[37]

In August 1979, the Provos supplied lethal confirmation of their enduring strength when a meticulously planned bomb attack killed eighteen British soldiers at Warrenpoint on the same day an IRA unit assassinated Lord Mountbatten during a holiday in Sligo. As Margaret Thatcher's new government ordered a review of security policy to determine what had gone wrong, the IRA was in bullish form. Its leaders saw no reason to contemplate another ceasefire until they were sure that Britain was getting out for good.

In April 1980, 'Brownie' returned to a familiar theme in the pages of *An Phoblacht*: 'A British withdrawal can be secured more quickly and in more favourable conditions if it is achieved not only because of the IRA's military thrust but also because resistance to British rule has been channelled into an alternative political movement.'[38] For all the time spent on Sinn Féin's revamped programme, the party was still a pale shadow of the IRA, with no real political weight and no chance of putting its radical policies into effect. However, the movement now stood on the brink of a dramatic breakthrough that would transform the balance of forces in Northern Ireland.

The issue that supplied this opening had been staring them in the face all along. When republican inmates in the H-Blocks began refusing to wear prison uniform, they set in motion a prolonged and hard-fought struggle that culminated in the death of ten hunger strikers during the summer of 1981. That struggle revived the fortunes of the republican movement and provoked the greatest crisis for British rule in Northern Ireland since the fall of Stormont nine years earlier. By then, Jimmy Drumm's call for mass resistance at Bodenstown in 1977 had been decisively answered. But we cannot draw a straight line between the new thinking of the Adams leadership and the dramatic events of the period that followed. At several crucial points, the Provos had to be coaxed reluctantly along the road that led them to their ultimate destination.

Strength in Unity

Soon after Drumm's speech at Bodenstown, Jim Gibney composed a letter from Crumlin Road jail, where he was being held on remand. Gibney saw the prison protest as a golden opportunity for 'rallying the people away from their inertia and apathy', but complained that the prisoners were not receiving enough support from the movement outside: 'Whilst not singling out any group in particular, I believe that unity on this issue is essential.'[39] Tact may have prevented Gibney from 'singling out' his own comrades for criticism, but the Provos had certainly shown little interest in mobilizing support for the prisoners, leaving the burden of such work to the Relatives Action Committees (RACs). According to People's Democracy, the RACs were 'unable to mobilize much more than the relatives of political prisoners and the hard-core activists of Sinn Féin and the Marxist groups'.[40] That weakness prompted Bernadette McAliskey and her Tyrone associates to organize an 'Anti-Repression Conference' in Coalisland at the beginning of 1978, in hope of expanding the campaign.

The former civil rights MP gave a sober assessment of where things stood almost a decade after NICRA's first march, reminding her audience that they represented a minority of the nationalist population.[41] People's Democracy called for a broad campaign in support of the prisoners that would not be restricted to supporters of the IRA, but Sinn Féin members greeted the proposal with suspicion.[42] The IRSP, which had its own prisoners involved in the protest, was more sympathetic, having been schooled in the idea of a 'broad front' by Seamus Costello before his death. Gerry Adams later admitted that the conference became a 'lost opportunity to build unity' because his own movement was still 'temperamentally and organizationally disinclined' to cooperate with other groups.[43] There was no hint of self-criticism from the Provos at the time. *Republican News* hailed the conference as a 'notable success', but warned against 'hasty thoughts of a "New Mass Resistance" comparable to that of the civil rights movement ten years ago. The clock cannot simply be turned back like that, much as People's Democracy and Bernadette McAliskey might wish it to be.'[44]

The work of building a campaign in support of the prisoners continued nonetheless. In August 1978, the RACs organized a march from Coalisland to Dungannon on the anniversary of NICRA's demonstration along the same route, laying claim to the civil rights heritage. Estimates of the turnout ranged from 10,000 to 25,000: a marked improvement on the 1968 march, which attracted a little over 2,000 people. Several veterans of the civil rights movement spoke at the rally, including Bernadette McAliskey, Eamonn McCann and Michael Farrell.[45] *Republican News* insisted that the protest was not just an expression of solidarity with the prisoners: 'It also confirms the continued massive support for the armed struggle being waged by the revolutionary Irish Republican Army.'[46] After the success of the first march, a coalition of left-wing groups called another demonstration, this time following the same path from Belfast to Derry that People's Democracy had traced a decade earlier. But Sinn Féin boycotted the event and condemned its organizers for registering the route with the RUC.[47]

Another row erupted in June 1979, when Bernadette McAliskey announced that she was contesting Northern Ireland's first European election on a platform supporting the prisoners. The Provos vehemently opposed her campaign: Gerry Adams warned that it would 'only confuse the nationalist people', and Martin McGuinness even heckled McAliskey with the aid of a megaphone as she canvassed in the Bogside.[48] On the eve of polling day, *An Phoblacht* railed against 'mosquito groups such as People's Democracy' who had rallied to McAliskey's banner: 'Perhaps they have opportunistically buried their principles in their eagerness to promote a candidate – Bernadette McAliskey – who they believe they can manipulate to give themselves a public voice independent of – and opposed to – the Republican Movement.'[49] The IRSP also called for a boycott of the poll, a measure of the distance travelled by Costello's party since 1975, when McAliskey had looked set to spearhead its electoral challenge in the North.

McAliskey's eventual score, 6 per cent, was respectable, although the SDLP candidate John Hume polled four times as many votes. PD saw the election as the start of a challenge to the SDLP's political hegemony among nationalists. Hume's margin of victory showed there was still a long way to go after 'years of anti-imperialist fragmentation, mistaken reliance on an armed campaign, and irresponsible sectarian behaviour'.[50] *An Phoblacht* was pleased to report that McAliskey had received fewer votes than her supporters were hoping for, thanks to a 'vigorous Sinn Féin boycott campaign'.[51] The paper accused PD of 'crossing the anti-EEC picket line' with its support for McAliskey – 'a mischievous act, and one which casts doubt on PD's sincerity when they call for unity among anti-imperialists'.[52]

However, after three years of foot-dragging, the Provos were about to endorse the proposal for a united front in support of the prisoners. Pressure from inside the H-Blocks may have been decisive. The IRA leadership wanted to dissuade the blanketmen from launching a hunger strike, but had to offer them some tangible signs of progress if that desperate gamble was to be avoided.[53] In October 1979, *An Phoblacht* passed on the movement's new line: 'Conditions placed by the Republican Movement in the past, for political-status campaigners to also support the armed struggle, no longer apply.'[54]

At a 'Smash H-Block' conference held in West Belfast that month, delegates elected a sixteen-person committee to organize a campaign of protest in support of the 'five demands' (civilian clothing, no prison work, free association with other prisoners, the right to organize leisure and educational facilities, and full remission of sentences). The committee naturally had a strong Provisional element, but also included representatives of People's Democracy and the IRSP.[55]

Over the next year, the National H-Block Committee channelled all its energies into publicity work, petitioning trade unions for support and organizing tours in the United States for its spokesmen. The committee's leading figures exposed themselves to real danger: in June 1980, loyalist paramilitaries killed two prominent activists, John Turnley of the Irish Independence Party and the IRSP's Miriam Daly. However, their efforts to rally public support proved unavailing. With no sign of a shift in British policy, Brendan Hughes led a group of seven IRA and INLA prisoners onto a fast that began in October 1980.[56]

The first protest in solidarity with the hunger strikers attracted 17,000 marchers onto the streets of Belfast: the kind of mobilization that had not been seen since the heyday of civil resistance in the early 1970s. In a report for the current affairs magazine *Magill*, Gerry Foley described the sight of Bernadette McAliskey overcome with emotion as she watched the crowds pass by: 'It was as if the civil rights movement that she knew eleven years ago had resumed its march.'[57] McAliskey herself, the most high-profile figure associated with the campaign, was lucky to survive an assassination attempt in January 1981 when a UDA hit squad riddled her with bullets. The attack was a perverse tribute to the central role McAliskey played in mobilizing support for the prisoners.

The first hunger strike ended in December 1980 without a clear agreement to address the grievances of the prisoners, exposing two tactical errors made by the prison leadership: all of the men had begun to refuse food simultaneously, and Hughes kept responsibility for decision-making even though he was taking part in the strike. One of the prisoners, Seán McKenna, proved to be physically weaker than his comrades and slipped into a coma. An offer of some kind appeared to be on the table, and Hughes decided to call off the protest rather than allow McKenna to die. There was still a window of opportunity at the beginning of 1981 when it might have been possible to resolve the stand-off in a way that allowed both sides to save face. However, the prisoners became convinced that the administration was bent on humiliating them and broke off negotiations.[58] They began preparing for a second hunger strike. This time, the prisoners would join the fast one by one, maximizing the impact of their sacrifice.

On the first day of March, Bobby Sands stood down as the IRA's commander in the Maze and began refusing food. Sands, soon to become the most iconic Provisional martyr of them all, had joined the IRA as a teenager in the early 70s. Convicted for possession of arms, he served time in the celebrated Cage 11 at Long Kesh, where Gerry Adams had begun to establish himself as one of the movement's leading strategists. After his release, Sands resumed his IRA career and before long was back in prison on another weapons charge, still in his early twenties.

Such experiences were typical of the blanketmen who now pitted themselves in a fight to the finish against the government of Margaret Thatcher. Thatcher's hostility to the republican cause had acquired a sharp personal edge when the INLA killed her friend Airey Neave two years earlier. It would require an unprecedented popular mobilization in support of the five demands to break her government's will to resist.

In the first week of the strike, an opportunity arose when the Nationalist MP Frank Maguire died suddenly, leaving his Fermanagh–South Tyrone seat vacant. Bernadette McAliskey was still recovering from the wounds inflicted by loyalist paramilitaries in January. She declared her willingness to run as a candidate in support of the prisoners, but promised to stand aside if one of the hunger strikers came forward in her place: 'I would work the shirt off my back for that prisoner and the other prisoners he is representing.'[59] On 9 April, the voters of Fermanagh–South Tyrone had a straight choice between Bobby Sands and the Unionist candidate Harry West. By a tight margin, they elected Sands to Westminster.

The Northern Ireland Office had been rather sanguine about the protests of the previous year, suggesting that popular indifference to their cause 'must have contributed to a sense of futility among the strikers'.[60] Shortly before the vote in Fermanagh–South Tyrone, civil servants reported that public interest in the strike 'still seems to be at a satisfyingly low level'.[61] The by-election put paid to that. It gave the Provos a tremendous political boost and shone a harsh, unflattering light upon the British government's record in Ireland.

Many supporters of the campaign assumed that Thatcher would now have to cut a deal with the prisoners. But she remained intransigent and Sands passed away in the prison hospital on 5 May. News of his death provoked violent clashes between young nationalists and the RUC throughout Northern Ireland. A newspaper report described the funeral on 7 May as 'the biggest demonstration of republican sympathy since the protest rally immediately after Bloody Sunday'.[62] Most alarmingly for London, demonstrations of support for the hunger strikers also took place in cities around the world. Dockworkers in the US refused to unload British ships for twenty-four hours, and the Portuguese parliament held a minute's silence in honour of Sands.[63]

The IRSP hailed the Fermanagh–South Tyrone by-election as 'a victory for the united front approach – by means of which members of different political organizations, and of none, can unite around the beliefs that they hold in common'.[64] The same could be said for the campaign as a whole. If the IRA leadership had insisted on making support for armed struggle into a precondition, its appeal would have been greatly reduced, and the hunger strikers might have gone to their graves without leaving any mark on Irish history. According to the RUC, there were at least 1,200 protests in Northern Ireland during the second hunger strike, attended by over 350,000 people. F. Stuart Ross, who has written the most comprehensive account of this upsurge, suggests that the mobilization of 1980–81 'dwarfed that of 1968 and 1969'.[65] Those who had put the idea of a united front campaign on the agenda in the first place – People's Democracy, Bernadette McAliskey, the IRSP – played a crucial role in making that happen.

Ten Men Dead

The far-left fringe, often dismissed by the Provos as irrelevant minnows, made another key intervention during the hunger strike. Local elections were scheduled for May 1981, and the British government resisted pressure to cancel the poll, fearing it would be seen as a victory for the Provos.[66] Sinn Féin had already decided to boycott the election, so People's Democracy and the IRSP stepped in to fill the vacuum and won two seats each in Belfast. For PD, it was especially important to challenge the West Belfast MP Gerry Fitt, who had urged Thatcher not to make any concessions to the prisoners: 'We cannot ignore quislings like Fitt nor can we render them irrelevant simply by mass mobilizations. They must be fought and defeated on their home ground.'[67] PD targeted Fitt and Paddy Devlin, another staunch opponent of the prisoners, knocking Fitt off the council altogether, while Devlin was lucky to survive with a much reduced vote. *An Phoblacht* took careful note of the 'remarkable' victories achieved by these shoestring campaigns: 'Had Sinn Féin or republican prisoners entered the field then the SDLP would have taken a sound enough knocking to have made nationalist collaboration a diminishing trade.'[68]

The Provos were steadily inching towards engagement with electoral politics, but they were still in no mind to question the armed struggle, and insisted that any campaign in support of the prisoners would require 'two sharply differing, but mutually reinforcing aspects: one peaceful, the other involving physical force'. Mass demonstrations, industrial action and lobbying of Nationalist politicians should be combined with 'popular street riots, the erection of barricades against the British forces, and other violent acts of civil disobedience building towards the establishment of no-go areas in the nationalist ghettoes; plus, of course, the armed action of IRA Volunteers.'[69] On the political front, their main goal was to force what republicans called 'the three cornerstones of the Irish establishment' – the Catholic bishops, the SDLP and the Dublin government – to come out in support of the prisoners.[70]

Thatcher's abrasive style made life a great deal harder for those who had been holding the line against the Provos since the conflict began. As the NIO's David Blatherwick observed at the beginning of June, the prime minister's speech on 28 May went down 'like a lead balloon'. The Catholic hierarchy 'ostentatiously avoided' Thatcher during her visit to Northern Ireland, on a tour which only managed 'further to alienate Catholics, and to cause even some moderate Protestants to wonder what we are at'. The prospects for containing nationalist anger grew dimmer by the day: 'Unless the hunger strike ends soon, probably before the next hunger strikers die and certainly before the beginning of the marching season, the situation will begin to deteriorate rapidly.'[71] When John Hume met with Humphrey Atkins, the secretary of state for Northern Ireland, he bitterly reproached Thatcher's government for 'treating the SDLP with contempt'. Hume feared that Sinn Féin would make an electoral breakthrough on the back of the protests and urged Atkins to negotiate with the prisoners.[72]

In his assessment of the strike, the British ambassador to Dublin, Leonard Figg, described it as 'one of the most difficult periods in Anglo-Irish relations for many years'.[73] The embassy had to deal with two different governments during the crisis. Fianna Fáil's Charles Haughey was in charge when Sands began his fast: Haughey privately assured Figg that he would do his best to help, but urged the British government to resolve the dispute as soon as possible by 'seeming to make concessions without actually doing so'.[74]

Garret FitzGerald of Fine Gael then became Taoiseach after a general election on 11 June. The poll gave the National H-Block/ Armagh Committee the chance to run a slate of prison candidates, winning two seats and over 40,000 votes. A stunning achievement for such a hastily improvised campaign, the result came as an unpleasant shock to FitzGerald and reinforced his desire to end the crisis. According to Figg, this was the point when tensions reached their peak. FitzGerald's overriding concern was the threat to domestic stability: 'The Irish Government's pressure on us to end the strike grew in proportion to their fears that they might not be able to control events and that the institutions of the state might collapse.'[75] That was precisely the dilemma with which the Provos had wanted to confront FitzGerald and his colleagues.

There was always a fundamental contradiction embedded in the H-Block campaign. Its activists wanted to end the phenomenon of 'spectator politics' for good, yet their campaign ultimately relied upon the mental fortitude and physical endurance of a tiny group of men in Long Kesh, whose willingness to risk death made it possible to organize the biggest protests Northern Ireland had seen since the early 70s. A self-sacrificing elite created the necessary conditions for the revival of mass action, before the collapse of their fast in September 1981 precipitated its decline. On 20 August the INLA's Mickey Devine became the tenth and last hunger striker to die, just as Sinn Féin's Owen Carron won the by-election triggered by the death of Bobby Sands.

'Red Mickey' had followed a winding path to Long Kesh, joining the first civil rights marches as a teenager in Derry and canvassing for Eamonn McCann in the Stormont election of 1969, before enlisting in the Official IRA with the rest of his young Labour comrades. He lined up with Seamus Costello when he launched the IRSP in 1975, along with the great majority of Derry Officials.[76] The IRSP put on a display of strength at Devine's funeral, the last real opportunity it would have to do so. The party's chairwoman Naomi Brennan described her martyred comrade as 'a revolutionary, a soldier, but above all a socialist', who 'realized that to have national freedom, we must have socialism, and that, also, to have any chance of socialism, we must have national freedom'. Brennan stressed the importance of united action in support of the prisoners: 'We have learnt by the mistakes of our revolutionary predecessors, and our campaign has been built on unity of all those who support the five demands. Such unity must not be taken lightly.'[77]

Behind the scenes, the picture was much less edifying. There had been a dispute on the National H-Block/Armagh Committee over the recent by-election, as the IRSP wanted Bernadette McAliskey to go forward and take her seat at Westminster if elected. The Provisionals had no desire to give an unpredictable maverick such an important platform and insisted on running their own man instead.[78] McAliskey's remarkable talents as an agitator had been a huge asset for the campaign, but the time was fast approaching for the Provos to leave their allies behind. Reporting on Owen Carron's victory, *An Phoblacht* announced that Sinn Féin would now be 'stepping firmly into the electoral arena, taking on the SDLP (already badly shaken by the events of recent months), and establishing its undisputed leadership of the nationalist people'. The paper told supporters to prepare for a war on two fronts: 'This new confidence within the Republican Movement, that now is the time – as never before – for its militant politics, is fully complemented by the IRA's continued ability to take on the military might of the British presence.'[79] The SDLP's Seamus Mallon lashed out at Thatcher after the result, suggesting that her government had 'almost destroyed the democratic process in Northern Ireland'.[80]

On 28 August, Carron held a meeting with Michael Alison, a junior minister at the Northern Ireland Office, to discuss the prisoners' fate. The minutes recorded a 'calm and friendly' discussion, at the end of which Alison 'expressed the hope that a situation would arise when Mr Carron felt that he could attend the House of Commons'.[81] But there was no sign of agreement. Fearing that the stand-off would continue indefinitely, the prison chaplain Denis Faul began urging family members to order medical assistance for their sons when they lost consciousness. This external intervention proved decisive in breaking the impasse. Over the weeks that followed, the hunger strike gradually collapsed, and Mickey Devine turned out to be the last fatality in Long Kesh.

The campaign's inability to push the 'three cornerstones' of Irish nationalism into supporting the prisoners was a crucial factor behind its defeat. The threat to stability feared by Garret FitzGerald never really materialized in the South. The largest disturbances came in July, when police officers blocked the route of a march in Dublin to prevent it from reaching the British embassy. A full-scale riot broke out, with bricks and bottles thrown at the police, who dispersed the protesters with a baton charge. Leonard Figg suggested that the clashes in Ballsbridge were 'clearly a turning point in popular support for the campaign'.[82] However, the mental gulf between northern nationalists and the southern population, far more evident in 1981 than it had been a decade earlier, was a much wider phenomenon than that, and proved to be an insuperable barrier for the movement.

Thatcher's government paid a heavy price for the victory it had secured. The IRA and INLA recruited a new generation of militants in the wake of the crisis, preserving their capacity to wage war for another decade. In his overview of the hunger strike for *An Phoblacht*, Peter Dowling insisted that British policy had given the IRA its greatest boost since internment, 'organizationally in terms of recruits, funds, "safe houses" and an expanded support base, and politically in terms of credibility and support at home and abroad'. Dowling picked out Sinn Féin's failure to run candidates in the local elections as the one true blunder of the campaign.[83]

The party leadership was now determined to make up for that omission at the earliest opportunity. As the hunger strike spluttered to a halt, a spokesman for the IRA tried to calm fears that the movement was going down the same road as the Officials: 'What was wrong with the "Sticks" was not just that they contested elections but that they had a totally incorrect analysis of the nature of British imperialism. They believed that the six-county state could be "democratized" from within.' There was no question of imitating Goulding's movement on the question that really mattered: 'The military struggle will go on with all the energy at our disposal.'[84]

Sinn Féin was ready to take advantage of a shift in nationalist opinion that David Blatherwick of the NIO gloomily described as 'a radicalization of politics in the urban minority': 'The young in particular are disillusioned with traditional politics and tend to regard conventional politicians as offering wrong answers to irrelevant questions.'[85] The Provos wanted to clear the decks for an electoral strategy and saw nothing to be gained by preserving an alliance with smaller groups that had their own ideas about the way ahead.

A poorly attended conference in October 1982 formally wound down the National H-Block/Armagh Committee. As PD observed, the decision simply ratified what was already happening on the ground: 'The underlying reality that faced these delegates was the collapse of the H-Block/Armagh campaign throughout the 32 Counties.'[86] The end of the prison protest had deprived the movement of its central focus, and it would be very difficult to find another issue with the same broad appeal. In any case, the Provos had no interest in keeping the alliance going, and without their support, there could be no united front of any value. It was the end of the road, and everyone at the conference knew it.

8

War by Other Means

A New Front

Sinn Féin's 1981 conference gave the leadership approval to contest every subsequent election, north and south. The first opportunity to test their dual strategy came in October 1982, just as the broad front against 'criminalization' was put out to pasture. Thatcher's Northern Ireland secretary, Jim Prior, had scheduled elections for a local assembly as part of a political initiative that he called 'rolling devolution'. Many nationalists feared that the British government was trying to restore Stormont by the back door, and the SDLP pledged to boycott Prior's assembly after the poll. This ill-fated scheme gave the newly energized Sinn Féin an ideal platform: the party won 10 per cent of the vote and five of its candidates were successful, including Gerry Adams, Danny Morrison and Martin McGuinness. The results were a sensational blow to British policy and gave Sinn Féin real substance as a political force.

In its analysis of the election, the Northern Ireland Office admitted that 'the existence of so considerable a Republican protest vote is disturbing'. Sinn Féin had absorbed the base of groups like People's Democracy and the Irish Independence Party, but also 'brought out a new element of hard-line nationalists who have previously boycotted elections' and 'maximized their support among young voters frustrated by economic and social conditions and angered by the constant harassment, as they see it, of the security forces'.[1] Government officials tried to find a silver lining in the party's success – 'involvement in politics may occupy people who might otherwise be busy with violence and could lead to divisions in the PIRA/Sinn Féin leadership' – but concluded that such divisions were unlikely to materialize. There was no precedent for a party of this kind performing so well in the United Kingdom: 'Open support for violence distinguishes Sinn Féin from all but the most extreme political groups.'[2] The Provos always rejected the claim that 'open support for violence' set them apart from the other political parties in the UK. But they would have been delighted to accept the characterization of Sinn Féin as a force like no other. With the sole exception of the *abertzale* movement in the Basque Country, no party with explicit ties to an armed insurgency has ever achieved such a degree of implantation in a liberal-democratic state.

For a time, it looked as if the Provisionals might sweep everything before them. The SDLP was their primary electoral target and seemed to be there for the taking. John Hume's party had never fully transcended its origins as the vehicle for a disparate group of politicians with their own constituency teams but no real activist base. In a preview of the 1983 Westminster election, Michael Farrell set out the factors that distinguished the two parties in Belfast and Derry. Sinn Féin's activists were 'young, unemployed, ex-prisoners' who 'live in the working-class ghettoes' and 'speak the people's language', in contrast to their nationalist rivals: 'The SDLP candidates are all middle-class. Three of the four candidates in Belfast are doctors.'[3] In private, the NIO's civil servants made similar observations: Sinn Féin was simply 'more astute and enthusiastic' than the SDLP in its approach to community politics, making its adversary look 'middle-class, middle-aged and out of touch'.[4] Farrell described the tireless constituency work of Sinn Féin advice centres, which far surpassed anything the SDLP could manage: 'Instead of waiting for complaints to come in, they have gone round the doors with a checklist of possible repairs or benefits – like beds, blankets or rent rebates – to which the people might be entitled.'[5]

There may have been a certain incongruity in the IRA's political wing making such carefully itemized claims upon the British state, but the results were plain for all to see on polling day in June 1983. Sinn Féin surpassed expectations, winning over 100,000 votes: one-third higher than its total the previous year. Most importantly, the party's share of the nationalist vote had increased from 35 to 43 per cent. Gerry Adams beat off competition from the SDLP's Joe Hendron and the incumbent Gerry Fitt to win in West Belfast, while Danny Morrison came within a hundred votes of victory in the Mid-Ulster constituency. Owen Carron lost his seat in Fermanagh–South Tyrone – the SDLP ran a candidate this time, dividing the nationalist vote – but overall, the result was a triumph for Sinn Féin, and its leaders were in exultant form.

When Adams sat down with Michael Farrell to discuss Sinn Féin's prospects after the election, the world seemed bright and full of promise. He was careful to insist that the IRA had no need for electoral validation, and rejected the idea that Sinn Féin's recent successes undermined the case for armed struggle against British rule: 'A movement that wants them out will either have to use force or the threat of force.'[6] However, there was no question that recent events had dramatically boosted republican self-confidence. Two IRA spokesmen also spoke to Farrell and explained that their perspective of a 'long war' lasting twenty years or more was now open to revision: 'If the Republican movement can capitalize on all the social discontent in the 26 Counties and continue the electoral successes it could be a lot shorter.'[7]

In November 1983, Adams formalized his control over the movement by replacing Ruairí Ó Brádaigh as Sinn Féin president at the party's Ard Fheis. Ó Brádaigh kept the private rancour of his tussle with the Adams faction under wraps, although he couldn't resist a parting shot across the bows, noting that his tenure as president had not witnessed any splits: 'Long may it remain so, as it will, provided we stick to basic principles.'[8]

Sinn Féin now had two clear objectives: to overtake the SDLP as the main voice of nationalist opinion in the North, and to carve out a political foothold in the South. Adams conceded that sympathy for northern nationalists would not be enough to win seats in the Dáil: 'You can't get support in Ballymun because of doors being kicked in by the Brits in Ballymurphy.' His party needed to develop a platform that could appeal to those angered by corruption and 'Thatcherite monetarist policies'. According to Adams, republicans also had to recognize that the majority of people in the South considered its institutions to be legitimate, whatever they might think themselves about the 'bastard state' that arose from the Treaty. His defence of Sinn Féin's abstentionist policy was distinctly underwhelming: 'While that remains the position I will support it.'[9] The rise of Sinn Féin deeply troubled Garret FitzGerald's government, which feared contagion across the border. FitzGerald responded by convening the New Ireland Forum, a gathering of constitutional nationalists intended to shore up the SDLP against its republican challenger.

There was another strand to the new Provo strategy that had the potential to carry its influence right into the heart of British politics. During the 1970s, organized support for British withdrawal had largely been confined to the extra-parliamentary left. The growth of Labour's Bennite current now held out the promise of a much more effective challenge to the bipartisan consensus on Northern Ireland. Adams told Michael Farrell that Sinn Féin had been trying to develop contacts with prominent Labour politicians such as Ken Livingstone, who was now in charge of the Greater London Council (GLC), Europe's biggest municipal authority.[10]

Livingstone himself saw a clear affinity between the two movements: 'If I had been born in West Belfast, I would have ended up in Sinn Féin.'[11] In his capacity as GLC chief, Livingstone invited Adams and Danny Morrison to visit London after Sinn Féin's triumph in the 1982 Assembly elections. The invitation provoked tabloid fury, and Margaret Thatcher's government imposed an exclusion order on the two men, preventing them from setting foot on British soil. Livingstone responded by travelling to Belfast as a guest of Sinn Féin. He argued strongly for Labour to commit itself to pulling out of Northern Ireland at the earliest possible date: 'We have to go into an election pledged to withdrawal within two years.'[12]

A few months before the Westminster poll of 1983, the NIO's David Blatherwick weighed up the chances that Sinn Féin might supplant the SDLP as the dominant force in nationalist politics.[13] Blatherwick found nationalist opinion to be characterized by 'frustration and helplessness': 'Catholics see in London a government which they believe to be dominated by chauvinistic and anti-Irish attitudes.' A growing number feared that any return to devolved rule would simply be a vehicle for unionist domination: 'Many ordinary Catholics appear to have concluded that the unionist leopard will not change his spots, that British governments will not grasp the nettle of unionist intransigence, as they see it, and that no "internal" solution is therefore possible.' This drift in nationalist thinking was 'not so much a reasoned decision to opt for Irish unity – many see the problems and dangers of unity and question the social norms of the Republic – but a reflection of their frustration over their inability to get what they want inside Northern Ireland'.

This was all music to Provisional ears. But Blatherwick's paper also found a potential crumb of comfort in the class divide among nationalists, which strongly influenced their political attitudes. In the Catholic ghettoes of Derry and Belfast, where rates of poverty and unemployment were still alarmingly high, 'people find it easy to believe that they would be no worse off, and maybe even better, in a united Ireland. Certainly, they can have little reason to believe that a resumption of devolved government, even on a power-sharing basis, would lead to a dramatic improvement in their standard of living.' This was no exaggeration: in 1981, the male unemployment rate for Northern Irish Catholics was higher than for any region or any other ethnic minority in the UK.[14] Having experienced political violence as part of their everyday lives for more than a decade, working-class nationalists could now, as Blatherwick observed, 'view with comparative equanimity the prospect that getting the "Brits" out of Ireland may mean more bloodshed, especially if it might solve the problem once and for all'.

The attitudes of their middle-class brethren were more complicated. Unemployment had not affected this social layer to the same extent: indeed, direct rule had 'largely removed from them the stigma of second-class citizens' and opened the door to public-sector employment for Catholic university graduates. Blatherwick still found middle-class Catholics to be 'deeply suspicious' of British and unionist attitudes, which made the idea of Irish unity more attractive from their perspective; however, 'because of their greater stake in the community they are far more disturbed than their working-class counterparts about the implications of continued violence'. They could still be weaned away from opposition to British rule if their political representatives secured a role in the administration of Northern Ireland: 'If not, the danger is that the Catholic community will lose interest in ordinary, constitutional politics; and even that the SDLP will lose heart and disintegrate.'

Boats and Boxes

Danny Morrison took on a distinctive role in the new Sinn Féin leadership team. His rhetorical style was blunt and provocative, in contrast to the measured, avuncular persona that Adams sought to cultivate. It was Morrison who coined the soundbite of the decade at the 1981 Sinn Féin Ard Fheis, when he asked the assembled delegates: 'Will anyone here object if, with a ballot paper in this hand and an Armalite in the other, we take power in Ireland?'[15] Soon after the 1983 election, he spoke at a rally in West Belfast to mark the anniversary of internment. Morrison gesticulated angrily at the helicopter that hovered over the crowd – 'the skies won't always be safe for the British pigs' – and offered British soldiers two routes out of Ireland: 'There is the boat and the box. We want them to take the boat. We are a peace-loving people and it is up to them.'[16]

Sinn Féin chose Morrison as its standard-bearer for the party's next big test, the European election of 1984. If the Provos could win a seat at the expense of John Hume, the implications for Irish politics would be earth-shattering. Morrison launched his campaign with confident predictions of victory, promising to use the assembly in Strasbourg to 'harangue the British government over plastic bullets, show trials and its illegal occupation of this part of our country'.[17] Even Hume's Unionist opponents were beginning to worry about his prospects. The UUP leader James Molyneaux had previously said there was no point trying to rescue the SDLP from 'the results of their own mistaken policies'.[18] But as the European election approached, Molyneaux gave the nod to a more diplomatic intervention by his party secretary Frank Millar, urging unionists to 'refrain in coming weeks from rhetoric of the kind which easily inflames fear and suspicion in our community', for this might simply help Sinn Féin leapfrog the SDLP – 'the ultimate nightmare for all the people of Northern Ireland'.[19]

The political cataclysm feared by Millar did not materialize on polling day. Hume fought a skilful campaign, presenting himself as a statesman who could work wonders for Northern Ireland on the international stage. As Ed Moloney observed, the SDLP leader channelled much of his energy into winning over 'that broad mass of Catholic voters often decried by Sinn Féin as "middle class" but who are in fact mostly employed, respectable, Church-going Catholics who are definitely working-class but who aspire to greater things for their sons and daughters'. Morrison's image as a 'Belfast street fighter' limited his appeal to this constituency.[20]

Sinn Féin's vote share – just over 13 per cent – was the same as in the previous year's Westminster election, albeit on a lower turnout. But Hume had increased the SDLP's score by 4 per cent, so the Provos were losing ground in the battle for nationalist hegemony. Moloney found party members to be 'openly despondent' about Morrison's performance at the count centre.[21] The overall winner was Ian Paisley, who topped the poll with a third of all votes cast. The SDLP's biggest concern was that Paisley's triumph and Hume's strong showing might discourage Thatcher from making any concessions to Irish nationalism when she responded to the New Ireland Forum's report.

Gerry Adams denied that Sinn Féin had reached a ceiling in its electoral ascent, but suggested that Morrison's vote reflected 'varying degrees of tolerance within the nationalist electorate for aspects of the armed struggle': those who voted for the SDLP, or

didn't vote at all, 'may have had some misgivings about IRA operations'.[22] Danny Morrison later expanded on those comments in an
interview with *Magill*. Morrison cited several factors that might
have contributed to Hume's success, from tactical voting by Alliance
Party supporters to the boons of incumbency. But he also put his
finger on a deeper problem for Sinn Féin: 'Perhaps it's not entirely
possible to totally harmonize the relationship between armed struggle and electoral politics.'[23]

Morrison was careful to stress that there could be no winding
down of the IRA campaign: 'Electoral politics will not remove
the British from Ireland. Only armed struggle will do that.'[24] His
insistence that 'all republicans' were united on that point masked a
bitter dispute that was unfolding behind closed doors, pitting Gerry
Adams against his former ally Ivor Bell.

Bell, who had been part of the delegation that met William
Whitelaw in 1972, supported Adams and his comrades as they took
control of the movement after the 1975 truce, and played a central
part in reorganizing the IRA along cellular lines.[25] Unlike Adams
and Martin McGuinness, Bell had not taken on a public role to
match his position in the IRA leadership. Now he was concerned
that Adams was diverting resources from the movement's coffers
to fund election campaigns. Bell and his associates also wanted
to loosen the restrictions on IRA activity that the leadership had
imposed for the sake of Sinn Féin's public image. Behind these
arguments lurked a suspicion that republican political growth was
bound to come at the expense of the armed struggle.

Facing a potential challenge from a dangerous adversary, Adams
moved quickly to arrange Bell's expulsion from the IRA. Bell's
former comrades warned him not to set up a breakaway faction
or join the INLA.[26] The tightly guarded affair stood as a warning
to Adams that he risked provoking a split if the IRA was not given
room to breathe. As 1984 drew to a close, republican sources
boasted that they had the manpower to return violence to the levels
of the early 1970s: all they lacked was the necessary arsenal.[27]

In the utmost secrecy, the IRA pressed ahead with a scheme to
import weapons from Libya that Bell had helped to initiate. The

Libyan connection gave fresh impetus to the IRA campaign just as Sinn Féin faced its first political setbacks. In the meantime, the Provos sent a defiant message to their opponents by planting a bomb at the Conservative Party conference in October 1984.

The Brighton attack claimed the lives of five people and came within a hair's breadth of killing Margaret Thatcher. The IRA revelled in the shock it had provoked and issued a statement baiting Thatcher and her colleagues: 'Today we were unlucky, but remember we only have to be lucky once. You will have to be lucky always. Give Ireland peace and there will be no more war.'[28] Whatever might be happening out of public sight, the message conveyed to the outside world by the IRA was one of uncompromising militancy. It would lay down its arms when Britain announced a date for withdrawal, and not a day before.

If there was no prospect of a ceasefire to clear the way for Sinn Féin's electoral advance, the Provos could still hope that British intransigence might drive nationalists into their arms. In November 1984, Thatcher responded to the New Ireland Forum's report by rejecting every option it had presented with undiplomatic candour. The SDLP's deputy leader Seamus Mallon reacted with fury to Thatcher's 'insulting', 'offensive' and 'racist' comments, while Gerry Adams claimed vindication for Sinn Féin: 'It must be a bitter disappointment to the SDLP and others who had hoped for a meaningful response.'[29] In the wake of the Forum controversy, politicians and civil servants embarked on a new round of Anglo-Irish talks to try and break the deadlock.

Meanwhile, Sinn Féin prepared itself for another test in the 1985 local elections. Adams was careful not to repeat Danny Morrison's mistake as the party launched its campaign, conceding that Sinn Féin had been 'ambitious' in its previous targets and suggesting that it might even lose votes this time.[30] His exercise in managing expectations proved to be a wise move. The SDLP's vote share fell back to its 1983 level, suggesting that John Hume's performance in the European election had been a personal achievement. But Sinn Féin also lost ground, so there was a 60:40 split between the two parties, below the level Sinn Féin had reached in 1983. The ceiling on Provo support was beginning to look like a permanent feature of Northern Irish politics.

When Adams addressed his party's annual conference in November 1985, he dismissed the Anglo-Irish talks as an attempt to isolate republicans and prop up the SDLP.[31] Within weeks, the two governments had announced the result of their deliberations, the Anglo-Irish Agreement (AIA). Claims that London and Dublin would now exercise joint sovereignty over Northern Ireland were based on a reckless misreading of the text.[32] The disputed region was to remain part of the United Kingdom for as long as a majority wished, but the Irish government now received a formal consultative role, with a permanent secretariat of civil servants to deal with issues like policing and discrimination.

Northern Ireland was no longer, in Thatcher's redolent phrase, 'as British as Finchley'. Unionist politicians responded angrily, resigning their Westminster seats to trigger a series of by-elections and calling for mass civil disobedience to overturn the agreement. John Hume was the only Northern Irish politician to have had any real influence on the talks, and the SDLP brandished the outcome as proof that its strategy could deliver.

Garret FitzGerald and his colleagues in the Irish government presented the AIA as a response to 'nationalist alienation'. But there was no homogeneous community with the same experience of alienation. For working-class Catholics who bore the brunt of violence, poverty and everyday harassment by the security forces, the agreement had limited appeal. For their middle-class counterparts, with ample reason for discontent but still much to lose if British withdrawal resulted in chaos, Hume's promise of incremental gains within the Anglo-Irish framework was likely to prove more attractive. The very fact of Unionist opposition, and Thatcher's willingness to face it down, made the agreement look more attractive to many nationalists. The campaign of resistance took many different forms, from big demonstrations to minor acts of non-compliance: four years later, the UUP's Ken Maginnis was still refusing to pay his television licence.[33] In spite of all these efforts, the hated agreement remained firmly in place.

Sinn Féin had to frame its response to the AIA carefully. Gerry Adams predicted that it would result in more loyalist violence against Catholics, and warned that there could be no peace without an end to partition. However, in describing the agreement as a 'carrot and stick' approach by Thatcher's government, he was keen to argue that any concessions stemming from it would be a response to Sinn Féin's political growth.[34] In private, NIO officials cheerfully acknowledged that Sinn Féin's breakthrough had been a vital stimulus: 'Our interest in fostering the SDLP as the party of constitutional nationalism increased; and that, indeed, was one of the objectives of the Anglo-Irish Agreement.'[35] Danny Morrison put forward a similar line to Adams, describing Thatcher's shift to a more conciliatory stance as a 'delayed reaction' to the Brighton bombing. Morrison insisted that Sinn Féin had never referred to the agreement as a 'sell-out', and accused the SDLP of wrongly attributing that view to his party so that it would have sole title to any nationalist gains.[36]

The Southern Strategy

The 1987 general election was the next major skirmish between the two nationalist parties, resulting in a clear triumph for the SDLP, which increased its vote share by 3 per cent, while Sinn Féin fell back again. Gerry Adams held onto his seat in West Belfast, but the SDLP outpolled Sinn Féin in all but two constituencies and won almost twice as many votes in total. The elections of 1984–85 had already suggested there would be a limit on Sinn Féin's expansion for as long as the armed struggle continued. The latest results powerfully reinforced that message. However, there could be no question of an IRA ceasefire, as the Adams leadership needed to buy the support of IRA Volunteers for a long-awaited move to abandon Sinn Féin's abstentionist policy. This was the very issue on which the Provos had broken with Cathal Goulding at the start of the conflict, so a great deal of care was needed in preparing for the shift.

Adams and his comrades learnt from Goulding's experience in two respects. First of all, they promised that Sinn Féin would never take its seats at Westminster or any revived Stormont assembly: Dublin's Leinster House was the only platform it would use. Secondly, they made sure to keep the debate over abstention boxed off from any question marks over the armed struggle. Not only would the war continue, the IRA would actually intensify its campaign, with the help of the Libyan arms shipments that had started to make their way into the country.[37] These promises of improved weaponry and greater autonomy for local units helped win the vote to ditch abstention at an IRA Army Convention in 1986.[38] Announcing the policy shift, an IRA spokesman promised there would be no let-up in its struggle against British rule.[39]

The IRA's decision gave Adams a vital asset as he faced his opponents in Dublin at the Sinn Féin Ard Fheis that November. Ruairí Ó Brádaigh was the spearhead of a traditionalist faction that opposed any change. All of the barely suppressed animosity between the old guard and those who had displaced them came to the surface, with talk of a split already trailed in the national media. Martin McGuinness scornfully dismissed Ó Brádaigh and his associates as a 'former leadership' who had never come to terms with their eclipse. He urged Sinn Féin members to keep faith with the 'true revolutionaries' of the IRA: 'If you walk out of this hall today the only place you are going is home. You will be walking away from the struggle.'[40] McGuinness was already settling into his role as the IRA's conscience, a bluff, plain-speaking militarist to offset the 'sleekedness' of his party leader.[41] The reputation he had earned by playing a hands-on role in IRA operations made him popular with the movement's grassroots, and his support for Adams in the debate was invaluable.[42]

Adams himself sought to rise above the polemical fray, acknowledging that many republicans had 'deep and justifiably strong feelings about abstentionism'. But he accused the Ó Brádaigh camp of trying to 'panic and intimidate' Sinn Féin members with talk of a split, and set out the case against abstention in emphatic terms: 'It is a massive mistake to presume that our republican attitude to

Leinster House is shared by any more than a very small section of our people, especially the citizens of this state.' By taking their seats in the Dáil, republicans could open up a new political front. For Adams, this was 'the only feasible way to break out of our isolation, to make political gains, to win support for our policies, to develop our organization and our struggle'.[43] He made full use of the Army Convention's recent vote to sway any doubters. The IRA was 'united in its determination to pursue the armed struggle', and those who denounced its new policy would have to turn their backs on republican prisoners in British jails.[44] Adams and his comrades had been keen to avoid a generational split by keeping veterans like Joe Cahill and John Joe McGirl on board. McGirl gave his full backing to the new line from the platform, insisting there could be no parallel drawn between Adams and Cathal Goulding: 'We have an army fighting sixteen years which will continue to fight until British rule is defeated.'[45]

The result was a decisive victory for Adams, as his supporters won the two-thirds majority needed to change the party's constitution. Ó Brádaigh and his comrades left the conference to set up a new organization, Republican Sinn Féin, which was still committed to the abstentionist policy. Their splinter group received the seal of approval from Tom Maguire, the only surviving member of the second Dáil elected in 1921. In private, the Provos warned Ó Brádaigh not to foment any split in the IRA's ranks.[46] His new party and its highly secretive military wing, the Continuity Army Council, would remain on the sidelines until the peace process of the 1990s gave Ó Brádaigh an opportunity to challenge the Adams leadership once again.

It wasn't long before Sinn Féin had the chance to put its new line into practice. In his conference speech, Adams suggested that the election after the next one would be the party's first serious test. He put the 'political pygmies of Leinster House' on notice to expect a strong challenge: 'For too long they have been allowed a monopoly upon what passes for politics in this part of Ireland and for too long a very sizeable section of Irish citizens have been denied the opportunity to shape and build a relevant, radical and principled alternative to partitionist rule.'[47] But that 'sizeable section of Irish citizens' proved to be elusive in the timeframe Adams had specified. There were two Irish general elections in 1987 and 1989. In the first, Sinn Féin won 1.9 per cent of the vote and no seats; in the second, it could only manage 1.2 per cent. The ramshackle Anti-H-Block campaign had won twice as many votes in 1981 as Sinn Féin did eight years later.

To compound the blow, 1989 was the greatest moment of triumph for the rebranded Officials in the South, just as they faced political oblivion north of the border. The Workers' Party had discarded most of its republican heritage during the 1980s in the hope of winning support from working-class Protestants. Having formerly denounced the RUC as 'a body of uniformed torturers', it now praised the force for its 'undoubted willingness' to enforce the law without communal bias.[48] The party programme called for a return to devolved government without power-sharing or the cross-border 'Irish dimension' insisted on by the SDLP. Workers' Party leaders blamed John Hume for the political log-jam, and suggested that the Anglo-Irish Agreement might be suspended so the Unionist parties would enter talks.[49] Such arguments made little impression on the Protestant electorate, as two of the party's leading intellectuals, Paul Bew and Henry Patterson, noted in a paper for their comrades: 'In the medium term we cannot hope for more than the interested attention of sections of the Protestant working class.'[50] But they were bound to raise hackles among the working-class nationalists who had supplied the Officials with a modest electoral base in the 1970s. In a survey conducted in 1985, 96 per cent of Protestants believed that the RUC carried out its duties 'fairly' or 'very fairly'; just 47 per cent of Catholics agreed.[51]

In effect, Cathal Goulding's movement had set out to build a working-class version of the bi-confessional, civic unionist Alliance Party, only to find that the realities of Northern Irish society militated against that project. The Alliance could base itself in a real if limited social constituency, to be found in prosperous suburban districts where middle-class Protestants and Catholics lived, worked and socialized together. Its vote share ranged from 5 to 15 per cent during the Troubles.[52]

There was no working-class equivalent of this social layer: communal polarization and segregation was at its most acute towards the bottom of the economic scale. The post-republican Workers' Party left the nationalist field to be tended by Sinn Féin and the SDLP, without doing anything to weaken the grip of the Unionist parties over the Protestant electorate. Throughout the 1980s, its vote fluctuated between 1 and 3 per cent, a handful of council seats the only reward for all the blood, sweat and tears invested by party activists. The NIO's Political Affairs Division was cruel but accurate in its assessment of the Officials after the 1983 election: 'They will continue their efforts to introduce class politics to the electorate but these will always be surrounded by a faint air of musical comedy.'[53]

For the Provos, there was nothing amusing about the apostasy of their former comrades, and they would have been happy to suppress the embattled sect altogether, if its members had not been able to call on their paramilitary shadow – known as 'Group B' – for protection.[54] But the Officials carved out a political niche south of the border, where the lack of republican baggage was an asset, not a liability. In 1989, the Workers' Party won 5 per cent of the national vote and seven seats in the Dáil. The European election that was held simultaneously saw the party's leader Proinsias De Rossa top the poll in Dublin. The personal vote for De Rossa, a veteran of the Border Campaign, was twice as large as the entire Provisional electorate. With Goulding's followers now occupying the ground Sinn Féin wanted to conquer in the South, just as the party found itself treading water in its northern heartlands, no amount of invective could dispel the sense of political stagnation as a new decade came into view.

'An end in itself'

Gerry Adams had claimed in 1986 that abstention was the main barrier to winning support from people who 'might otherwise be open to our policies on all other issues'.[55] But it was the IRA campaign that really stood in Sinn Féin's path. Whatever latent sympathy there might be for republican goals, public opinion in the South was overwhelmingly hostile to the armed struggle. A series of kidnappings and bank robberies in the mid 1980s, some of which resulted in the death of Irish soldiers and policemen at the hands of IRA Volunteers, greatly sharpened that mood. Sinn Féin leaders railed against what they saw as the hypocrisy of Dublin's political class. Danny Morrison reminded Garret FitzGerald that his own father, the 1916 veteran Desmond FitzGerald, had fought for Irish independence 'with a Thompson machine gun in one hand and a ballot paper in the other'.[56] Morrison followed up that remark with a blistering pamphlet, *The Good Old IRA*, itemizing the atrocities committed by republicans during the War of Independence, in order to 'confront those hypocritical revisionists who winsomely refer to the "Old IRA" whilst deriding their more effective and, arguably, less bloody successors'.[57]

The Good Old IRA painted such a black picture of the 'Tan War' that some have described it as a pioneering exercise in revisionist historiography.[58] Morrison's goal was not, of course, to discredit the republicans of yesteryear, but to show his readers that 'no struggle involves a clean fight'.[59] But his central argument that Northern Irish nationalists 'live under arguably worse conditions in terms of repression than did all of Ireland in the pre-1921 period', and that the case for armed struggle was as valid today as it had ever been, made no impact on its intended audience.[60] Historians might agree that there was no yawning gulf between the methods of the old IRA and those used by the Provos. The need for logical consistency troubled politicians in Dublin much less. The War of Independence had been fought long ago and given them a state of their own with all the trappings of sovereignty. The Provo campaign now posed a threat to the interests of that state, and they wanted it to end as soon as possible. There was no substantial body of opinion in the South that took a different view.

The IRA still had the means to keep on fighting for a long time to come. Colonel Gaddafi's regime in Libya had promised them a remarkable gift: 240 tons of sophisticated weaponry, including heavy machine guns, surface-to-air missiles and a huge stock of Semtex explosive.[61] A special IRA team managed to bring about half of this material into the country by sea before French police captured the largest shipment off the Atlantic coast in October 1987. The big question now for the Provo leadership was whether they should use this windfall to dramatically escalate their campaign, in the hope of precipitating a terminal crisis for British rule in Ireland.

The IRA's main objective throughout the conflict was to kill members of the British security forces. From that perspective, there had been a marked decline in its capacity for lethal violence. Five hundred and seventy-nine soldiers and policemen lost their lives in the 1970s, the vast majority at the hands of the IRA, but the number of deaths fell to 342 in the following decade. These bald figures concealed a more important shift as 'Ulsterization' took effect. Losses suffered by the British Army had fallen sharply, from 349 to 124, but there was hardly any drop for the locally recruited forces (230 deaths to 218). From 1975 to 1988, there were only two years when the Army took more casualties than the RUC and the UDR. For five consecutive years in the mid 1980s, Army deaths were in single figures.[62]

To a large extent, the Provos were fighting a war of attrition against the Protestant community in arms. They had to face charges of sectarian bigotry, especially when IRA Volunteers killed off-duty members of the UDR at their homes or places of work. Even if they shrugged off such accusations, IRA leaders could hardly deny that 'Ulsterization' had placed a formidable buffer between their campaign and the British government. Politicians in London would not have to face their own Vietnam, with the families of dead soldiers urging them to withdraw from a country whose fate meant nothing to them. If anything, the loss of sons and fathers made Northern Irish Protestants more determined to support the war against the IRA.

One response to this impasse might be to suddenly change gear and catch the British Army on the hop. Republicans weighed up the merits of their own 'Tet Offensive', inspired by the seminal moment

in the Vietnam War when NLF guerrillas abandoned their usual
hit-and-run tactics and tried to hold territory from static positions.
According to one IRA Volunteer, 'the idea was to take and hold
areas in Armagh, Tyrone and Fermanagh and to force the British
either to use maximum force or to hold off.'[63] Another republican source described a plan to 'take on the Army at roads and at
fortifications with fifty to sixty IRA members involved at a time',
using the anti-aircraft missiles obtained from Libya to shoot down
helicopters.[64] By denying the British Army safe use of the skies, the
Provos would force it to rely on ground transport to supply its
bases, leaving it vulnerable to ambush with the new weapons in the
IRA's arsenal.[65]

Ed Moloney's account of this proposal, easily the most comprehensive, draws heavily upon off-the-record interviews with
republican dissenters who accused Gerry Adams and his associates of sabotaging the IRA campaign to prepare the ground for
a ceasefire. The Libyan weapons and the 'Tet Offensive' form the
centrepiece of this latter-day *Dolchstoßlegende*: according to the dissidents, elements in the Provo leadership deliberately compromised
the last arms shipment before it reached Irish shores, scuppering the
plans for a 'big bang' by removing the crucial element of surprise.[66]

This version of events glosses over a fundamental point: what
would have happened if the IRA had actually gone ahead with the
plan? According to Moloney, republicans were hoping to repeat
the experience of the early 1970s by goading their opponents into
a counter-productive response.[67] If that was the case, then the IRA
was on the brink of repeating Brian Faulkner's mistake in 1971 by
ignoring the fact that circumstances had changed dramatically since
the last round.

On a purely technical level, it would have been much easier for
the British government to strike a blow against the IRA by intern-
ing its members without trial. Having kept the organization under
close surveillance since the conflict began and penetrated its ranks
with informers, they would have had a much better idea of who to
arrest and where than in the early 70s. If the authorities in Dublin
had decided to act simultaneously – and there was a much better

chance of that happening than in 1971, given the thaw in Anglo-Irish relations – the IRA would have found itself under severe pressure. Pitched battles between IRA units and British troops were also bound to take a heavy toll. It would have been a stiff challenge to preserve the organizational skeleton needed to train and equip any new layer of recruits, even if that layer had been forthcoming.

More importantly, the broader political context had changed beyond recognition since 1971. When British soldiers took the first internees to Long Kesh, it was at the behest of a Unionist government propped up by military force that had faced countless demonstrations by nationalists over the past three years. Now, Stormont was long gone, and the British government had pushed through its most recent political initiative in spite of ferocious Unionist opposition. Popular mobilization by nationalists had subsided after the hunger strikes, and Sinn Féin's electoral advance was grinding to a halt. Public opinion in the South was indifferent to the IRA's cause, if not actively hostile.

There was no reason to think that republicans could reverse these unfavourable trends with an all-or-nothing gamble. One senior Provisional suggested that the outcome would have been 'six months' intense fighting, with heavy casualties on both sides', but no prospect of victory at the end of the line.[68] If the Adams leadership really did sabotage the 'Tet Offensive', they most likely saved the IRA from a messy defeat that would have been a poor return on two decades of struggle and sacrifice.

There was a more limited escalation of the IRA campaign in the late 1980s, making use of the Libyan weapons that had slipped through the net. Army losses increased to their highest levels since the 1970s, with twenty-three soldiers killed in 1988 and twenty-four the following year. But the British state also had the capacity to raise its game. The Army killed nineteen IRA members in the space of a year, including an eight-man unit wiped out by the SAS at Loughgall in May 1987.[69] The ambush in Tyrone was damaging enough, but the IRA could at least hope to turn the disaster to good account by transforming its dead Volunteers into martyrs for the cause.

However, no silver lining could be found in the IRA's worst setback of the time. In November 1987, a Provo bomb exploded during a Remembrance Day ceremony in Enniskillen, killing eleven civilians, all of them Protestant. There was a furious popular backlash, especially in the South, where Sinn Féin had been hoping to establish a foothold.

Soon after the bombing, the US journalist Kevin Kelley published a new edition of his highly sympathetic book about the Provos, with some words of commendation from Gerry Adams on the cover. Kelley added an epilogue on 'the need for non-violence', arguing that republicans were 'bound to lose more than they will gain by continuing indefinitely on their present course', and would do better to adopt new methods of struggle: 'Sit-downs, "illegal" marches, refusal to pay rates, rents or fines, destruction of public records, and complete non-cooperation with all agencies and officials of the state – each of which would presumably result in mass arrests – might well stir international opinion and the British conscience in ways that bombs in London and bullets in Belfast demonstrably do not.'[70] There were powerful echoes here of the case for civil resistance as a substitute for armed struggle that People's Democracy had made a decade earlier, when the Provos brushed such arguments impatiently aside.

Another warning about the perils of republican militarism came from the fate of the INLA, which seemed to have entered its death throes. A new chief of staff, Dominic McGlinchey, held the organization together in rough-and-ready fashion for a few years in the 1980s, while the political wing of Seamus Costello's movement continued to wither on the vine. McGlinchey had won a fearsome reputation as a Provisional commander in south Derry before the Provos expelled him for indiscipline. When the IRSP's paper interviewed McGlinchey in 1983, while he was on the run from the Irish police, the INLA leader dutifully noted the party's importance in giving 'political leadership on the class struggle in Ireland' and spoke of his interest in left-wing ideology, 'from Fanon and Cabral to Guevara and Mandel'.[71]

But McGlinchey's own practice was unmistakably that of a traditional republican militarist, and he masterminded a series of high-profile attacks. After the Irish authorities captured him in 1984, the INLA's quarrelsome factions began preparing for all-out war.[72] One splinter group broke away to form the Irish People's Liberation Organization (IPLO) and ordered the rump INLA to disband. When their former comrades disregarded those instructions, a grisly vendetta ensued, claiming the lives of twelve people before it staggered to a halt.

The victims of the feud included Thomas 'Ta' Power, who had been trying to promote some fresh political thinking since his release from prison. A document written by Power gave a scathing description of the INLA's 'macho' internal culture and asked whether the movement had backed itself into a corner: 'We get no analysis, we get no strategy outside the basic [military] confrontation – it eventually becomes an end in itself simply due to the fact that they don't know any other strategy.'[73]

Repeating the arguments made by Bernadette McAliskey and her allies a decade earlier, Power urged his comrades to 'put politics in command' by establishing the supremacy of the IRSP over its military wing. Supporters of the IPLO faction gunned him down before he had any chance to put these ideas into effect. The INLA somehow survived the onslaught launched by its former comrades, but could not transcend the macho militarism that Power had castigated. One consequence of the feud was to incapacitate a potential rival for the Provos, just as they were putting out feelers for a new political initiative that might cause ructions inside the IRA.

9

Down a Few Rungs

'The risk of being defeated'

In the summer of 1988, Sinn Féin sat down for talks with the SDLP to see whether a 'national consensus on Irish unification', as Gerry Adams put it, could be forged.[1] The discussions began soon after a chaotic sequence of events that thrust Northern Ireland onto the global news agenda once again. In March, an SAS unit shot dead three IRA members preparing a bomb attack in Gibraltar whose leader, Mairéad Farrell, was already a hero for republicans. It soon became clear that Farrell and her comrades were unarmed when the soldiers opened fire, a revelation that generated intense controversy, coming after previous 'shoot-to-kill' incidents involving the SAS.

The Provos mounted a show of strength at the funeral service in Belfast ten days later. But the mourners came under attack from a loyalist paramilitary, Michael Stone, who tossed grenades and fired repeatedly at the crowd, killing three people before he was overpowered. At the funeral of one of Stone's victims, two British soldiers dressed in plain clothes suddenly drove into the procession. The crowd assumed they were loyalists bent on another attack: the soldiers were dragged from their car, beaten and shot by the IRA before the security forces could intervene.

The killing of the two soldiers provoked a torrent of hostile commentary on the republican movement and the communities that sustained it. Speaking at a republican rally in the same Milltown cemetery that Michael Stone had attacked weeks earlier, Martin McGuinness denounced this 'hysterical welter of condemnation and abuse of the decent people of West Belfast'. McGuinness also lashed out at 'so-called constitutional-nationalist politicians and pro-British bishops' who had 'given moral succour and advice to the British war machine' with their polemics against the IRA.[2] However, his party was now willing to break bread with those politicians in the hope of finding common ground.

There had been some ideological fine-tuning to clear the way for Sinn Féin's approach to the SDLP. In his 1986 book *The Politics of Irish Freedom*, Adams suggested that the pressures of electoral competition had 'unnecessarily brought out some of the class differences between ourselves and the SDLP', and expressed his hope for 'some kind of general unity, in which both parties would agree to disagree on social and economic issues and maximize pressure on points of agreement'.[3] Adams had already spoken of 'the dangers of ultra-leftism' at Sinn Féin's 1983 Ard Fheis: 'Republicans have a duty to beware of any tendencies which would narrow our demands and our base.'[4] Now he returned to the theme, dismissing 'the ultra-left view, which counterposes republicanism and socialism and which breaks up the unity of the national independence movement by putting forward "socialist" demands that have no possibility of being achieved until real independence is won'.[5]

Adams quoted James Connolly's biographer Desmond Greaves in defence of this 'stageist' line on the Irish revolution. It was ironic to find Greaves, whose protégés Roy Johnston and Anthony Coughlan *An Phoblacht* had once assailed as communist infiltrators, now being cited as an authority in republican circles.[6] Sinn Féin leaders worried that an influx of new left-wing members from groups like People's Democracy after the hunger strikes was alienating more conservative sections of their base. At Bodenstown in 1986, McGuinness tried to calm troubled waters: 'Not every person who argues new positions is a trendy lefty, and not everyone who advocates traditional republicanism is a right-wing traditionalist.'[7]

Debates about the stages theory of revolution were mainly of interest to the ideological cognoscenti, but when Sinn Féin delegates voted to adopt a pro-choice policy at the 1985 party conference, that was a very different matter. The Fine Gael politician Michael Noonan attacked Sinn Féin for adopting a stance that would 'extend the definition of legitimate targets to unborn children', and the SDLP made great play of the issue during election campaigns.[8]

Adams warned Sinn Féin activists that the party's line on abortion was an electoral liability:

> We need to avoid issues which are too local, partial or divisive. This is not to say that we should be anti-feminist. On the contrary, I am proud to say we are not. It is a question of using political judgement in taking up issues and never adopting positions which weaken the overall thrust of the movement towards national freedom.[9]

Although Adams disclaimed any wish to overturn the current policy, his real attitude was perfectly clear, and the party soon ditched its pro-choice line. The dispute over Sinn Féin's abortion policy laid down a marker. The party leadership welcomed members from a left-wing background who had no 'republican taboos' – as one Adams ally, Joe Austin, put it – and could be relied on to support its political innovations.[10] But these new recruits would not be allowed to push the leadership further than it wanted to go. By establishing a clear hierarchy of objectives, with national independence taking priority over socialism or feminism in the movement's strategy, Adams left himself with plenty of leeway as he began reaching out to conservative nationalists.

In his first exchange of documents with John Hume's party, Gerry Adams argued that the IRA campaign had been 'beneficial to the political aspirations of the nationalist community', not least by strengthening the SDLP's position in talks. He emphasized that Sinn Féin was 'totally opposed to a power-sharing Stormont assembly', and accused the SDLP of encouraging the British government to believe that a settlement along those lines was within reach: 'Our struggle and strategy has been to close down each option open to the British until they have no other option but to withdraw.'[11] Opening the debate for his party, John Hume rejected Sinn Féin's view that partition was the result of British interference. For Hume, a British withdrawal without prior unionist consent could only result in carnage: 'Each section of the community would seize its own territory and we would have a Cyprus/Lebanon-style formula for permanent division and bloodshed.'[12]

Conflicting ideas of what 'self-determination' entailed were the main stumbling block to agreement between the two parties. In its response to Hume, Sinn Féin insisted that 'nationalists and democrats cannot concede a veto to unionists over Irish reunification.' There was a subtle change of emphasis when discussing the arrangements that would have to be made *after* Britain announced it was going to withdraw from Northern Ireland: 'There must be due provision for the rights of northern Protestants and every effort made to win their consent. By adopting such a policy the British would be joining the persuaders.'[13] But overall, this was a restatement of long-held republican principles that could not be reconciled with Hume's analysis of the conflict. When the discussions wrapped up without agreement, Adams issued a statement criticizing the SDLP for its claim that Britain was no longer opposed to Irish unity: 'To confer neutrality on the British Government would be to confer neutrality on the Turkish Government whose military invasion has partitioned the island of Cyprus.'[14] In a new book published soon after the talks, the Sinn Féin leader railed against 'so-called constitutional nationalists' who were 'prepared to accept the legitimacy of the state so long as the section of the Catholic population whose interests they represent are incorporated into it'.[15]

Adams still argued that the exercise had been 'good for the morale of the hard-pressed nationalist community which would clearly support joint action on their behalf'.[16] However, there seemed to be little chance of such unity materializing after John Hume launched a withering attack on the Provos at his party conference in November, branding them as 'fascists' who had 'killed six times as many human beings as the British Army, thirty times as many as the RUC and 250 times as many as the UDR'.[17] A few weeks later, Sinn

Féin's Tom Hartley and Martin McGuinness joined a small group of demonstrators at Burntollet for the twentieth anniversary of the People's Democracy march. Bernadette McAliskey told the marchers they were 'still on the road' after many years of struggle, and insisted there could be no peace in Ireland 'so long as this country is divided and partitioned and governed by the British'.[18] Some of her audience must have wondered if they would be returning to Burntollet in another two decades to face the same depressing vista.

Several hints at a change in strategy could be detected over the following year. In January 1989, Gerry Adams stressed that IRA violence was a tactical question, not a matter of principle: 'It is up to those who don't believe it's legitimate to come up with alternatives.' At the Sinn Féin Ard Fheis later that month, he urged IRA Volunteers to be 'careful and careful again' in seeking to avoid civilian casualties, and Martin McGuinness announced that the IRA leadership had disbanded a unit in west Fermanagh for unethical behaviour.[19]

As Ed Moloney pointed out soon afterwards, Adams and McGuinness were effectively setting the IRA a test it would never be able to meet: 'If the Army, the UDR and the RUC with all their training, discipline and practice make "mistakes" – as they have consistently done down the years – how much more likely is it that the IRA will too?' Thanks to 'localized sectarianism, the brutalization of a twenty-year war, plain incompetence and the inability of any guerrilla organization to fight a civilian-friendly campaign while hurting its enemy', the clean war sought by the Sinn Féin leadership was 'probably undeliverable'.[20]

Delegates at the 1989 Ard Fheis voted in favour of a motion calling for an 'all-Ireland anti-imperialist mass movement' that would bring together 'the broadest range of social and political forces'. Gerry Adams described the proposal as a formal acknowledgement that Sinn Féin could not win on its own. The only speaker to oppose it directly was Donegal's Johnnie White, a veteran activist who had been commander of the Derry Officials at the time of Bloody Sunday, when Martin McGuinness was his Provisional counterpart. White said that he had no problem with the idea of a broad front in principle, but didn't like the subtext he discerned behind the motion: 'Who are we trying to attract – members of the SDLP and Fianna Fáil?'[21]

The results of Northern Ireland's European election later that year drove home the urgency of a new venture from the Provos. In 1984, Danny Morrison had been hoping to supplant John Hume; this time, the SDLP leader simply crushed Morrison, winning almost three times as many votes. Combined with Sinn Féin's dire performance in the South, this was clear evidence that the party's rise had stalled.

The waning fortunes of its allies on the British political scene compounded the malaise. In June 1989, a conference of Tony Benn's Socialist Movement greeted Gerry Adams with a standing ovation.[22] However, Neil Kinnock and his associates had long since defeated Benn's attempt to transform the Labour Party. As one journalist observed, Kinnock saw engagement with Irish republicans 'in the same context as support for gays, lesbians and black sections – precisely the kind of policies which he perceives as major vote-losers'.[23]

The Bennite MP Jeremy Corbyn infuriated his leader by inviting Adams to speak at a fringe meeting in Brighton during the Labour Party conference, which was due to be held in the same hotel the IRA had bombed five years earlier. But Labour's Northern Ireland spokesman Kevin McNamara spoke trenchantly against a motion calling for British withdrawal.[24] Labour's policy of 'unity by consent', reaffirmed by McNamara, placed it closer to the SDLP than to Sinn Féin.

At every turn, doors appeared to be slamming shut. In August 1989, Adams chaired a public meeting in West Belfast to discuss the legacy of the civil rights protests. His close ally Jim Gibney drew up a gloomy balance sheet: 'I don't believe that the political philosophy that has emerged from the struggle over the last twenty years has the capacity any more to motivate people.' If the republican movement didn't find some way out of its current impasse, Gibney warned, 'you actually run the risk of being defeated'.[25]

Hume–Adams

As the new decade began, Sinn Féin members took part in the launch of the Irish National Congress (INC). The trade unionist Matt Merrigan, who joined Bernadette McAliskey on the INC's executive, described it as 'an attempt to build a movement of the oppressed and deprived'.[26] A few weeks later, speaking at the Sinn Féin Ard Fheis, the party's chairman Séan MacManus rejected 'the one-sided concept of a republican ceasefire'. But the steady trickle of criticism for IRA operations continued: Richard McAuley warned that the IRA 'must realize it damages the national liberation struggle'.[27] One notable absence from the conference was Danny Morrison, following his arrest a few weeks earlier at a house where the IRA was holding a police informer. Morrison subsequently received an eight-year prison sentence, transforming Sinn Féin's leadership triumvirate into an Adams–McGuinness duopoly, just as the party was about to enter a crucial period in its evolution.[28]

An important republican ally that appeared to be going from strength to strength had clearly inspired the INC's choice of name. The 1990 Ard Fheis heard electrifying news that the apartheid regime in South Africa was planning to lift its ban on the African National Congress. Gerry Adams hailed the announcement, which would 'give great comfort to those groups and organizations throughout the world struggling to achieve national self-determination'.[29] Sinn Féin had always supported the Irish Anti-Apartheid Movement, whose chairman, the exiled ANC militant Kader Asmal, brushed aside an attempt by Garret FitzGerald to have the party excluded from its ranks.[30] However, it was only after Asmal's death in 2011 that the full extent of his ties with the republican movement came to light in a posthumous memoir. At Asmal's request, Gerry Adams had arranged for ANC guerrillas to be trained by the IRA in the late 1970s, and IRA members subsequently carried out reconnaissance on the ANC's behalf for one of its most successful operations, the bombing of the Sasol oil refinery near Johannesburg.[31] Adams was in no position to boast about this enterprise in public, but his party could always be sure of a warm welcome from ANC leaders as they entered the corridors of power.

South Africa offered an intriguing template for the Provos, with a guerrilla movement unable to secure outright victory entering a process that was to some extent fluid and indeterminate in order to achieve its goals by other means. They discreetly reopened a backchannel for communication with the British government that had been dormant since the hunger strikes.[32] Thatcher's Northern Ireland secretary Peter Brooke supplied food for thought with an interview acknowledging that the IRA could not be defeated militarily.[33] This matched what the NIO was saying in private. An assessment of the IRA's strengths and weaknesses from February 1990 suggested that it still had 'a sufficient pool of "volunteers", mainly, but not exclusively, drawn from the lower strata of the deprived urban Roman Catholic working class', along with an adequate supply of 'weapons, explosives and money', to persist with its campaign. There was no prospect of a swift military victory: 'It seems more likely that the key factor in the ending of terrorist violence in Northern Ireland will be an acceptance by the PIRA/Sinn Féin leadership (which may be forced upon them by the wider nationalist community) that such violence has shown itself to be futile.'[34]

The secretary of state soon backtracked from one historical allusion that suggested a willingness to pull out of Northern Ireland altogether: 'Let me remind you of the move towards independence in Cyprus, and a British minister stood up in the House of Commons and used the word "never" in a way which within two years there had been a retreat from that word.'[35] Brooke insisted that he had been talking about the possibility of talks with Sinn Féin, not a British withdrawal. He followed this up with a major speech insisting that Britain had no 'selfish strategic or economic interest' in keeping hold of Northern Ireland. The British government sent the Provos an advance copy of the text.[36] In public, Gerry Adams responded by urging Brooke to act over the heads of the unionists: 'The argument that the consent of this national minority, elevated into a majority within an undemocratic, artificially created state, is necessary before any constitutional change can occur is a nonsense.'[37]

Of course, there was one clear difference between the Provos and their ANC comrades. No serious observer could deny that the majority of South Africans supported the ANC, although the voting laws of the apartheid system prevented it from registering that support at the ballot box. In contrast, about one-third of the nationalist population in the North voted for Sinn Féin, and barely a sliver of the southern electorate supported the party.[38] Speaking at Bodenstown in June 1992, Jim Gibney frankly acknowledged this shortcoming: 'We know and accept that this is not 1921 and that at this stage we don't represent a government-in-waiting. We're not standing in the airport lounge waiting to be flown to Chequers or Lancaster House; we have no illusions of grandeur. Idealists we are, fools we are not.'[39]

Gibney left the timeframe for Irish unity open-ended, suggesting that British withdrawal 'must be preceded by a sustained period of peace and will arise out of negotiations'. There was no mention here of the demand for withdrawal to be completed in the lifetime of a British parliament. He asked if republicans were fated to remain 'hostages to an immediate past because of all the pain, suffering and commitment; to past views expressed, trenchantly, which in time solidified into unyielding principles'.[40] Those who understood Gibney's role in the movement as an outrider for Gerry Adams immediately grasped the significance of his intervention.[41] Sinn Féin also hinted at flexibility about deadlines and transitional arrangements in its document 'Towards A Lasting Peace in Ireland', which Gibney described as 'another stage in the maturing process' for republicans.[42]

A reassessment of Sinn Féin's attitude towards the unionist community had partly inspired this shift. There was a distinct softening of the movement's rhetoric, with much emphasis on the need to win 'the greatest possible consent' to constitutional arrangements for a new Ireland (but no endorsement of the 'consent principle' as such). The Derry activist Mitchell McLoughlin criticized the lack of empathy for unionists in republican circles, and broke a taboo against criticism of the IRA's campaign: 'One objective reality which must be faced is that many IRA activities from the northern Protestant perspective are perceived to be sectarian.'[43]

However, the main purpose of Sinn Féin's revisionism was to build bridges with the SDLP and the Irish government. 'Towards a Lasting Peace' urged those political actors to 'forcefully and continually represent the interests of the nationalist people' on the international stage.[44] Just a few years earlier, Gerry Adams had spoken of 'driving a wedge between the leadership of Fianna Fáil and the SDLP on the one hand and their members and rank-and-file supporters on the other', warning that 'unless the most radical social forces are in the leadership of the independence struggle then inevitably it must fail or compromise'.[45] But his party now played down the social fractures in the nationalist community as much as it could. Most importantly, the republican leadership indicated their willingness to end the IRA's war – 'an option of last resort' – if there was a 'consistent constitutional strategy to pursue a national democracy in Ireland'.[46]

Behind the scenes, they were preparing to move further still. The private discussions Adams had been conducting with John Hume and the Fianna Fáil leader Charles Haughey from the late 1980s were intended to forge a pan-nationalist consensus that would inevitably require Sinn Féin to move closer to the perspective of its would-be allies. When the talks began, Adams did have some grounds for hoping that Fianna Fáil might be induced to meet the Provos halfway in the event of a ceasefire. Haughey had cultivated a hard-line, nationalist image from the opposition benches in the 1980s, opposing the Anglo-Irish Agreement.[47] Fianna Fáil's team were closer to Sinn Féin in their analysis of British policy than the SDLP had been at the 1988 talks.[48] But Haughey softened his line on the agreement after returning to office in 1987, and his administration stayed close to John Hume. In October 1991, Hume worked with Irish officials to draw up the text of a declaration for the two governments to endorse that would, he hoped, give the IRA enough room to halt its campaign.[49]

Sinn Féin's first alternative draft in February 1992 tried to water down Hume's emphasis on unionist consent, merely acknowledging that 'the exercise of the democratic right to self-determination by the people of Ireland as a whole *would best be achieved* with the agreement and consent of the people of Northern Ireland', and committing the British government to bring about Irish unity 'within a period to be agreed'.[50] This was still compatible with republican orthodoxy, albeit expressed in unfamiliar language.

But four months later, Sinn Féin endorsed a fresh draft – known as the 'Irish Peace Initiative' or simply 'Hume–Adams' – that took the movement right out of its comfort zone: 'The British Government accepts the principle that the Irish people have the right collectively to self-determination, and that the exercise of this right *could take the form* of agreed independent structures for the island as a whole.'[51] This was to be balanced by a symmetrical commitment from Dublin, with the Taoiseach accepting, in the light of Northern Irish experience, that 'stability and well-being will not be found under any political system which is refused allegiance or rejected on grounds of identity by a significant minority.' Self-determination by the Irish people 'as a whole' would have to be 'exercised with the agreement and consent of the people of Northern Ireland'.[52]

Although there was still a certain ambiguity in the wording, the most plausible reading of Hume–Adams was that it maintained the guarantee for unionists, but transferred its location from London to Dublin. The Irish government would grant the North's unionist majority the right to block constitutional change, and republicans would find that easier to swallow than the existing veto upheld by Britain.[53] There was no commitment to British withdrawal: the exercise of self-determination 'could take the form of agreed independent structures', but then again it might not.

According to Gerry Adams, the IRA leadership approved this document as the basis for a possible ceasefire.[54] If so, the members of the Army Council had either shifted away from established orthodoxies, or did not fully grasp the import of what they were endorsing. Combined with the public signs of flexibility in Gibney's Bodenstown speech and 'Towards a Lasting Peace', the Provos had taken the first major step that would lead towards an IRA ceasefire and the Good Friday Agreement of 1998.

The Final Phase

The military stalemate facing the IRA in the early 90s was an obvious spur towards such ideological revisionism. In September 1988, an IRA spokesman assured Eamonn Mallie that its struggle was now entering the 'final phase': 'The next eighteen months to two years will be critical because the IRA has the resources and will then know if it has the capacity to end it.'[55] This turned out to be a shrewd analysis, if not in the way intended. After the spike of 1988–89, losses inflicted by the IRA dropped sharply again. From 1991 to 1994, forty-two members of the security forces were killed in total, fewer than in 1988 alone.[56] In January 1992, Colonel Derek Wilford, the commander of 1 Para on Bloody Sunday, made a surprising reappearance on the massacre's twentieth anniversary, comparing Northern Ireland to Aden and calling for the withdrawal of British troops: 'It would be a victory for common sense.'[57] But such exhortations were increasingly rare.

The IRA had mixed results when it tried to broaden the scope of its war. A policy that branded civilians who worked on Army and RUC bases as 'legitimate targets' reached its nadir in January 1992, when an IRA bomb killed eight Protestant construction workers. Facing charges of sectarianism, the Provos might retort that they had also targeted Catholics who worked for the security forces, but this would simply remind their critics of the infamous 'human bomb' attack launched by the Derry IRA in October 1990, when they forced a local man who worked for a military canteen to drive a van packed with explosives into an Army checkpoint.[58]

A renewed campaign in Britain did more to boost the IRA's morale. Its Volunteers revelled in the technical proficiency of a mortar attack that came close to wiping out John Major's cabinet in January 1991, and a new tactic of planting 'blockbuster' devices in the heart of London's financial centre inflicted more economic damage than two decades of bombing in Northern Ireland. An *Irish Times* round-up of the IRA's activity in 1992 noted the paradox: security-force casualties were at an all-time low, but its bombing campaign had been more effective than at any time since the Troubles began.[59] In April 1993, a one-tonne bomb devastated Bishopsgate, causing more than a billion pounds in damage and forcing the City of London to impose a new security cordon in the hope of preventing further attacks. With the City now bidding to overtake New York as the world's financial capital, the IRA had found a new weakness to exploit in the defences of its adversary.

However, the 'blockbusters' had their own inherent limitations, as the margin between success and failure was very fine. Every time the Provos phoned in a warning, they took the risk of mass casualties if the police were unable to clear the area in time. In March 1993, journalist Mary Holland suggested that it was 'beginning to look almost inevitable that one day soon the IRA, by accident or design, is going to cause a major disaster in a British city'. She warned that the bombings would not have the desired effect on public opinion in Britain, which was 'too fragmented' to rally behind a demand for withdrawal from Northern Ireland: 'To effect such a dramatic change the IRA would need, quite deliberately, to sanction acts of terrorism against innocent civilians on a scale which its own supporters would not stomach.'[60]

Within weeks, a Provisional bomb had killed two children at a shopping centre in Warrington: perhaps not as bad an outcome as Holland had feared, but bad enough to provoke an angry backlash in Ireland and Britain alike, with protests against the IRA on the streets of Dublin. The main political impact of the 90s bombing campaign may have been on the IRA itself. It made it easier for the Provos to claim that they were moving towards a ceasefire from a position of strength as an 'undefeated army', not suing for peace from their enemies.

Republican pride was a source of great irritation to the IRA's opponents, but there could be no doubting its importance in the approaching endgame. Danny Morrison's prison journal offers a useful window into the leadership's thinking at the time.[61] In

September 1990, he suggested that republicans were now determined to achieve 'something substantial' instead of 'glorifying past
defeats', which would only be possible if 'everybody agrees to come
down a few rungs'.[62] A letter to the journalist David McKittrick
from September 1991 urged him to empathize with IRA Volunteers
as 'human beings who are in trenches, whose rationale may often
appear elusive or inexplicable but who feel they have no other
choice', and who would 'have to feel that a settlement was just and
that their opponents were making compromises also'.[63] In another
message to McKittrick the following January, Morrison denied that
he was 'so stupid as to believe that republicans can win at the negotiating table what they haven't won on the battlefield'.[64] In tone as
much as content, it was a far cry from the bombastic triumphalism
of a decade earlier.

Writing to Gerry Adams in October 1991, Morrison suggested
that the IRA could 'fight on forever' without facing outright defeat:
'Of course, that isn't the same as winning or showing something for
all the sacrifices.'[65] He drew his thoughts together in an article for
An Phoblacht after the UK general election of 1992, when Adams
lost his West Belfast seat to the SDLP. Morrison feared there would
now be 'a big temptation, because of frustration and alienation,
for many republicans to abandon even their limited faith in politics and place all their trust in armed struggle'. That 'emotional
reaction' would be a huge mistake: 'The whole purpose of opening
up a political front in the first place was because of the acknowledgement that the purely military struggle was being isolated and
marginalized and could not on its own win.'[66]

The main thrust of his argument pointed in the opposite direction: 'If the IRA does not raise the quality of its campaign the
struggle could go on forever, and if it cannot raise the quality of its
campaign it should consider the alternative.'[67] Republicans should
'never allow the situation to decline to the extent that we face such
a decision from the depths of an unpopular, unseemly, impossible-
to-end armed struggle or from the point of brave exhaustion'.[68]
According to Morrison, the paper's editor turned down his article,
despite agreeing with much of its content, because 'it would have

been seized upon by our opponents'.[69] He later suggested it was too early for such arguments to appear in the republican press: with Gibney's Bodenstown speech already in the pipeline, IRA Volunteers would have seen it as a kite-flying exercise for the leadership.[70]

Some opponents of the IRA have claimed there was another crucial factor behind its shift away from armed struggle. As the Provos began inching towards a ceasefire, the loyalist paramilitaries stepped up their campaign after a period of relative inactivity: between 1983 and 1987, loyalists killed fifty people; between 1988 and 1994, they killed 224. By 1992, the UVF and the UDA were killing more people than the IRA.[71] Now that the republican movement had an identifiable public face, it was easier for the loyalist groups to target Sinn Féin activists, but, as before, the majority of their victims were randomly selected Catholic civilians. In 1993, a leading Unionist politician, John Taylor, suggested that the escalation of loyalist violence was establishing a 'parity of fear' between Protestants and Catholics in Northern Ireland, making a peace settlement more likely.[72] After the IRA called its ceasefire, Taylor argued that the loyalists should be credited with having made 'a significant contribution to the IRA finally accepting that they couldn't win'.[73] The paramilitaries themselves made similar assertions about the impact of their campaign.[74]

Sinn Féin spokesmen insisted at the time that the loyalist groups were receiving generous assistance from the security forces.[75] British government spokesmen dismissed talk of 'collusion' as republican propaganda, but the case of Brian Nelson made it harder to credit such blanket denials. Nelson, who worked for the Army's secretive Force Research Unit (FRU), had become the UDA's director of intelligence and played a central part in the assassination of Pat Finucane, a high-profile lawyer who defended IRA suspects.

Nelson's role as a government agent gradually came into public view as the investigation into Finucane's killing progressed. Under pressure from John Major's government, the prosecution struck a plea bargain with Nelson, ensuring he would not face cross-examination at his trial.[76] Nelson's commanding officer Gordon

Kerr – identified as 'Colonel J' in media reports – took 'personal moral responsibility' for the actions of his subordinate, describing Nelson as a man who was 'very loyal to the system' and earning him a reduced sentence.[77] It later became obvious that Kerr had misled the court about Nelson's role in the UDA. With the full knowledge of his handlers, the FRU agent had reorganized the group's intelligence files to improve its targeting and arranged for a massive arms shipment to be brought into Northern Ireland in 1988.[78] Those weapons proved to be invaluable for the recharged loyalist campaign that followed.

The Finucane case remains emblematic to this day because it illustrates so many aspects of collusion: the enabling role of agents from different arms of the state (FRU, RUC Special Branch); failure to act on knowledge, before and after the fact; and the part played by government ministers, both in jeopardizing Finucane's life and in arranging the subsequent cover-up. Much of what we know about Brian Nelson, and about the wider picture of collusion, dates from the period after the IRA ceasefire, when a series of reports exposed the seamy side of Britain's counter-insurgency.[79] But knowledge of the basic facts had already percolated widely when the killings were at their peak. As Eamonn McCann observed in November 1993: 'Stop anybody at random on the Falls or in the Bogside and ask about the "Nelson Affair", and there's a fair chance you will be told in detail about the UDA man Brian Nelson, "Colonel J", the killing of Catholics, the South African arms and so forth.'[80]

In nationalist communities, the perception that the security forces were giving loyalist paramilitaries a helping hand intensified the mood of fear that John Taylor believed to have such a salutary effect. Echoing Taylor, the historian Paul Bew has suggested that collusion and peace talks should be seen as two aspects of 'one, mutually reinforcing process'.[81] The problem with such arguments, quite apart from their moral implications, is that the initial reassessment of republican strategy preceded the high point of loyalist violence in the early 90s. So did the sense of political inertia on which that reassessment was based. If the republican leadership had possessed any good reason to believe that victory was close at hand, the threat posed by the UVF and the UDA might have appeared to them in a very different light, as an evil that would have to be endured.

Reconciling the Irreconcilable

News of the Hume–Adams initiative leaked out in April 1993, in a story broken by Eamonn McCann. The two nationalist leaders kept the 'Irish Peace Initiative' under wraps, although their first public statement on the talks hinted heavily at its contents: 'The exercise of self-determination is a matter for agreement between the people of Ireland. It is the search for that agreement and the means of achieving it on which we will be concentrating.' Shortly afterwards, Adams urged the British government to support the end of partition 'in the shortest possible time consistent with obtaining maximum consent', having identified 'the steps that would be needed to get Northern majority consent to Irish reunification'. Adams did not spell out any mechanism for establishing 'Northern majority consent', although Hume insisted that a peace settlement would have to be approved by dual referendums, north and south, 'to reassure the unionist people that we mean what we say when we talk of agreement'.[82]

Republican spokesmen sent out mixed messages about the movement's bottom line over the following months. Tom Hartley, a member of the so-called 'kitchen cabinet' driving Sinn Féin's peace strategy, dismissed a paper from the British Labour politician Kevin McNamara that envisaged joint sovereignty between London and Dublin as 'tinkering at the edges'.[83] When an interviewer asked Gerry Adams about the same idea three months later, the Sinn Féin president tested out a verbal formula that his party would deploy frequently as the peace process gathered momentum. Adams put his own position on the record – 'I have ruled out joint sovereignty as a solution' – but immediately pivoted towards a more flexible stance: 'How could you rule out discussing it? That would be ridiculous.'[84]

Ed Moloney later compared this rhetorical strategy to 'a footballer who disapproves of the off-side rule but agrees to play all the same'.[85] The journalist Geraldine Kennedy received a detailed briefing on the Hume–Adams document in October 1993 and had no trouble grasping its significance: 'For the first time, Sinn Féin, with the full backing of the Army Council of the IRA, accepts the principle of unionist consent to any change in the constitutional status of Northern Ireland.'[86] According to Adams, a positive response to the document from the British government would be enough for an IRA ceasefire.[87]

In the meantime, Hume and the new Fianna Fáil Taoiseach, Albert Reynolds, had been trying to redraft the June 1992 paper to make its language more acceptable to the Unionist parties and the British government.[88] A separate negotiating channel between republicans and John Major's government confirmed that London had no intention of announcing a timetable for withdrawal, even one that extended over the space of a generation. A message from the British side in March 1993 made the position clear:

> The British Government cannot enter a talks process, or expect others to do so, with the purpose of achieving a predetermined outcome, whether the 'ending of partition' or anything else. It has accepted that the eventual outcome of such a process could be a united Ireland, but this can only be on the basis of the consent of the people of Northern Ireland.[89]

From a traditional republican perspective, this restatement of the 'unionist veto' ensured that any talks would indeed have a predetermined outcome: the continuation of British rule for an indefinite period. If Adams and his inner circle had still been committed to a straightforward 'Brits Out' agenda, this would have been the moment to pull the plug on the whole process, but instead they persisted.

There were enough straws in the wind to indicate that a significant change in republican policy was in the offing, and talk of an IRA ceasefire gathered pace. Such optimism coexisted eerily with signs of worsening conflict. Loyalist paramilitaries denounced the Hume–Adams 'pan-nationalist front' and began targeting SDLP members in a bid to scupper the talks.[90] The SDLP politician Joe Hendron, who had replaced Gerry Adams as West Belfast's MP, told reporters that there was now pervasive fear in the Catholic ghettoes: 'Hit squads can seemingly roam about the city murdering at random, as a consequence of limited or no security-force presence in the areas from which they launch their murderous attacks.'[91] Just as speculation about a truce reached fever pitch, an IRA spokesman promised to 'exact a price' from the loyalists, but insisted that his organization would 'under no circumstances play into British hands by going down the cul-de-sac of sectarian warfare'.[92]

Within a fortnight, an attempt by republicans to wipe out the UDA leadership had gone disastrously wrong, raising the spectre of all-out civil war. The IRA's Belfast Brigade planted a bomb in a fish shop on the Shankill Road below an office that the UDA had been using as a meeting place: the device went off prematurely, killing nine Protestant civilians and injuring dozens more. In revenge for the bombing, loyalist gunmen killed fourteen people, including eight victims of a 'spray job' in a crowded bar. The two governments embarked on a frantic round of political manoeuvres to dispel the sense that Northern Ireland was on the brink of catastrophe.

Events moved at a dizzying pace, with politicians and diplomats shuttling back and forth in a process that ultimately led to the Downing Street Declaration of December 1993.[93] The Sinn Féin leadership, having done so much to get the ball rolling, now found themselves watching from the sidelines. The Shankill bombing was the immediate cause of their political isolation, but even without that calamity, it was always likely that the final drafts of a 'joint declaration' would emerge in such a fashion. As soon as the Provos decided to rely upon John Hume and Albert Reynolds to strengthen their negotiating position, they accepted the risk of being presented with a fait accompli.

The text of the Declaration drew upon the Hume–Adams document, but whittled down some of its key elements.[94] In particular, it ditched the idea of a positive commitment to Irish unity, with the

British government no longer promising to 'use all its influence and energy to win the consent of a majority in Northern Ireland' for steps in that direction.[95] The constitutional guarantee that Hume–Adams had transferred to Dublin remained in its present location: 'The British Government agree that it is for the people of the island of Ireland alone, by agreement between their two parts respectively, to exercise their right of self-determination on the basis of consent, freely and concurrently given, North and South, to bring about a united Ireland, if that is their wish.'[96]

Eamonn Mallie and David McKittrick described that 'serpentine paragraph' as 'a masterpiece of diplomatic ambiguity' that 'reconciled the irreconcilable'.[97] But the reconciliation was achieved at a discursive level, not a substantive one. The NIO minister Michael Ancram had good reason to depict it as 'a pretty Orange document in Green language'.[98] In the terms used by Walter Bagehot to analyse the British constitution, the dignified parts of the Declaration were Green, while its efficient parts were Orange.

It would be harder for Gerry Adams to sell the Declaration to the IRA as the basis for a ceasefire, but the alternative was to break with Sinn Féin's negotiating partners, and the republican leadership had gone too far down the pan-nationalist road to contemplate that. Instead of rejecting the Declaration outright, Adams played for time by asking the British government for 'clarification'. His claim to have found a discrepancy between statements by John Major and Albert Reynolds was disingenuous. In truth, the two leaders had been spinning the text of the Declaration for the benefit of their respective audiences, using very different language to describe the same essential point: there could be no change in Northern Ireland's constitutional status without the consent of a majority.[99] While Sinn Féin delayed its response to the Declaration, Adams set off on a trip to the United States whose main purpose was to demonstrate the political benefits that would accrue from a ceasefire.

Unlike most guerrilla movements of the late twentieth century, the Provisionals had always looked west rather than east for support: before the Libyan arms shipments of the 1980s, by far the greater part of the IRA's arsenal came from Irish-American sympathizers.

The collapse of the Soviet Union thus had no immediate relevance to the Provos.[100] The broader crisis of the international left, affecting movements that had been a real source of inspiration for republicans, was a different matter. In 1989, when Jim Gibney warned his comrades that they were facing the spectre of defeat, he described 'creative Marxism' as the 'liberating philosophy' that was 'capable of bringing people out of the apathy which they are sunk under'.[101] However, in the cramped political environment of the early 1990s, there was little chance of Gibney's movement embracing Marxism of any variety.

Danny Morrison's rejected article for *An Phoblacht* two years earlier had taken the electoral defeat of the Sandinistas in Nicaragua as its starting point. Morrison saw that setback as a triumph for brute American force.[102] But the tendency for movements like the Sandinistas and the PLO to seek an accommodation with the sole remaining superpower found a strong echo in the new republican peace strategy. Adams reached out to Irish-American politicians and businessmen like Bill Flynn with close ties to the US foreign policy establishment.[103] These new contacts gave the republican leadership another reason to put hard-left rhetoric in cold storage. Questioned about his burgeoning relationship with the Clinton Administration, Gerry Adams gave a phlegmatic response: 'You can have right-on, politically correct opinions, but, if I may say so, the correct left position must be to bring an end to British rule in Ireland.'[104]

On his return from Washington, Adams played down talk of a ceasefire in public while putting the last pieces together behind the scenes. In July 1994, he listed 'issues of immediate concern' that a peace process would need to address, from which the demand for British withdrawal was conspicuously absent.[105] Later that month, a Sinn Féin delegate conference in Donegal formally rejected the Downing Street Declaration, but the party's leader insisted that the peace process was 'very much alive'.[106] In a letter to Adams, the lawyer Paddy McGrory, who had represented several prominent republicans, cut to the heart of the matter: 'The most important decision is not acceptance or rejection of the Declaration, but a decision as to whether more is likely to be gained for the republican

cause by armed struggle than might be won by political means.'
McGrory argued that an IRA ceasefire would 'garner a rich harvest
of support for the republican movement, such as it has not known
for decades', while carrying on with the war would bring only isolation: 'The tide is at the flood, and is beginning to ebb. This is the
hour.'[107] Adams and his 'kitchen cabinet' clearly agreed.

10

Endgame

The Picador Approach

An IRA ceasefire duly followed on 31 August 1994, recipro-
cated weeks later by the loyalist paramilitaries. A document
circulated to IRA Volunteers on TUAS – 'Tactical Use of Armed
Struggle' – set out the rationale for a truce: 'Republicans at this
time and on their own do not have the strength to achieve the end
goal.' The priority now was to 'construct an Irish nationalist consensus with international support'. The paper suggested that such
a consensus could be based on a number of principles – 'partition
has failed', 'structures must be changed', 'no internal settlement',
etc. – but acknowledged that there were 'differences of opinion' on
how those principles should be applied, such as 'an interpretation
of what veto and consent mean'. Basic questions about the meaning
of consent and self-determination, which had been fundamental to
the conflict for the past quarter-century, thus became matters of
secondary importance. It may well have been, as the document suggested, 'the first time in twenty-five years that all the major Irish
nationalist parties are rowing in roughly the same direction'.[1] But it
was the Provos who had turned their boat around.

Gerry Adams spelled out the shift in perspective the following
year. According to Adams, the British government's current position would not prevent 'constitutional change or political advances

which fall short of dismantling the union from going ahead without the consent of a majority in the North'.[2] By implication, political advances which *did* go beyond that point were off the agenda. The Sinn Féin leader was now aiming for a settlement with strong cross-border institutions that could be presented as a first step towards Irish unity.

In the meantime, reforms should be carried out to ensure 'equality of treatment' for nationalists in Northern Ireland. Adams claimed that such measures would 'erode the very reason for the existence of that statelet'.[3] Republican critics of Adams had repeatedly compared him to Cathal Goulding over the previous decade – a suggestion that he found deeply wounding, as those who made it intended.[4] In this case it could be said, without polemical distortion, that the movement's leadership had reverted to the civil rights strategy of the late 60s. Then as now, republicans argued that a successful reform programme would leave Northern Ireland with no long-term future.

The main question was whether Adams and his allies could hold the movement together on the basis of this revisionist agenda. Observing the reaction to the ceasefire in Provisional strongholds, Eamonn McCann detected 'a sense of relief, or more accurately of release, from a burden which people had found harder to bear than they'd been able to acknowledge', with no desire for the war to go on: 'There are some who have doubts about what's on offer in return, but no powerful faction has emerged to argue that continuation of armed action is the best way to win more.'[5]

In the long run, IRA Volunteers would find it very difficult to swim against the current of nationalist opinion, but there was no guarantee they would heed it in the timeframe that Sinn Féin's peace strategy required. However much it reflected wider political realities, the ceasefire had clearly been leadership-driven, with the decision made by the seven-man Army Council.[6] The TUAS document acknowledged that 'communication up and down the organization has been patchy' and promised to do better from now on.[7]

John Major's government insisted on the decommissioning of IRA weapons as a precondition for Sinn Féin's entry into talks.

British officials who had been involved in contacts with the republican movement saw this as a reckless gambit. Quentin Thomas of the NIO believed that Major's demand 'kept inviting the Sinn Féin leadership to confront those within their movement who they did not want to confront for perfectly normal political reasons', while the MI6 veteran Michael Oatley tartly described it as the 'picador approach' to peace negotiations: 'No doubt, if sufficient barbs are thrust into its flanks, the animal will eventually, with reluctance, charge. The picadors can then claim that the beast was always a ravening monster.'[8] In contrast, Albert Reynolds moved quickly to bring Sinn Féin inside the tent, hosting a meeting with Adams and John Hume within weeks of the ceasefire.

As ever, the IRA's inner life could only be glimpsed through a glass darkly. One well-informed reporter, Suzanne Breen, saw 'immense trust' in the Adams leadership when the ceasefire began, provided it kept peace overtures within certain limits. An IRA Volunteer in Belfast told Breen that 'intelligence-gathering, fund-raising and other activities' would carry on as before: 'If it was a question of us handing over arms, we'd oppose it. But that's not on the agenda.'[9] Twelve months later, she still found the ceasefire to be 'rock-solid', with 'no immediate threat of an internal split', but widespread dissatisfaction in the lower ranks of the movement.[10] By the start of 1996, Breen was warning that trouble might lie ahead: 'The IRA's opponents are paying a small price for the ceasefire. They can afford to be more magnanimous in victory.'[11]

The decommissioning stand-off was the main issue for republicans, but there had been other developments to put the ceasefire under strain. When the Reynolds government collapsed in December 1994, a new coalition headed by Fine Gael's John Bruton took its place. Bruton made no bones about his hostility to 'pan-nationalism'; worse still from a republican perspective, his government included Proinsias De Rossa's new vehicle Democratic Left, which had ditched the Marxist ideology of the Workers' Party but retained all of its animosity towards the Provos.

For their part, sceptics pointed to evidence of ongoing IRA activity, in particular a botched robbery that claimed the life of a post

office worker in November 1994. The IRA leadership admitted that
its members were responsible for the killing, but insisted that the
Army Council had not sanctioned the operation.[12] IRA units also
shot dead several alleged drug dealers in Belfast during the ceasefire, using the cover name 'Direct Action Against Drugs'.

In the summer of 1995, rioting broke out in nationalist areas
after two controversial events: John Major's decision to release a
British soldier who had been convicted of murder, and the RUC's
decision to push an Orange march through the predominantly
Catholic Garvaghy Road in Portadown. The Ulster Unionist MP
David Trimble joined hands with Ian Paisley as they completed the
parade, insisting there had been no deal with the Garvaghy Road
residents.[13] Trimble's role in the controversy helped him ascend to
the UUP leadership in September 1995.

After years in which he was known primarily as an IRA leader,
Martin McGuinness had begun to emerge as a politician with a
profile to rival that of Gerry Adams. His reputation as an uncompromising militarist might have led one to expect a strained
relationship between the two men, but there was little sign of that
in public. Indeed, that hard-line image proved to be a vital asset
for Adams, making it easier to sell the compromises that his strategy was bound to entail. When push came to shove, the contrast
between the two Sinn Féin leaders appeared to be largely a matter
of style and personality, masking the deeper political convergence
between them.

On the first anniversary of the truce, McGuinness reproached
the British government for its 'begrudging and negative response'.[14]
The controversy over IRA weapons overshadowed further evidence of the change in Sinn Féin's position. Not for the last time, a
republican leader tried to snatch a semblance of victory from the
jaws of retreat by redefining basic political concepts.[15] McGuinness
railed against 'London's acceptance of the unionist veto over talks',
insisting that 'no group can be allowed a veto on change'.[16] This
minimalist recasting of the 'unionist veto' would allow Sinn Féin to
claim victory when it secured entry to all-party talks, even if that
veto as republicans traditionally understood it was a foundation

stone of the entire process. 'Change' was every bit as malleable a term, since British governments had already accepted that Unionist politicians could not veto reforms that fell short of ending partition.

The balance of forces inside the IRA eventually tipped in favour of the sceptics, after more foot-dragging from John Major, and a massive bomb in London's Canary Wharf shattered the ceasefire in February 1996.[17] The subsequent campaign now looks like a strange parenthesis in the history of the movement, prosecuted by a leadership that had no desire to abandon the peace process altogether, with little activity inside Northern Ireland, and successful operations like Canary Wharf and the bombing of Thiepval barracks punctuated by major setbacks.

The IRA's Easter statement in April 1996 simply called for all-party talks that would 'allow for the core issues at the heart of this conflict to be addressed'.[18] But the militarist tendency would have been happy to go back to basics, as Brendan O'Brien observed: 'There *were* those who argued for a single-minded Brits Out offensive, with a view to extracting what they had previously failed to extract, namely a British commitment to withdraw. The advocates of this course were prepared to jettison the community-based support, built up over twenty years, even jettison the Sinn Féin connection.'[19] If this faction had taken control of the movement, all bets would have been off.

The Adams leadership kept its strategy alive by seeing off the dissident challenge at an Army Convention in November 1996.[20] Fortified by this victory, they faced a special party conference in Athboy later that month. Although the conference was held behind closed doors, a transcript of the speech given by Gerry Adams soon leaked out. Adams made his distrust of Sinn Féin's erstwhile 'pan-nationalist' allies clear: 'It would be far better if we were bigger than them. We could ignore them.' He also hinted at the possibility of a breach between Sinn Féin and the IRA: 'Whatever the Army does is the Army's business and people can have whatever views they want about that. But let us not use the Army in whatever it does as an excuse for us not to make peace.'[21] However, the Convention's outcome had made the prospect of a split much less likely.

The most controversial part of his speech concerned the issue of Orange marches. The second confrontation on the Garvaghy Road in July 1996 was far more dramatic than the previous year's stand-off, with loyalists setting up roadblocks throughout Northern Ireland and a huge crowd massing at Drumcree to force the parade through. When the RUC's Chief Constable Hugh Annesley reversed the decision to impose a ban, the relish of his officers in clearing nationalist protesters off the streets was all too evident.[22] Adams credited the entire affair, which had made the RUC and the Unionist parties appear in the worst possible light, to 'three years of work' by republican activists: 'Fair play to the people who put that work in. And they are the type of scene changes that we have to focus in on and develop and exploit.'[23] Unionist politicians seized on these remarks as proof that Sinn Féin had confected the opposition to Orange parades for its own benefit.

In fact, Adams had exaggerated his party's influence: as events were to show, the Sinn Féin leadership was in no position to give orders to the Garvaghy Road Residents Group or its spokes-man, Breandán MacCionnaith.[24] But there was a deeper irony to his comments that the critics appear to have missed. As the thir-tieth anniversary of NICRA's first venture from Coalisland to Dungannon approached, the question of street marches once again took centre stage in the politics of Northern Ireland. The movement Adams had joined after the republican split used NICRA's protest campaign as the launchpad for a war that went on for much longer than anyone could have anticipated. Some IRA activists wanted to exploit 'Drumcree 2' in similar fashion to recharge their move-ment's batteries for another generation.[25] In contrast, Adams cited the 'community resistance' of the Garvaghy Road as proof that, while the war might be over, the struggle would continue.

The Unwinnable War

Over the next few months, the pieces began falling into place for a second ceasefire. In May 1997, Tony Blair's Labour Party trounced

John Major's Conservatives in the UK general election. Sinn Féin's vote share in Northern Ireland rose from 10 to 16 per cent, with seats for Gerry Adams in West Belfast and Martin McGuinness in Mid-Ulster. A few weeks later, Fianna Fáil's new leader, Bertie Ahern, returned his party to government in Dublin, while Sinn Féin won its first seat for a southern constituency since the Border Campaign. Blair and Ahern went on to provide continuity of leadership in the two states for the next decade. The new Taoiseach had criticized John Bruton during the election campaign for his handling of the peace process; Blair maintained a 'bipartisan' line in public while Major was still in power, but soon indicated that Sinn Féin could enter talks without decommissioning by the IRA.[26]

A second ceasefire came into effect in July, and Sinn Féin signed up to a set of principles drafted by the US mediator George Mitchell, committing the party to 'exclusively peaceful means of resolving political issues' and 'total disarmament of all paramilitary organizations' in the framework of an eventual settlement.[27] Adams led a Sinn Féin delegation into talks soon afterwards. Paisley's DUP withdrew in protest, but David Trimble kept his party in the mix, while refusing to engage directly with Sinn Féin.[28]

Acceptance of the Mitchell Principles proved to be the final straw for Michael McKevitt, the IRA's quarter-master general, who had spearheaded the challenge to Adams. After another Army Convention in October 1997 that strengthened the hand of the leadership, McKevitt and his supporters broke away to form a group known as the 'Real IRA'.[29] McKevitt's new organization soon acquired a political shadow, the 32 County Sovereignty Movement, that accused Sinn Féin of betraying republican principles. But the effect of his departure was to splinter the internal opposition to Sinn Féin's new approach.

Two small parties represented the loyalist paramilitaries at the talks: the UDA's political mouthpiece, the Ulster Democratic Party, and the Progressive Unionist Party, aligned with the UVF. After the DUP's exit, their presence alongside Trimble's party satisfied the need for at least half of the Unionist electorate to be involved in the process. These groups proved to be more flexible than their bigger rivals on the terms of a peace settlement, so long as the Union remained in place. Infuriated by this accommodating stance, the UVF's Mid-Ulster commander Billy Wright tried to lead his comrades back to war, setting up his own organization, the Loyalist Volunteer Force (LVF), after the UVF expelled him in 1996.[30]

Wright's death inside the Maze prison in December 1997 sparked off a round of sectarian killings by the LVF and its UDA allies, but the loyalist ceasefire ultimately held. The shooting of Wright was the main intervention by a largely inactive INLA while the talks were in progress, although some INLA activists worked with McKevitt's Real IRA to carry out bomb attacks.[31]

Tony Blair had scrapped Labour's 'unity by consent' policy after becoming the party's leader and removed its chief advocate, Kevin McNamara, from his position on the front bench. He used his first speech in Northern Ireland as prime minister to deliver a warm endorsement of the Union.[32] Blair's administration was no more willing to play the role of 'persuader for unity' than its predecessor had been. On the short-term question of decommissioning and Sinn Féin's entry into talks, the new governments gave Gerry Adams exactly what he needed. However, the Heads of Agreement paper they published in January 1998 had a much weaker 'all-Ireland' element than the Framework Documents produced by Major and John Bruton in 1995.[33] The republican leadership had lowered its sights and was prepared to accept cross-border institutions with substantial powers in lieu of a united Ireland; now, even that objective looked to be slipping away as the final stage of negotiations began.

After a flurry of last-minute brinkmanship, the parties agreed on the text of the Good Friday Agreement (GFA) in April 1998.[34] The Downing Street Declaration had already laid down the broad parameters for a deal, leaving various secondary elements to be haggled over. In simple terms, the SDLP got most of what it wanted over power-sharing arrangements, David Trimble got most of what he wanted over cross-border structures, and Sinn Féin got most of what it wanted over decommissioning and prisoner releases. The republican negotiating team ditched its opposition to a new regional assembly, and watched Trimble secure the hollowing out of a paper on North–South institutions.[35] But they kept the time-table for the release of prisoners down to two years, and made sure there was no requirement for decommissioning in advance of Sinn Féin's entry into government.

Trimble seems to have expected Sinn Féin to leave before the talks were over, relieving him of the need to sell a package that would put republicans in a power-sharing administration.[36] If so, he underestimated the party's determination to remain inside the tent, even at the price of major ideological concessions. In order to secure his flank against internal opposition, Trimble extracted a letter from Tony Blair at the last minute, promising measures to exclude Sinn Féin from the regional government if decommissioning did not begin 'straight away'.[37] As the academic Padraig O'Malley pointed out, the text of the GFA itself did not impose any such obligation on Sinn Féin; that was what the party's leadership had signed up to, not a bilateral commitment from Blair to the UUP.[38] Ian Paisley geared up to oppose the Agreement in any case, accusing Trimble of selling out to the Provos.

At the Sinn Féin Ard Fheis in May 1998, Gerry Adams was careful not to oversell the GFA, describing it as 'another staging-post on the road to a peace settlement' rather than a settlement in its own right: 'British rule has not ended. Neither has partition. That is why our struggle continues.'[39] Adams strengthened his case for a 'Yes' vote by welcoming the 'Balcombe Street Gang' onto the stage to receive a ten-minute standing ovation. The men, who had spent the last two decades in British jails after carrying out a series of bomb attacks in the 1970s, were on day release after their recent transfer to Portlaoise prison. Their presence reminded delegates that the Agreement would bring the IRA's prisoners home and helped secure an overwhelming vote to endorse it, clearing the way for Sinn Féin to take its seats in a new Northern Ireland Assembly.[40] Adams concluded his speech with a new tactical emphasis: 'We go into this next phase of struggle armed only with whatever mandate we receive, armed only with our political ideas and our vision of the future.'[41]

Nationalist support for the GFA was sky-high: the overwhelming majority of Northern Irish nationalists voted in favour, and there was a 95 per cent 'Yes' vote in a simultaneous plebiscite south of the border. But just 57 per cent of unionists endorsed the deal.[42] Most unionists reacted with horror to the performance staged by the Sinn Féin leadership in Dublin, which weakened David Trimble's position in the referendum campaign. Hard as it might be for their opponents to accept, the republican movement needed something to sweeten the pill after signing up to a political framework it had rejected out of hand for decades. The federalism of Éire Nua and the abstentionist policy never mattered as much to the northern Provos grouped around Gerry Adams as they did to their estranged comrade Ruairí Ó Brádaigh. But a firm belief that the state in Northern Ireland could never be reformed was absolutely central to their ideology. Now they would be haggling over the extent of such reforms for an indefinite period.

In total, the IRA accounted for nearly half of those killed between 1966 and 2001: over 1,750 people. Just over one in two of the organization's victims fitted its own definition of legitimate targets (soldiers, police and prison officers, or loyalist paramilitaries).[43] By the standards that the IRA set for itself, its war ended in failure.

That outcome was both predictable and predicted from an early stage. Northern Ireland was a small, densely populated area on the fringe of Western Europe, with no mountains or jungles for guerrillas to shelter in. But the challenges that the region's physical geography posed were ultimately less important than its social geography. Guerrilla movements need popular support to overcome the military advantages enjoyed by their opponents, yet the IRA faced implacable opposition from the unionist majority throughout the conflict. If the whole of Northern Ireland had been like West Belfast or South Armagh, the Provisionals could easily have won. In that scenario, of course, partition would never have been viable in the first place. The surprising thing is not that the Provos eventually compromised on their demands, but that they managed to avoid outright defeat.

Internal critics of Gerry Adams had warned that his electoral strategy would undermine the IRA from the moment it got off the ground.[44] But it could well be argued that Sinn Féin's political growth in the 1980s extended the war beyond its natural lifespan, by giving the movement's leadership reason to hope it could still win. After all, the dual campaign from 1981 to 1994 comfortably outlasted the 'pure' military struggle of the 1970s, and went on for much longer than any previous republican insurgency, from the 'Tan War' to Operation Harvest. Once Sinn Féin hit its electoral ceiling, it should have been clear that republicans would find victory elusive. From that point on, it was a question of securing the best deal they could achieve.

Facing charges of betrayal from republican splinter groups, Adams and his comrades had one trump card: a widespread belief that armed struggle was a political dead end, even if the fruits of Sinn Féin's alternative strategy left much to be desired. Richard O'Rawe, an IRA veteran who fell out with the republican leadership in the most acrimonious way, still defended their change of course without hesitation: 'Of course I support the peace process. Like or dislike Gerry Adams, he has to be given credit for ending the unwinnable war.'[45]

Michael McKevitt's Real IRA dealt a hammer-blow to republican militarism in August 1998 when it planted a bomb in Omagh that killed twenty-nine civilians: the worst individual atrocity of the entire conflict. Having threatened to build up a head of steam, the group had little choice but to call a ceasefire in the wake of the carnage, although its uncompromising perspective suggested that it would eventually return to war. As long as the 'dissidents' were bent on restarting an unpopular armed campaign that had no prospect of forcing Britain to withdraw, there was little chance they would pose an effective political challenge to the Provos.

'Crablike towards their goal'

The period since 1998 is still very hard to view in a long-term perspective. The making and remaking of the Good Friday Agreement has been in progress for almost as long as the IRA's armed struggle, without completing the transition from current affairs to history. Due to the limited availability of sources, any judgement on the post-conflict years must be rather tentative. Even so, we can identify some crucial landmarks, and examine some of the underlying factors beneath the surface of events. As both supporters and opponents would agree, this was a time in which Sinn Féin and the IRA remained absolutely central to the politics of Northern Ireland, forcing the other players to respond to their initiatives whether they liked it or not.

In the afterglow of the 1998 referendum, many observers expected that David Trimble's Ulster Unionists would go on to dominate the region's political life in tandem with the SDLP. But Trimble's insistence on prior decommissioning – 'no guns, no government' – blocked the speedy formation of a power-sharing executive. The impasse dragged on for several years, while reports of continued IRA activity, from Colombia to Castlereagh, began to accumulate. Trimble's authority as the leader of Unionism steadily drained away, and he dismissed eventual moves by the IRA on decommissioning as inadequate for his political needs. In the meantime, republican and loyalist prisoners won their freedom, and a commission headed by the Conservative politician Chris Patten delivered a report on police reform that Unionists greeted with fury.

The political stalemate did Sinn Féin little harm at the ballot box, and the party overtook the SDLP for the first time in the UK general election of 2001. When Paisley's DUP surpassed the Ulster Unionists in regional elections two years later, Tony Blair and Bertie Ahern sought to broker a compromise between the new communal hegemons, at first to little avail. But in September 2005, after coming under intense pressure, the IRA announced the full decommissioning of its arsenal. Two years later, Sinn Féin concluded a deal with Ian Paisley to form a power-sharing government that became a lasting feature of the political scene.

Describing what happened is straightforward enough; accounting for why it happened is a much trickier business. In public and in private, the Sinn Féin leadership had a simple explanation for the slow pace of decommissioning after 1998: their overriding fear of a split. Critics dismissed that claim out of hand, and chided Blair for his alleged reluctance to call Sinn Féin's bluff. In Britain, a cluster of journalists and academics associated with hawkish, right-wing think tanks took up these arguments, already commonplace among anti-agreement Unionists.[46]

But a writer with a very different political outlook, Ed Moloney, also became a forceful spokesman for the 'appeasement' thesis. According to Moloney, Adams and his comrades could have begun decommissioning 'very soon after the Good Friday Agreement was ratified', having secured their control over the IRA. Instead, they opted to stall in pursuit of electoral advantage, an approach that 'divided and destabilized mainstream unionism, rendered their SDLP rivals almost irrelevant, and polarized Northern Ireland politics to the advantage of the extremes'.[47] The two governments were 'naive, not to mention foolish' in their stance towards the IRA: Blair in particular, Moloney suggested, 'would concede virtually anything that was asked of him'.[48] Given the importance of decommissioning for the whole course of events after 1998, this argument deserves careful scrutiny.

It is useful to compare Moloney's picture of Blair and Ahern as IRA dupes with the account of the peace process supplied by Blair's chief of staff, Jonathan Powell. Powell sympathized with the need for Gerry Adams and Martin McGuinness to 'move crablike towards their goal, in cautious and gradual steps, never revealing in full to the movement their eventual destination'. There was, he believed, a convergence of interests between his government and the Provo leadership, since they were both determined to avoid an IRA split: 'We did not want to have to make peace lots of times with republican splinter groups. We wanted to do it once.'[49]

For Powell, determining where Sinn Féin's bottom line actually lay was an art, not a science, and there was no particular virtue in testing them to the limit 'just for the pleasure of feeling we had got the deal at the lowest possible price'.[50] Ed Moloney described the ultimate reward for such patience very well: 'Since it was the IRA's own leaders who were winding up the armed struggle, it was coming to an end with a certainty and finality that no amount of security successes could have guaranteed.' Moreover, the political price being asked in return would have been considered 'impossibly modest' just a few years earlier.[51]

Although Powell did not say so explicitly, Blair's attitude towards the IRA clearly owed something to his commitments elsewhere. The period bookended by the Good Friday Agreement and the decommissioning statement of 2005 saw British forces deployed in action on a scale unknown since the last days of empire. With an almost messianic zeal, Blair held up armed struggle as the path to liberation for oppressed peoples, from the Balkans to Afghanistan and Iraq. Powell does not appear to have noticed the irony: his memoir scolds Martin McGuinness for 'cheekily' criticizing the bombing of Afghanistan – 'he should know a thing or two about bombing campaigns, we thought' – but there is no hint of self-awareness when Powell recalls Blair nipping out of crisis talks to strong-arm the Chilean president before a crucial vote on Iraq.[52] Those who accused Blair of pandering to the Provos were often keen supporters of his strategy in the Middle East.[53] They were reluctant to admit that the flip side of military boldness in Basra or Helmand was a more cautious approach in South Armagh.

Ed Moloney detected 'an intriguing clue as to how the IRA leadership really regarded Blair' in papers seized by police officers investigating an alleged republican spy ring: 'One document referred to the British Prime Minister by his IRA code-name: "The Naïve Idiot".'[54] If word of this got back to Downing Street, Blair might well have chuckled at such self-aggrandizing bravado. The pay-off for his 'naivety' was the freedom to dispatch troops to far-flung locations without having to worry about exposing the British state's soft underbelly. By one estimate, at least one-third of the IRA membership still consisted of 'internal dissidents' after the Real IRA split.[55] From Blair's perspective, keeping those sceptics under the thumb of Gerry Adams was a bargain-basement approach to counter-insurgency.

It is hard to imagine that a fresh republican campaign could have matched the Provisional war of the 1970s and 80s, much less that it could have succeeded where the Provos failed. But violence on a more limited scale would still have destabilized the region and obliged the British government to commit forces on the home front, just as the 'war on terror' was entering its most ambitious phase. Blair's line on decommissioning looks more like a calculated trade-off between policy objectives than the product of gullibility.

If the supposed fear of large-scale defections had been no more than a cynical ploy used by Adams to strengthen his movement's bargaining position, we might have expected word of this to reach the highest levels of government. After all, one Sinn Féin activist on the fringe of the party's inner circle, Denis Donaldson, was subsequently revealed to be a British agent. Powell's account suggests genuine uncertainty about the balance of opinion within the IRA.[56] The future release of state papers may reveal that Powell's colleagues knew more than he let on.

But the work of journalists with good republican sources tends to confirm the wisdom of a cautious attitude. In January 2000, Suzanne Breen identified decommissioning as one compromise that the IRA's grassroots could not stomach: 'It has touched a deep chord. The vast majority are firmly opposed to even a token hand-over.' She predicted that any move in that direction by the movement's leadership would supply a major boost to the Real IRA: 'The mood in the general nationalist community is firmly against a return to conflict but the republican base remains more ambiguous.'[57]

Two years later, Breen argued that it was still necessary for the Army Council to allow intelligence-gathering and weapons training to continue, even at the price of political embarrassment for Sinn Féin, 'in order to keep their base occupied'.[58] At the beginning of 2003, as speculation mounted that the Provos were going to stand their units down for good, she found 'caution, disbelief and some resignation' among IRA Volunteers in Belfast. Her report suggested that the salami tactics used by Adams to marginalize his opponents had paid off.

One IRA member told Breen that the movement was now 'too far down the road to turn back', even though he was unhappy with the outcome of the peace process: 'I thought we would be heading towards a united Ireland. I'd have called anyone a liar who had suggested we would sit in Stormont or disarm, let alone wind up.' Another 'disillusioned Provisional' had no intention of linking up with the dissidents: 'They are not seen as alternatives. The only place for people like me to go is home.'[59] Breen still detected 'considerable discontent within IRA grassroots, particularly in Tyrone and Fermanagh' a few months later.[60] The Sinn Féin leadership may well have exaggerated the strength of internal opposition as a negotiating tactic, but they did not invent it altogether.

There is also an unacknowledged tension in Moloney's own account of these years. The final catalyst for wholesale decommissioning in 2005 came from two events that were extremely damaging for Sinn Féin: the Northern Bank robbery in December 2004, for which the IRA was immediately held responsible, and the brutal killing of Robert McCartney after a row with IRA members in a Belfast pub. The circumstances of the bank heist suggested that it must have had prior approval from the Army Council, unlike McCartney's murder.[61]

According to Moloney, McCartney's death was 'an unforeseeable event whose subsequent handling nonetheless assisted the move towards final decommissioning'. But the Northern Bank robbery was something more calculated, 'an operation approved by the IRA's political leadership in the knowledge that its consequences would force the organization to contemplate far-reaching measures'.[62]

Whether or not this hypothesis is correct, it can hardly be reconciled with the rest of Moloney's argument. If the republican leadership had had a free hand to decommission the IRA's entire arsenal from 1999 onwards, there would have been no need for them to compromise Sinn Féin's position by giving the IRA a rope with which to hang itself later on.

Spinning Plates

The overall impression we get from Moloney's narrative is that Sinn Féin approached the period after 1998 with a carefully thought-out strategic master plan. It appears much more likely that they improvised in response to events, knowing roughly where they wanted to end up but ducking and weaving along the way. An apt metaphor for the challenge facing them came from Moloney himself, who once compared the way Sinn Féin was handling the weapons issue to 'that old circus act in which a juggler tries to keep an ever-growing number of plates spinning atop rows of bamboo poles'.[63]

Ironically, Gerry Adams used a very similar image when discussing the republican peace strategy: 'As any juggler worth his balls knows, keeping more than two in the air at the same time requires a lot of focus and concentration.'[64] Adams and his comrades certainly wanted to extract the maximum political advantage from disposing of the IRA's arms, but they also had real difficulties in bringing their supporters to that point. In much the same way, David Trimble exploited a genuine threat to his own leadership from within the UUP to lobby for concessions from Blair's government.[65]

In Moloney's version of the juggling metaphor, it was only a matter of time before things went wrong for its subject: 'Eventually he overreaches himself, tries to spin one plate too many and the rest begin to fall.' That moment came in the early months of 2005, after Robert McCartney's death and the Northern Bank robbery. If the Provisional leadership did possess the authority to order full decommissioning back in 2003, a move at that point would have left Sinn Féin with a stronger hand to play than after the September 2005 statement. Trimble's waning political fortunes had encouraged republican hesitancy, as his advisor Steven King acknowledged: 'Perhaps a card or two had to be kept back just in case they were in negotiations with the DUP in a few years' time.'[66] But in the end, the Provos still had to surrender their most valuable bargaining chip before attempting to strike a deal with Paisley. Sinn Féin's decisive entry into government came from a position of weakness and political isolation.

The long stalemate over decommissioning obscured the fact that Sinn Féin was becoming an increasingly conventional political party. The Provos had been the purest example of an anti-systemic movement in Western Europe: not only did they possess their own army, which doubled as a community police force, they also had their own media, entertainment industry and even transport system (the 'black cabs' of West Belfast). When Gerry Adams argued for Sinn Féin to scrap its abstentionist policy back in 1986, he referred in passing to the question of 'electoralism as a means of revolutionary struggle', which had 'affected all struggles in areas where parliaments with universal suffrage exist'. Sinn Féin's link to the IRA campaign was, he argued, the true guarantee of its revolutionary character.[67] As the party finally severed that link, the full extent of its transformation since the 1980s should have been readily apparent.

One activist, Féilim Ó hAdhmaill, had expected a return to 'the mass mobilizations of the civil rights period, producing a type of republican intifada' after the IRA ceasefire.[68] But the only real example of that came from the community protests against Orange marches in the late 1990s. The mobilization of the Garvaghy Road residents in Portadown was a clear-cut success: in spite of heavy pressure from David Trimble, reinforced behind the scenes by Tony Blair, they secured the banning of the march in 1998, and all subsequent efforts to overturn that ban proved fruitless.[69] By 2004, as Jonathan Powell observed, the Drumcree march was a 'dead letter'.[70] Away from flashpoints like Drumcree, however, there was little room for mass participation in Sinn Féin's new struggle.

Northern Ireland probably had more elected representatives per capita than any region in Europe, and a remarkably high proportion of Sinn Féin's activist base became involved in electoral work, whether directly as councillors and Assembly members or indirectly as research assistants, constituency workers, etc. A much smaller group managed the high politics of the peace process: very often it would be just Gerry Adams and Martin McGuinness, or even Adams alone, who took part directly in negotiations.[71] The enervating, stop-start, 'Groundhog Day' character of the talks led to widespread apathy, as Suzanne Breen observed in 2003: 'Most people have simply switched off. In pubs, taxi depots and cafés, in-depth analysis focuses on the race for the English Premiership, not that for the peace deal. The strategies of Sir Alex Ferguson and

Arsene Wenger arouse much more interest than those of Gerry Adams and David Trimble.'[72]

Back in the 1970s, 'Brownie' and his comrades had proclaimed the need to eliminate 'spectator politics' and mobilize the republican base. Now the peace process had created a new form of spectator politics, and it was losing the battle for audience share.

If Sinn Féin had become a rather conventional vote-winning machine, it was at least a very efficient one. The party's vote in regional elections rose from 16.7 per cent in 1998 to 23.5 per cent in 2003 and 26.2 per cent four years later, largely at the expense of the SDLP. By 2007, it had 63 per cent of the nationalist vote. Although there was some attrition in traditional strongholds, Sinn Féin remained completely hegemonic in West Belfast, taking five of the constituency's six Assembly seats that year with 70 per cent of the total poll. The party had made deep inroads into the middle-class Catholic electorate without forfeiting its original base. Republicans were naturally delighted to overtake the SDLP, but that pleasure must have been tinged with a nagging recognition that they had stolen much of its political wardrobe. After vowing to overthrow the state for so many years, the Provos were now trying to manage and reform it as best they could on behalf of the nationalist minority, just as the SDLP had originally set out to do.

Sinn Féin's claim to have changed its methods but not its goals rested on a few slender reeds. One was the argument that the GFA's tightly ring-fenced cross-border institutions would somehow unleash a 'transitional dynamic' leading inexorably to Irish unity.[73] This belief had little objective basis, as Fianna Fáil's chief ideologue Martin Mansergh pointed out: 'There is no evidence, let alone inevitability, from international experience that limited cross-border cooperation necessarily leads to political reunification.'[74] In 2005, a careful analysis by Jonathan Tonge found the binational aspects of the Agreement to be 'woefully thin'.[75] British sovereignty may not have been as intrusive as before, but when vital interests were at stake, its undiluted character became readily apparent.

Security reform was one such interest. In 2001, Blair's government appointed the Canadian judge Peter Cory to investigate several killings where there were strong suspicions of state collusion, including the murder of Pat Finucane. Cory recommended a public inquiry into Finucane's death, warning that it 'could be seen as a cynical breach of faith' if Blair demurred.[76] While there was never any question of the British state dismantling its own security machine, an inquiry would have been a symbolic act of decommissioning, turning the page on a very ugly chapter in that machine's history. However, the untrammelled investigation that Cory called for never took place. It was one thing to reconstitute the RUC as the Police Service of Northern Ireland (PSNI), after watering down some of Chris Patten's ideas for reform to keep the process within safe limits.[77] A wide-ranging inquiry that was bound to implicate 'mainland' institutions like the Army and MI5 was a very different matter. The British state settled down for a grinding war of attrition, doing its best to keep evidence of collusion out of the public domain.[78] That made it harder for Sinn Féin to support the PSNI, a precondition for its entry into government with the DUP, although the party leadership eventually got its way over the issue at the 2007 Ard Fheis.[79]

The other source of consolation for the Provos was their political growth in the South, which appeared to lend substance to an all-Ireland vision. Having won its first seat in 1997, Sinn Féin took five in 2002, then surged past the Irish Labour Party with 11 per cent of the vote in the European election two years later. Sinn Féin's southern representatives included men like Caoimhghín Ó Caoláin and Seán Crowe, who had been republican activists since the hunger strikes, and the IRA veteran Martin Ferris, reputedly a member of the Army Council when he claimed a seat for the party in Kerry.[80] But its successful candidate for Dublin's Euro-constituency, Mary Lou McDonald, came from a new generation, a 'peace process levy' to supplement the 'H-Block levy' of the 1980s.

Southern politics provided the main outlet for Sinn Féin's residual leftism, as the only electoral niche available lay on the Labour Party's left flank. This was a much softer variety of left-wing politics than that of the 1980s, swapping Third World liberation movements for Nordic social democracy as a source of inspiration.[81] It was still a distinctive message in a state dominated by centre-right parties, and Sinn Féin looked set to grow in the general election of 2007.

As polling day approached, the party announced that it was 'ready for government, north and south'.[82] The Dublin TD Aengus Ó Snodaigh argued that a republican presence around the cabinet table in both Irish states would help create 'a truly national government'.[83] This argument leaned heavily on one of the main cross-border institutions, the North/South Ministerial Council, which brought together ministers from both jurisdictions to discuss matters of common concern. While the presence of Sinn Féin representatives from either side of the border would certainly have had great symbolic value for republicans, strictly speaking it would make no difference to Northern Ireland's constitutional status. Once again, the road to Irish unity was being paved with wishful thinking.

Sinn Féin's only plausible route into government was as a junior coalition partner for one of the centre-right parties, most likely Fianna Fáil. The party leadership had seen off motions at the previous year's Ard Fheis that sought to exclude that option.[84] Now they abruptly ditched a plan to raise corporation tax in order to ease their passage towards government office.[85] Having sacrificed principle for power, Sinn Féin found itself with neither. The party increased its vote share slightly but lost one of its five seats, and was in no position to drive a bargain of any sort with Fianna Fáil. A conservative newspaper columnist, Noel Whelan, expressed his satisfaction at the outcome: 'Whereas in Northern Ireland, Sinn Féin is now a catch-all party dominant on the nationalist side, in the Republic it has been, and it now appears will continue to be, a niche party on the far-left, ardent-republican end of the spectrum.'[86] Throughout the peace process, the republican leadership had relied upon an image of dynamism and forward thrust to keep its supporters motivated in the face of constant U-turns.[87] Now, with the IRA off the stage and Sinn Féin's electoral growth becalmed, there was no mistaking the sense of historic closure.

Epilogue

Towards the Republic?

In one of the most penetrating studies of Sinn Féin's development, published soon after the 2007 election, Kevin Bean identified a malaise that was much deeper than any polling setbacks. For Bean, what distinguished the Provos from revisionist predecessors like Fianna Fáil or the Officials was 'not just the mood of defeat, but the sense of collapse and terminus'. Republicanism now seemed to be 'intellectually exhausted, giving the appearance of an ideological project that has run its historical course'.[1] In the decade since that book appeared, Sinn Féin has certainly managed to restore a sense of forward momentum on the electoral front. But has it been able to kick-start the republican project itself? Was the 'underlying loss of historical confidence' no more than a passing phase?[2]

If the period since 1998 still resists any long-term assessment, the same point holds with even greater force for the last decade of Irish history, as the impact of the Great Recession has unsettled the usual patterns, just as it has disrupted political life throughout Europe and the wider world.[3] A new balance has yet to emerge on either side of the Irish border, and it would be reckless to predict where Irish politics is likely to stand when it does. But even in the midst of a hurricane, knowing something about the nature of a ship and its crew makes it easier to predict whether it will reach its ultimate destination. Sinn Féin and the wider republican tradition of which it is part entered the crisis with some basic political characteristics whose importance has not diminished since 2008.

The most ambitious attempt to change the party's ideological coordinates since the Good Friday Agreement came from another product of the 'peace process levy', Eoin Ó Broin. Ó Broin, a middle-class Dubliner, joined Sinn Féin in the mid 90s and spent several years as a councillor in Belfast before returning to his home town, where he eventually became a TD in 2016. In the wake of the 2007 election, he criticized the party's drift towards the centre ground: 'Sinn Féin does not belong there and should not be in the business of trading fundamental redistributive policies in the hope of short-term electoral gain. That's a kind of politics we should leave to Fianna Fáil.'[4]

Ó Broin followed this up with a wide-ranging historical study of attempts to marry the republican tradition with left-wing politics.[5] He associated two main strands of left republicanism with the figures of James Connolly and Liam Mellows. For Connolly, a Marxist who spent his whole life in the workers' movement, the struggles for socialism and national independence formed one indivisible whole; for Mellows, with his Fenian roots, class politics could serve as a booster shot to keep republican hopes alive. His left turn during the Civil War had been 'a tactical shift, not an ideological one'.[6]

As Ó Broin went on to argue, the Provos clearly stood in the tradition of Mellows, not Connolly. He criticized the 'stageist' line of Gerry Adams that held up Irish unity as 'Sinn Féin's "primary objective", with democratic socialism relegated to the status of an "ultimate objective"'. This ensured that Sinn Féin's brand of left-wing politics, 'relegated to a future point in the struggle, would always be underdeveloped, as the more immediate needs of the national struggle took precedence'.[7] Ó Broin urged his comrades to 'abandon the key ideological formulation that has underpinned left republicanism since Mellows' and 'end the hierarchy of objectives implied in the party's ideology, policy and strategy'.[8] It was a compelling indictment, but given the weight of Sinn Féin's history, and the organizational ballast that held it in place, there was never much chance that the party leadership would take it to heart. It would be a lot easier to respond to the setback of 2007 with 'a tactical shift, not an ideological one', tacking their sails to the left without attempting to rebuild the entire craft.

That was precisely what happened after the financial crash of 2008 that plunged the southern economy into a deep crisis.[9] A rising tide of disaffection lifted all purportedly left-wing boats as support for Fianna Fáil collapsed. Gerry Adams urged the Irish Labour Party to join a 'new alignment' that could end 'the dominance in this state of two large conservative parties'.[10] Labour, now led by a former Workers' Party TD, Eamon Gilmore, predictably spurned that offer. An anti-austerity platform delivered Labour's best ever result in the 2011 election, surpassing Fianna Fáil for the first time with almost 20 per cent of the vote, while Sinn Féin took 10 per cent and fourteen seats, establishing its strongest foothold in southern politics since the break with Éamon de Valera in the 1920s. Gilmore immediately took Labour into a coalition with Fine Gael to implement the same austerity programme that had cost Fianna Fáil most of its support. Five years later, Labour followed its electoral high point with a precipitous fall.

Sinn Féin continued to grow, almost doubling its vote in the European election of 2014 and coming within touching distance of Fianna Fáil and Fine Gael. The party's bid to channel the anti-austerity mood had a strong parliamentary focus: when a major protest movement against water charges developed from the autumn of 2014, it was unwilling to endorse calls for civil disobedience. Trotskyist parties with origins in the same milieu that once spawned People's Democracy made all the running on that front, forcing Sinn Féin to adopt a stronger line. The hard-left groups also posed searching questions about the party's new strategy, which still allowed for a governing alliance with the centre right, as long as Sinn Féin had the greater number of seats.[11] The same reluctance to try and make the political weather was apparent at a later stage, when a powerful campaign for abortion rights took shape in the South. Sinn Féin delayed adopting a clear pro-choice position for so long that it was in danger of being overtaken by Fianna Fáil and Fine Gael.

Sinn Féin's left turn reached its peak in the first half of 2015, when the victory of Syriza in the Greek elections inspired talk of a new left-wing surge across the periphery of the Eurozone. As the Sinn Féin MEP Martina Anderson told the party's Ard Fheis that year: 'In Athens it's called Syriza, in Spain it's called Podemos, in Ireland it's called Sinn Féin.'[12] The Sinn Féin leadership could not be held responsible for the capitulation of Syriza under pressure from the Troika later that year, any more than they could be blamed for Labour's coalition manoeuvre in 2011.[13] But their response to the rout in Athens was to shy away from a clash with the 'Berlin Consensus' that had inflicted so much social suffering on Ireland and Greece alike. Sinn Féin's disappointing performance in the 2016 general election – a little under 14 per cent, well below its polling average for the previous year – greatly reinforced that tendency. The party's 2017 Ard Fheis changed its policy on coalition, clearing the way for a junior partnership with Fine Gael or Fianna Fáil once again.[14]

Just as a window of opportunity for republicans appeared to be closing in the South, events in Britain suddenly flung one open in the North. To the surprise of many, Sinn Féin's partnership with the DUP lasted for the best part of a decade. Ian Paisley hadn't done a very good job of preparing his supporters to accept a deal with the old enemy, and his seeming bonhomie with Martin McGuinness was too much for many DUP activists to swallow. Paisley's deputy Peter Robinson, formerly seen as a pragmatic balm for his leader's persecuting zeal, soon eased 'the Big Man' into retirement with the promise of a tougher line.[15]

The power-sharing administration inspired no great love in either community. In 2015, the journalist Susan McKay described a political culture that seemed to 'lurch from crisis to crisis with scarcely more than a shrugging of shoulders, a raising of eyebrows, a disheartened smirk', and the dysfunctional assembly at its heart: 'Petitions of concern, which were built into the Good Friday Agreement to prevent the voting-in of sectarian measures, are widely used simply to block anything the other side wants to do.'[16] But the regional government survived a whole series of events that might have sunk a more conventional lash-up, including the 2014 arrest of Gerry Adams for his alleged role in the murder of Jean McConville, a Belfast woman killed by the IRA in 1972.[17]

The real source of disruption came from the centre of the United Kingdom, not its periphery. When the Conservatives returned to power in London after the crash, it was only a matter of time before they extended their austerity programme across the water, and there was a prolonged stand-off over welfare cuts in 2014–15 that threatened to collapse the power-sharing institutions. The long-term impact of the Great Recession on British politics was then just starting to take effect.

In 2015, the Labour Party elected Jeremy Corbyn, a stalwart of the Bennite left, as its new leader. While Corbyn's opponents used his historical ties with Sinn Féin as a line of attack, in practical terms, his policy of support for the Good Friday Agreement was little more than would be expected from any Labour politician.[18] More significant for the fate of Northern Ireland was the presence of men like Michael Gove and Boris Johnson in David Cameron's cabinet, with strong roots in the *Daily Telegraph*–Policy Exchange nexus that had denounced the GFA as a sell-out to Irish nationalism.

In 2016, Gove and Johnson spearheaded a successful drive to take Britain out of the European Union, without appearing to remember that the United Kingdom had another segment called Northern Ireland. The DUP, now led by Arlene Foster, also supported the Leave campaign, while its Unionist rivals joined Sinn Féin and the SDLP in the Remain camp. The region voted to stay in the EU by a 56–44 margin, which made no difference to the outcome given the vast preponderance of English votes. In general, the strongest Remain votes were in majority-nationalist areas, with the greatest support for Leave in unionist strongholds, although it was clear that a significant minority of unionists had ignored the DUP's counsel.

Most of the commentary on the implications of Brexit for Northern Ireland focused on the question of its land border with the South. While that was certainly an important issue, the upsurge of chest-thumping British nationalism that followed the vote posed a more immediate problem for the region. The outcome soured an already fraught relationship between Martin McGuinness and Arlene Foster, and the DUP leader then finished the job by refusing to take responsibility for mismanagement of a renewable-heating scheme that will impose a crippling financial burden. The Sinn Féin–DUP partnership fell apart at the beginning of 2017 as McGuinness announced his resignation. Shortly afterwards, Cameron's successor Theresa May called a snap general election, lost her parliamentary majority, and had to rely on support from Foster's party to stay in power.

At time of writing, there is no certainty about the outcome of Britain's journey towards Brexit, let alone the political impact it will have on either side of the Irish Sea. Sinn Féin clearly sees potential in the issue to win support for a united Ireland. We can trace no predictable, linear route from Northern Ireland's Remain vote to Irish unity. However, it has at the very least introduced an element of flux to the existing constitutional arrangements that was hard to imagine just a few years ago. The possibility of movement towards Irish unity is bound to pull Sinn Féin back towards the nationalist side of its political character, already more important to the party than a left-wing platform that remains – in the words of Eoin Ó Broin – 'ambiguous, underdeveloped and at times contradictory'.[19]

2017 witnessed another milestone in the 'normalization' of Sinn Féin, as the death of Martin McGuinness and retirement of Gerry Adams saw two younger women with no IRA backgrounds, Mary Lou McDonald and Michelle O'Neill, take the reins. In itself, this generational shift need not be a conservative step: if there is one lesson to be drawn from the IRA's history, it is that the whiff of cordite offers no lasting guarantee of radicalism. But in practice, McDonald and O'Neill are likely to continue a long journey towards the centre ground traversed by so many republicans in the past. Those who still aspire to the kind of change that the most radical elements in that tradition dreamed of will have to look elsewhere.

Acknowledgements

I'm very grateful to my colleagues at *New Left Review* – Susan Watkins, Kheya Bag, Emma Fajgenbaum, Tom Hazeldine, Midori Lake and Rob Lucas – for all of their support, and for picking up the burden of my editorial duties while I took time off to finish the writing of this book. Leo Hollis shepherded it into print for Verso with great tact, and hopefully stopped me from drifting too far down a number of rabbit holes. The book draws heavily upon my doctoral thesis, which was funded by the Irish Research Council, and I want to acknowledge their generous support.

I owe a debt to many researchers in the field of Irish history whose work is indispensable for any understanding of this period. I especially want to thank Kevin Bean, John Borgonovo, Sarah-Anne Buckley, Matt Collins, David Convery, Brian Hanley and Donal Ó Drisceoil for their comments, advice and encouragement with this project. Any remaining errors are my own, of course.

I owe another debt to countless friends and comrades who have discussed the events that this book covers with me over the years. They include Kevin Brannigan, Colm Breathnach, Darren Cogavin, Des Derwin, Paul Dillon, Oisin Gilmore, Mark Grehan, José Antonio Gutiérrez, Bernie Hughes, Kevin Keating, Paul Kerwick, Fintan Lane, Stephen Lewis, Alan MacSimoin (an example to all of us, who sadly passed on soon after I completed the manuscript), Sam McGrath, Tommy McKearney, Scott Millar, Paul Moloney,

Cian O'Callaghan, Aindrias Ó Cathasaigh, Fergus O'Hare, Gearóid Ó Loingsigh, John O'Neill, Kevin Quinn, James Redmond, Frank Scalzo, Helena Sheehan, Kevin Squires and Brian Trench. Brendan Harrison deserves particular thanks, both for putting me up on trips to Belfast and for helping me to understand this period long before I started researching it formally. The late Father Joseph Brennan would have spotted an echo of his classes in the book's opening chapter; it's a great pity that I didn't get a chance to send it to him. Invaluable support came from Mary O'Flynn, Laura Shudell, Holly Loftus, Ciara Kennedy, Frank and Shane McGuinness, and above all from my parents, Mary and Johnny, to whom I dedicate this book.

Notes

Introduction

1. Bernadette Hayes and Ian McAllister, 'Public Support for Political Violence and Paramilitarism in Northern Ireland and the Republic of Ireland', *Terrorism and Political Violence*, vol. 17, no. 4, 2005, pp. 600–1.
2. Brendan O'Leary, 'Mission Accomplished? Looking Back at the IRA', *Field Day Review*, vol. 1, 2005, pp. 233–4.
3. Christopher Paul et al., *Paths to Victory: Detailed Insurgency Case Studies*, Washington, DC 2013, p. 329.
4. Ministry of Defence, *Operation Banner: An Analysis of Military Operations in Northern Ireland*, Army Code 71842, July 2006, Foreword. The author of those words, Sir Mike Jackson, was an officer in the regiment that killed fourteen civilians in Derry in January 1972.
5. Ian Cobain, *Cruel Britannia: A Secret History of Torture*, London 2012; *The History Thieves: Secrets, Lies and the Shaping of a Modern Nation*, London 2016.
6. Tom Nairn, *The Break-Up of Britain: Crisis and Neo-Nationalism*, London 1977.
7. V. I. Lenin, *National Liberation, Socialism and Imperialism: Selected Writings*, New York 1968, p. 130 (emphasis in original).

1. The Long War

1. Barry Flynn, *Soldiers of Folly: The IRA Border Campaign 1956–1962*, Cork 2009, p. 197.
2. Ibid., pp. 200–1.
3. Nancy Curtin, *The United Irishmen: Popular Politics in Ulster and Dublin 1791–1798*, Oxford 1994, p. 21.
4. Nancy Curtin, 'The transformation of the Society of United Irishmen into a mass-based revolutionary organization, 1794–6', *Irish Historical Studies*, vol. 24, no. 96, November 1985, pp. 476–84.
5. Curtin, *The United Irishmen*, pp. 136–9.
6. James Quinn, 'The United Irishmen and social reform', *Irish Historical Studies*, vol. 31, no. 122, November 1998.
7. Curtin, *The United Irishmen*, p. 170.
8. James Quinn, 'Theobald Wolfe Tone and the historians', *Irish Historical Studies*, vol. 32, no. 125, May 2000; Francis Shaw, 'The Canon of Irish History: A Challenge', *Studies*, vol. 61, no. 242, Summer 1972.
9. Christine Kenealy, *Repeal and Revolution: 1848 in Ireland*, Manchester 2009.
10. Owen McGee, *The IRB: The Irish Republican Brotherhood from the Land League to Sinn Féin*, Dublin 2005, pp. 28–9.
11. Donal McCartney, 'The Church and the Fenians', *University Review*, vol. 4, no. 3, Winter 1967.
12. Shin-Ichi Takagami, 'The Fenian rising in Dublin, March 1867', *Irish Historical Studies*, vol. 29, no. 115, May 1995.
13. T. W. Moody and Leon Ó Broin, 'The IRB Supreme Council, 1868–78', *Irish Historical Studies*, vol. 19, no. 75, March 1975, p. 314.
14. Donald Jordan, 'John O'Connor Power, Charles Stewart Parnell and the centralization of popular politics in Ireland', *Irish Historical Studies*, vol. 25, no. 97, May 1986.
15. McGee, *The IRB*, pp. 66–9.
16. Ibid., pp. 120–36.
17. Matthew Kelly, '"Parnell's Old Brigade": the Redmondite–Fenian nexus in the 1890s', *Irish Historical Studies*, vol. 33, no. 130, November 2002.
18. James McConnel, '"Fenians at Westminster": the Edwardian Irish Parliamentary Party and the legacy of the New Departure', *Irish Historical Studies*, vol. 34, no. 133, May 2004.
19. McGee, *The IRB*, pp. 298–9.
20. Ronan Fanning, *Fatal Path: British Government and Irish Revolution 1910–1922*, London 2013, pp. 32–40.

21. Diarmaid Ferriter, *A Nation and Not a Rabble: The Irish Revolution 1913–1923*, London 2015, p. 107.

22. D. George Boyce, *Nationalism in Ireland*, London 1995, pp. 295–9.

23. Ferriter, *A Nation and Not a Rabble*, p. 108.

24. Conor McCabe, 'Irish Class Relations and the 1913 Lockout', in David Convery, ed., *Locked Out: A Century of Irish Working-Class Life*, Sallins 2013, pp. 10–12.

25. Emmet O'Connor, 'The age of the red republic: the Irish left and nationalism, 1909–36', *Saothar*, no. 30, 2005, p. 74.

26. Emmet O'Connor, *A Labour History of Ireland 1824–2000*, Dublin 2011, pp. 91–5.

27. Fanning, *Fatal Path*, pp. 46–7.

28. Graham Walker, *A History of the Ulster Unionist Party: Protest, Pragmatism and Pessimism*, Manchester 2004, pp. 36–8.

29. Fanning, *Fatal Path*, pp. 110–14.

30. Charles Townshend, *Easter 1916: The Irish Rebellion*, London 2005, pp. 39–46, 52–3.

31. Ferriter, *A Nation and Not a Rabble*, p. 169; Townshend, *Easter 1916*, pp. 78–80.

32. Aindrias Ó Cathasaigh, ed., *James Connolly: The Lost Writings*, London 1997, pp. 185–92, 194–7, 201–4.

33. Desmond Greaves, *The Life and Times of James Connolly*, London 1972, pp. 371–93; Kieran Allen, *The Politics of James Connolly*, London 1990, pp. 134–60.

34. Fearghal McGarry, *The Rising: Ireland: Easter 1916*, Oxford 2010, pp. 213–26.

35. Michael Laffan, *The Resurrection of Ireland: The Sinn Féin Party 1916–1923*, Cambridge 1999, pp. 113–21.

36. Fiona Devoy McAuliffe, 'Workers Show Their Strength: The 1918 Conscription Crisis', in Convery, ed., *Locked Out*.

37. Laffan, *The Resurrection of Ireland*, pp. 164–5.

38. Ferriter, *A Nation and Not a Rabble*, p. 156.

39. Charles Townshend, *The Republic: The Fight for Irish Independence*, London 2013, pp. 157–9, 165–71.

40. Fanning, *Fatal Path*, pp. 241–2.

41. Laffan, *The Resurrection of Ireland*, pp. 282–3, 310–18.

42. Townshend, *The Republic*, pp. 100, 144–8.

43. Michael Hopkinson, *The Irish War of Independence*, Dublin 2002, pp. 177–97.

44. Michael Laffan, *The Partition of Ireland, 1911–1925*, Dublin 1983, p. 64.

45. Fanning, *Fatal Path*, pp. 217–21.

46. John McGarry and Brendan O'Leary, *Explaining Northern Ireland: Broken Images*, Oxford 1995, pp. 36–9.
47. Ferriter, *A Nation and Not a Rabble*, pp. 249–50.
48. Fanning, *Fatal Path*, pp. 293–4, 307.
49. Michael Hopkinson, *Green Against Green: The Irish Civil War*, Dublin 2004, pp. 32–3.
50. Townshend, *The Republic*, p. 362.
51. Ferriter, *A Nation and Not a Rabble*, pp. 260–2; Townshend, *The Republic*, pp. 404–6.
52. Hopkinson, *Green Against Green*, pp. 36–8; Laffan, *The Resurrection of Ireland*, pp. 350–5.
53. Ronan Fanning, *Éamon de Valera: A Will to Power*, London 2015, pp. 133–8.
54. Gavin Foster, 'Class dismissed? The debate over a social basis to the Treaty split and Irish civil war', *Saothar*, no. 33, 2008.
55. O'Connor, *A Labour History of Ireland*, pp. 105–6.
56. Aindrias Ó Cathasaigh, 'Getting with the programme: Labour, the Dáil and the Democratic Programme of 1919', *Red Banner*, no. 35, March 2009, pp. 30–1.
57. Hopkinson, *Green Against Green*, p. 52.
58. Townshend, *The Republic*, p. 432.
59. Ibid., pp. 442–3.
60. Emmet O'Connor, *Reds and the Green: Ireland, Russia and the Communist Internationals 1919–43*, Dublin 2004, p. 67.
61. O'Connor, *Reds and the Green*, pp. 71–4.
62. Townshend, *The Republic*, pp. 446–7.
63. Laffan, *The Resurrection of Ireland*, p. 355.
64. Diarmaid Ferriter, *The Transformation of Ireland 1900–2000*, London 2004, pp. 294–5.
65. Brendan O'Leary and John McGarry, *The Politics of Antagonism: Understanding Northern Ireland*, London 1993, p. 108.
66. John Bowman, *De Valera and the Ulster Question, 1917–73*, Oxford 1982.
67. Ferriter, *The Transformation of Ireland*, p. 296; Cormac Ó Gráda, *A Rocky Road: The Irish Economy since the 1920s*, Manchester 1997, p. 91.
68. Conor McCabe, *Sins of the Father: The Decisions That Shaped the Irish Economy*, Dublin 2013, pp. 74–82.
69. Paul Bew, Ellen Hazelkorn and Henry Patterson, *The Dynamics of Irish Politics*, London 1989, pp. 145–6.
70. O'Connor, *Labour History of Ireland*, p. 140.
71. Fanning, *Éamon de Valera*, p. 155.

72. D. R. O'Connor Lysaght, '"Labour Must Wait": The making of a myth', *Saothar*, no. 26, 2001.

73. Richard Dunphy, *The Making of Fianna Fáil Power in Ireland, 1923–1948*, Oxford 1995.

74. Fanning, *Éamon de Valera*, pp. 187–98.

75. Ó Gráda, *A Rocky Road*, p. 109; McCabe, *Sins of the Father*, pp. 22–7.

76. Brian Hanley, *The IRA, 1926–1936*, Dublin 2002, p. 16.

77. O'Connor, *Reds and the Green*, pp. 128, 170–3.

78. Richard English, 'Socialism and republican schism in Ireland: the emergence of the Republican Congress in 1934', *Irish Historical Studies*, vol. 27, no. 105, May 1990, p. 51.

79. Ibid., pp. 54–6.

80. Richard English, *Armed Struggle: The History of the IRA*, London 2003, pp. 52–3, 60–5.

81. Joe Lee, *Ireland 1912–1985: Politics and Society*, Cambridge 1989, pp. 301–2.

82. Robert White, *Out of the Ashes: An Oral History of the Provisional Irish Republican Movement*, Dublin 2017, p. 34.

83. Ibid., p. 39.

84. Flynn, *Soldiers of Folly*, p. 197.

2. Fish through a Desert

1. Billy McMillen, 'The Role of the IRA, 1962–1967', in Des O'Hagan, ed., *Liam MacMaolain: Separatist, Socialist, Republican*, Belfast 1976, p. 1.

2. *An tÓglách*, October–November 1967.

3. George Gilmore, *Labour and the Republican Movement*, Dublin 1966.

4. *United Irishman*, July 1967.

5. Kieran Conway, *Southside Provisional: From Freedom Fighter to the Four Courts*, Dublin 2014, p. 15.

6. Brian Hanley and Scott Millar, *The Lost Revolution: The Story of the Official IRA and the Workers' Party*, 2010, p. 25.

7. Matt Treacy, *The IRA, 1956–69: Rethinking the Republic*, Manchester 2014, p. 15.

8. Peter Taylor, *Provos: the IRA and Sinn Féin*, London 1997, pp. 45–6.

9. *Irish Times*, 4 January 2014.

10. *United Irishman*, September 1965.

11. Ibid., July 1967.

12. NAI D/T 98/6/495.
13. Ibid.
14. Henry Patterson, *The Politics of Illusion: A Political History of the IRA*, London 1997, p. 116.
15. *United Irishman*, July 1966.
16. Ibid., July 1968.
17. Hanley and Millar, *The Lost Revolution*, pp. 84–5, 88–90, 97–8.
18. Treacy, *The IRA, 1956–69*, p. 109.
19. Cathal Goulding, 'The New Strategy of the IRA', *New Left Review*, November–December 1970, p. 57.
20. Niamh Puirséil, *The Irish Labour Party, 1922–73*, Dublin 2007.
21. O'Leary and McGarry, *The Politics of Antagonism*, pp. 113–14.
22. Henry Patterson and Eric Kaufman, *Unionism and Orangeism since 1945: The Decline of the Loyal Family*, Manchester 2007, p. 5; O'Leary and McGarry, *The Politics of Antagonism*, p. 114.
23. Ibid., p. 123.
24. Ibid., pp. 131–2.
25. Patterson and Kaufman, *Unionism and Orangeism*, pp. 56–7.
26. O'Leary and McGarry, *The Politics of Antagonism*, p. 127.
27. Graham Ellison and Jim Smyth, *The Crowned Harp: Policing Northern Ireland*, London 2000, pp. 21–31.
28. O'Leary and McGarry, *The Politics of Antagonism*, pp. 129–31; John Whyte, *Understanding Northern Ireland*, Oxford 1990, p. 56.
29. Bob Rowthorn and Naomi Wayne, *Northern Ireland: The Political Economy of Conflict*, Cambridge 1988, p. 35.
30. Ellison and Smyth, *The Crowned Harp*, p. 36.
31. Rowthorn and Wayne, *Northern Ireland*, p. 209.
32. O'Leary and McGarry, *The Politics of Antagonism*, p. 131.
33. Walker, *A History of the Ulster Unionist Party*, pp. 108, 112, 154–5.
34. Henry Patterson, *Ireland Since 1939: The Persistence of Conflict*, London 2007, p. 44.
35. Liam O'Dowd, Bill Rolston and Mike Tomlinson, *Northern Ireland: Between Civil Rights and Civil War*, London 1980, p. 12.
36. Walker, *A History of the Ulster Unionist Party*, p. 105.
37. Simon Prince and Geoffrey Warner, *Belfast and Derry in Revolt: A New History of the Start of the Troubles*, Newbridge 2012, p. 51.
38. Paddy Devlin, *Straight Left: An Autobiography*, Belfast 1993, p. 132.
39. Walker, *A History of the Ulster Unionist Party*, p. 151.
40. Paul Bew, Peter Gibbon and Henry Patterson, *Northern Ireland 1921–1996: Political Forces and Social Classes*, London 1996, p. 176.
41. *Sunday Times* Insight Team, *Ulster*, London 1972, p. 47.

42. Gerry Adams, *The Politics of Irish Freedom*, Dingle 1986, p. 12; McMillen, 'The Role of the IRA, 1962–1967', p. 8.

43. Rosita Sweetman, *'On Our Knees': Ireland 1972*, London 1972, p. 195. GHQ: General Headquarters, commanders appointed by the IRA's chief of staff.

44. Prince and Warner, *Belfast and Derry in Revolt*, pp. 55–8.

45. McMillen, 'The Role of the IRA, 1962–1967', p. 5.

46. *United Irishman*, May 1965.

47. Ibid., January 1967.

48. Members of the Irish community in Britain set up the Connolly Association in the 1940s to promote left-wing and republican ideas. Greaves was the editor of its newspaper, the *Irish Democrat*, for many years.

49. Desmond Greaves, *Northern Ireland: Civil Rights and Political Wrongs*, London 1969.

50. Communist Party of Northern Ireland, *North Ireland: For Peace and Socialism*, Belfast 1952, p. 12.

51. Brian Dooley, *Black and Green: The Fight for Civil Rights in Northern Ireland and Black America*, London 1998, p. 106.

52. Hazel Morrissey, 'Betty Sinclair: A Woman's Fight for Socialism, 1910–1981', *Saothar*, no. 9, 1983.

53. *United Irishman*, September 1968.

54. Gerry Adams, 'A republican in the civil rights campaign', in Michael Farrell, ed., *Twenty Years On*, Dingle 1988, p. 44.

55. Gerry Foley, *Ireland in Rebellion*, New York 1970, p. 23.

56. Adams, *The Politics of Irish Freedom*, pp. 13–14.

57. Purdie, *Politics in the Streets*, p. 135.

58. PRONI HA/32/2/27.

59. Steve Bruce, *Paisley: Religion and Politics in Northern Ireland*, Oxford 2009, pp. 80–9.

60. Patterson and Kaufman, *Unionism and Orangeism*, p. 72. In fact, the IRA had no plan to organize large-scale disturbances on the fiftieth anniversary of the Easter Rising that year, but Unionist leaders like Clark assumed that they must have been preparing something.

61. *United Irishman*, November 1966. Bennett, who came from a Protestant background, had joined the Communist Party during the Second World War and worked alongside Desmond Greaves in the Connolly Association. He wrote an influential column for Dublin's *Sunday Press* under the pen name 'Claude Gordon', focusing on the misdeeds of Stormont, and took part in the discussions that led to NICRA's launch.

62. Prince and Warner, *Belfast and Derry in Revolt*, pp. 75–8.

63. Peter Taylor, *Loyalists*, London 1999, p. 43.
64. Conor Cruise O'Brien, *States of Ireland*, London 1974, p. 193.
65. Adams, *The Politics of Irish Freedom*, p. 15.
66. *United Irishman*, December 1967.
67. The clearest summary of this perspective can be found in the 'Freedom Manifesto' issued by the Official republicans at the beginning of 1970: *United Irishman*, February 1970.
68. PRONI HA/32/2/27.
69. Prince and Warner, *Belfast and Derry in Revolt*, pp. 36–7.

3. Points of No Return

1. Prince and Warner, *Belfast and Derry in Revolt*, p. 85.
2. Simon Prince, *Northern Ireland's '68: Civil Rights, Global Revolt and the Origins of the Troubles*, Dublin 2007.
3. O'Leary and McGarry, *The Politics of Antagonism*, p. 121.
4. Niall Ó Dochartaigh, *From Civil Rights to Armalites: Derry and the Birth of the Irish Troubles*, Basingstoke 2005, pp. 37–9.
5. Purdie, *Politics in the Streets*, p. 229.
6. Ó Dochartaigh, *From Civil Rights to Armalites*, p. 18.
7. PRONI HA/32/2/26.
8. McMillen, 'The Role of the IRA 1962–67', p. 9.
9. Roy Johnston, *A Century of Endeavour: A Biographical and Autobiographical View of the Twentieth Century in Ireland*, Dublin 2003, p. 236.
10. McMillen, 'The Role of the IRA 1962–67', p. 9.
11. Ó Dochartaigh, *From Civil Rights to Armalites*, p. 18.
12. PRONI HA/32/2/26.
13. PRONI CAB/4/1406.
14. *Disturbances in Northern Ireland: Report of the Commission appointed by the Governor of Northern Ireland*, Belfast 1969, para. 44 (hereafter *Cameron Report*).
15. *Cameron Report*, paras 186, 213.
16. Ibid., para. 54.
17. Eamonn McCann, *War and an Irish Town*, London 1993, p. 91.
18. *Cameron Report*, para. 165.
19. Ibid., paras. 102–16
20. McCann, *War and an Irish Town*, p. 99.
21. Prince, *Northern Ireland's '68*, pp. 164–7.
22. Ó Dochartaigh, *From Civil Rights to Armalites*, pp. 25–7.

23. PRONI CAB 9B/205/7.

24. PRONI CAB/4/141/3.

25. PRONI CAB 9B/309/1.

26. Ibid.

27. Ibid.

28. PRONI CAB 9B/205/8.

29. Patterson, *Ireland Since 1939*, pp. 206–8; Prince, *Northern Ireland's '68*, p. 193.

30. *Cameron Report*, para. 195.

31. Liam Baxter et al., 'Discussion on the Strategy of People's Democracy', *New Left Review*, May–June 1969, p. 8.

32. In 1966, Farrell had spoken on behalf of an Irish student organization at a left-wing congress in Vienna and successfully proposed a motion demanding 'immediate repeal' of the Special Powers Act: *United Irishman*, July 1966.

33. Michael Farrell, 'Long March to Freedom', in Farrell, ed., *Twenty Years On*, p. 56.

34. Bernadette Devlin, *The Price of My Soul*, London 1969, pp. 117–18.

35. McCann, *War and an Irish Town*, p. 295.

36. Paul Arthur, *The People's Democracy 1968–73*, Belfast 1974, pp. 38, 43.

37. Devlin, *Straight Left*, pp. 92–3.

38. PRONI HA/32/2/26.

39. *Sunday Times* Insight Team, *Ulster*, p. 64.

40. Ibid., pp. 66–7.

41. Ó Dochartaigh, *From Civil Rights to Armalites*, pp. 29–30, 35–6.

42. *Cameron Report*, para. 100.

43. O'Brien, *States of Ireland*, pp. 165–6; Joe Lee, *Ireland 1912–1985: Politics and Society*, Cambridge 1989, pp. 422–3; Taylor, *Loyalists*, p. 56; Patterson, *Ireland Since 1939*, pp. 204–7; Prince, *Northern Ireland's '68*, pp. 194–211.

44. Daniel Finn, 'The Point of No Return? People's Democracy and the Burntollet March', *Field Day Review*, vol. 9, 2013.

45. *Cameron Report*, para. 101.

46. People's Democracy, *Comments on Cameron*, Belfast 1969, para. 39.

47. *Cameron Report*, para. 183.

48. Liam de Paor, *Divided Ulster*, London 1971, p. 182. McCann was not actually a member of People's Democracy at the time, but Cameron treated him as such throughout his report, and he was certainly a well-known associate of the march organizers.

49. *Cameron Report*, para. 96.

50. Ibid., para. 195.

51. Dooley, *Black and Green*, pp. 55–6.

52. Patterson, *Ireland Since 1939*, p. 203.

53. O'Brien, *States of Ireland*, p. 148 (emphasis in original). Of course, O'Brien was quite wrong to imply that 'Dixie' had settled down to a 'fairly peaceful' trajectory of racial reform after Eisenhower sent in troops to enforce desegregation. SNCC organized the march from Selma to Montgomery almost a decade later, after its activists had endured years of murder, torture and arbitrary arrest at the hands of southern police forces and their civilian accomplices, while the federal government stood idly by: Howard Zinn, *SNCC: The New Abolitionists*, Cambridge, MA 2002, pp. 263–7.

54. Farrell seems not to have anticipated the IRA's revival. In a pamphlet published towards the end of 1969, he attacked 'militant anti-partitionists' who wanted to impose a united Ireland by force, but the people Farrell had in mind were a coterie of Fianna Fáil politicians in the South: 'The anti-partitionists' alternative to the use of British troops to put down the Protestant extremists is the use of the Irish Army.' Farrell did not raise the possibility that the northern Catholic ghettoes might produce their own anti-partitionist army: Michael Farrell, *Struggle in the North*, Belfast 1969, p. 32.

55. PRONI CAB/9/B/205/8.

56. PRONI CAB/4/1425.

57. Ibid.

58. PRONI CAB/4/1427.

59. Arthur, *The People's Democracy*, p. 119. Republicans described PD's agnostic stance towards the Irish border as a 'pernicious doctrine': *United Irishman*, March 1969.

60. Arthur, *The People's Democracy*, p. 49.

61. Walker, *A History of the Ulster Unionist Party*, pp. 171–2.

62. Taylor, *Loyalists*, pp. 59–61.

63. PRONI HA/32/3/1.

64. Ó Dochartaigh, *From Civil Rights to Armalites*, p. 40.

65. Dooley, *Black and Green*, pp. 65–6.

66. Baxter et al., 'Discussion on the Strategy of People's Democracy', p. 6.

67. Eamonn McCann, 'Derry: Who's Wrecking Civil Rights?' (1969).

68. Ronan Fanning, 'Playing It Cool: The Response of the British and Irish Governments to the Crisis in Northern Ireland, 1968–9', *Irish Studies in International Affairs*, vol. 12, 2001, p. 71.

69. Ó Dochartaigh, *From Civil Rights to Armalites*, pp. 101–4.

4. Law and Disorder

1. At the time, Sinn Féin had no seats to take, so the question of attendance was purely hypothetical.
2. Taylor, *Provos*, p. 66.
3. Hanley and Millar, *The Lost Revolution*, p. 125.
4. Gerry Adams, *Before the Dawn: An Autobiography*, Dingle 1996, p. 104.
5. Goulding, 'The New Strategy of the IRA', pp. 57–8.
6. McMillen, 'The Role of the IRA 1962–1967', p. 11.
7. Hanley and Millar, *The Lost Revolution*, pp. 133–4.
8. McMillen, 'The Role of the IRA 1962–1967', p. 11.
9. Goulding, 'The New Strategy of the IRA', p. 59.
10. Ibid.
11. Adams, *Before the Dawn*, p. 104.
12. Sweetman, 'On Our Knees', p. 155.
13. Patrick Bishop and Eamonn Mallie, *The Provisional IRA*, London 1988, pp. 92–3, 115.
14. Malachi O'Doherty, *Gerry Adams: An Unauthorized Life*, London 2017, pp. 44–5.
15. Adams, *The Politics of Irish Freedom*, pp. 8–13.
16. Adams, 'A Republican in the Civil Rights Campaign', pp. 49–50; *Before the Dawn*, pp. 121–9. This conclusion is based to some extent on reading between the lines, since Adams has never discussed his role as an IRA commander.
17. Jim Monaghan, interview, 11 August 2011.
18. Sweetman, 'On Our Knees', p. 160.
19. Kevin Kelley, *The Longest War: Northern Ireland and the IRA*, London 1988, pp. 128–9.
20. Sweetman, 'On Our Knees', p. 155.
21. Prince, *Northern Ireland's '68*, pp. 103–5.
22. Hanley and Millar, *The Lost Revolution*, p. 262.
23. *Ar Aghaidh le Sinn Féin*, Dublin 1968; Foley, *Ireland in Rebellion*, pp. 29–31.
24. This version of events first appeared in the *United Irishman*, and was then compiled in two pamphlets: *Fianna Fáil: The IRA Connection* and *Fianna Fáil and the IRA* (n.d.).
25. *Fianna Fáil and the IRA*, p. 27.
26. Taylor, *Provos*, p. 62; Bishop and Mallie, *The Provisional IRA*, pp. 130–1.
27. Taylor, *Provos* p. 63.
28. *United Irishman*, January 1970, September 1970.

29. Ibid., March 1970.

30. Mike Milotte, *Communism in Modern Ireland: The Pursuit of the Workers' Republic Since 1916*, Dublin 1984, p. 278.

31. Communist Party of Ireland, *A Democratic Solution*, Belfast 1971.

32. Gerard Murray and Jonathan Tonge, *Sinn Féin and the SDLP: From Alienation to Participation*, London 2005, pp. 10–13.

33. Fanning, 'Playing It Cool', p. 72. Callaghan's habit of talking about Northern Ireland 'as if we were some sort of external territory' enraged Chichester-Clark. He would not have been reassured by the comments of the British foreign secretary, Michael Stewart, when his Irish counterpart called for the Apprentice Boys march to be banned: 'A similar problem had arisen in Bermuda recently.' Ibid., pp. 71–2.

34. Ibid., pp. 75–6.

35. Patterson and Kaufman, *Unionism and Orangeism*, pp. 78, 95, 102–3, 111.

36. Prince and Warner, *Belfast and Derry in Revolt*, p. 221.

37. *Operation Banner: An Analysis of Military Operations in Northern Ireland*, paras 803–4.

38. Peter Taylor, *Brits: The War Against the IRA*, London 2002, p. 32.

39. *Sunday Times* Insight Team, *Ulster*, p. 142.

40. McCann, *War and an Irish Town*, p. 126.

41. Ó Dochartaigh, *From Civil Rights to Armalites*, pp. 121–3.

42. The derisory harvest of reform by the end of 1971 is summarized well in *Sunday Times* Insight Team, *Ulster*, pp. 300–1.

43. Ó Dochartaigh, *From Civil Rights to Armalites*, pp. 136–40.

44. NAI D/T 2001/6/513.

45. *Operation Banner*, para. 538.

46. Taylor, *Provos*, pp. 73–4; Bishop and Mallie, *The Provisional IRA*, p. 158.

47. PRONI CAB/9/G/89/2.

48. Thomas Hennessy, *The Evolution of the Troubles 1970–72*, Dublin 2007, pp. 28–31.

49. *Sunday Times* Insight Team, *Ulster*, p. 206.

50. Taylor, *Provos*, pp. 75–8.

51. *Sunday Times* Insight Team, *Ulster*, pp. 226–7.

52. Ó Dochartaigh, *From Civil Rights to Armalites*, p. 184.

53. McCann, *War and an Irish Town*, p. 131.

54. *United Irishman*, January 1970.

55. Ibid., April 1970.

56. *Sunday Times* Insight Team, *Ulster*, pp. 215–17.

57. Hanley and Millar, *The Lost Revolution*, p. 157.

58. Colm Campbell and Ita Connolly, 'A Model for the "War Against Terrorism?" Military Intervention in Northern Ireland and the 1970 Falls Curfew', *Journal of Law and Society*, vol. 30, no. 3, September 2003.

59. Paddy Devlin, *Straight Left: An Autobiography*, Belfast 1993, p. 134.

60. *Operation Banner*, para. 829.

61. *United Irishman*, June 1971.

62. Hanley and Millar, *The Lost Revolution*, p. 159.

63. PRONI CAB/4/1535. The bill in question resulted in one unsuccessful prosecution of a loyalist by the end of 1971.

64. Ciaran de Baróid, *Ballymurphy and the Irish War*, London 2000, pp. 49–57.

65. Ed Moloney, *Voices from the Grave: Two Men's War in Ireland*, London 2010, pp. 70–1.

66. McCann, *War and an Irish Town*, pp. 129–30.

67. Prince and Warner, *Belfast and Derry in Revolt*, p. 185; Ó Dochartaigh, *From Civil Rights to Armalites*, pp. 152–4.

68. McCann, *War and an Irish Town*, p. 135.

69. *Sunday Times* Insight Team, *Ulster*, pp. 227–9.

70. Prince and Warner, *Belfast and Derry in Revolt*, pp. 156–7.

71. Tommy McKearney, *The Provisional IRA from Insurrection to Parliament*, London 2011, pp. 98–9.

72. Lorenzo Bosi, 'Explaining Pathways to Armed Activism in the Provisional Irish Republican Army, 1969–1972', *Social Science History*, vol. 36, no. 3, Fall 2012.

73. David Sharrock and Mark Devenport, *Man of War, Man of Peace: The Unauthorized Biography of Gerry Adams*, London 1997, p. 38.

74. Adams, *Before the Dawn*, pp. 43–4.

75. Fionnuala O'Connor, *In Search of a State: Catholics in Northern Ireland*, Belfast 1993, pp. 294–5.

76. Conway, *Southside Provisional*, pp. 67–71.

77. Taylor, *Brits*, p. 316.

78. *Irish Times*, 19 April 1972.

79. *Irish Times*, 12 May 1971; *An Phoblacht*, March 1970.

80. *Irish Times*, 11 February 1971.

81. *Éire Nua: The Social and Economic Programme of Sinn Féin*, Dublin 1972, pp. 55–6, 3–4.

82. Conway, *Southside Provisional*, p. 52.

83. Conway, whose Southern, middle-class background and grounding in student politics were entirely untypical of his fellow Volunteers, joined the Provos after being rejected by the Official IRA and rose to become their director of intelligence. He developed his own Marxist

rationale for seeing the Provos as the more radical of the two factions: *Southside Provisional*, p. 21.

84. *Irish Times*, 19 April 1972.
85. Taylor, *Brits*, p. 58.
86. Patterson and Kaufman, *Unionism and Orangeism*, p. 116.
87. Ibid.
88. *Sunday Times* Insight Team, *Ulster*, p. 260.
89. *United Irishman*, May 1971.
90. Bishop and Mallie, *The Provisional IRA*, pp. 141–3.
91. Ó Dochartaigh, *From Civil Rights to Armalites*, pp. 209–10.
92. PRONI HA/32/2/51.
93. Michael Farrell, 'Long March to Freedom', in Farrell, ed., *Twenty Years On*, p. 63.
94. John Gray, interview, 29 January 2011; 'Farrell, 'Long March to Freedom', p. 63.
95. *Free Citizen*, 23 July 1971.

5. The Year of Civil Resistance

1. The *United Irishman* editor Seamus Ó Tuathail smuggled out some of the first reports from Crumlin Road prison, to be published in the *Irish Times*. Another detainee, the People's Democracy activist John McGuffin, later wrote a full-length book on the use of torture by the Army: *The Guinea Pigs*, London 1974.
2. Cobain, *Cruel Britannia*, pp. 138–47.
3. Ian Cobain, 'Ballymurphy shootings: 36 hours in Belfast that left 10 dead', *Guardian*, 26 June 2014.
4. Hanley and Millar, *The Lost Revolution*, p. 166.
5. Margaret Urwin, *A State in Denial: British Collaboration with Loyalist Paramilitaries*, Cork 2016, p. 28.
6. Ibid., p. 94.
7. Patterson and Kaufman, *Unionism and Orangeism*, p. 137.
8. Taylor, *Brits*, pp. 67–8; Roy Foster, *Luck and the Irish: A Brief History of Change, 1970–2000*, London 2008, pp. 114–15.
9. Devlin, *Straight Left*, p. 157.
10. NAI DFA/2003/17/304.
11. Eamonn McCann, *Bloody Sunday in Derry: What Really Happened*, Dingle 1992, pp. 51–2.
12. Hanley and Millar, *The Lost Revolution*, pp. 170–1.
13. *Sunday Times* Insight Team, *Ulster*, p. 264. Brian Faulkner later claimed that Farrell and the other PD members arrested were also

IRA Volunteers, without saying which faction he had in mind: 'Many members of the IRA have belonged, or indeed still belong, to the Sinn Féin movement or the Republican organizations or to bodies like the People's Democracy or the Northern Ireland Civil Rights Association. If a person is interned, however, it is solely because he is directly associated with the IRA.' PRONI D/2890/5C/1.

14. Rosa Gilbert, 'No Rent, No Rates: Civil Disobedience Against Internment in Northern Ireland, 1971–1974', *Studi irlandesi: A Journal of Irish Studies*, no. 7, 2017, p. 27.

15. Gilbert, 'No Rent, No Rates', pp. 27–9.

16. Terry Robson, 'Workerism and Republicanism: The Seduction of Armed Struggle', in Pauline McClenaghan, ed., *The Spirit of '68: Beyond the Barricades*, Derry 2009, pp. 116–17.

17. McCann, *War and an Irish Town*, p. 151.

18. Gilbert, 'No Rent, No Rates', p. 28.

19. *Unfree Citizen*, 14 January 1972.

20. Patterson, *Ireland Since 1939*, p. 222.

21. *United Irishman*, December 1971.

22. Gilbert, 'No Rent, No Rates', p. 32.

23. NAI DFA/2003/13/6.

24. NAI DFA/2003/13/7.

25. NAI D/T/2002/8/483.

26. PRONI HA/32/2/54.

27. In January 1972, Roy Johnston announced his resignation from Goulding's movement after the assassination of Unionist politician John Barnhill by the Official IRA. He joined the Communist Party soon afterwards: *Irish Times*, 18 January 1972.

28. *Irish Times*, 25 October 1971.

29. *United Irishman*, October 1971.

30. *Starry Plough*, 30 April 1973.

31. *United Irishman*, January 1972.

32. Taylor, *Provos*, p. 134.

33. *United Irishman*, January 1972.

34. Ibid., September 1971.

35. *Irish Times*, 19 July 1971.

36. Sweetman, 'On Our Knees', p. 157

37 *Free Citizen*, 28 May 1971; *Unfree Citizen*, 14 January 1972.

38. Baxter et al., 'Discussion on the Strategy of People's Democracy', pp. 11–12. Eamonn McCann objected strenuously to the term 'Catholic power'; Farrell explained that he meant it to be humorous.

39. *Unfree Citizen*, 15 October 1971.

40. Ibid.

41. People's Democracy, *People's Democracy: What It Stands For, Its Attitudes*, Dublin 1972, p. 10.
42. Adams, *Before the Dawn*, p. 215.
43. *United Irishman*, January 1972.
44. *Irish Times*, 3 January 1972.
45. Ibid., 19 January 1972.
46. McCann, *Bloody Sunday in Derry*, pp. 62–63.
47. *Irish Times*, 24 January 1972.
48. Ibid., 26 January, 31 January 1972.
49. Ibid., 29 January 1972.
50. Ó Dochartaigh, *From Civil Rights to Armalites*, pp. 279–84.
51. *Irish Times*, 31 January 1972.
52. Murray Sayle, 'Bloody Sunday Report', *London Review of Books*, 11 July 2002. Sayle composed his report with Derek Humphry for the *Sunday Times* within days of the massacre, but legal concerns blocked its publication for another thirty years.
53. *Irish Times*, 2 February 1972.
54. White, *Out of the Ashes*, pp. 88–91.
55. *Irish Times*, 7 February 1972.
56. NAI DFA/2003/17/284.
57. NAI DFA/2003/13/22.
58. *Bloody Sunday, 1972: Lord Widgery's Report of Events in Londonderry, Northern Ireland, on 30 January 1972*, London 2001, pp. 97–100.
59. *United Irishman*, February 1972.
60. Eamonn McCann, 'Twisting the Truth about Bloody Sunday', *Socialist Worker*, 16 June 2011.
61. Sayle, 'Bloody Sunday Report'; Eamonn McCann, *What Happened in Derry*, London 1972, pp. 11–12.
62. *Unfree Citizen*, 3 March 1972. The *Sunday Times* Insight Team confirmed the plausibility of this account: 'The magistrates' courts were so clogged with cases hinging upon military testimony that the court-building in Chichester Street looked daily more like a barracks than a hall of justice.' *Ulster*, p. 288.
63. *Unfree Citizen*, 3 March 1972.
64. Ibid., 8 October 1971.
65. *United Irishman*, May 1972.
66. Ibid., June 1972.
67. *Starry Plough*, no. 4, May–June 1972. The Officials also had to fend off some Red-baiting from their republican rivals, who described an abortive plan to establish street committees in 'Free Derry' as a plot to impose 'Moscow-style communism'. The *Plough*'s reply gave

a sense of the terse humour that characterized the paper: 'When we advocated street committees we did not mean that neighbour should spy on neighbour. If any of our supporters have taken steps to plant sophisticated electronic bugging devices in the kitchen next door, please stop it. That is not what we meant. All those experimenting with micro-dots can knock it off, and anyone who has a high-powered telescope poking out of his bathroom window can get rid of it. That was not the idea.'

68. McCann, *War and an Irish Town*, pp. 162–6.
69. NAUK CJ 4/195.
70. *United Irishman*, June 1974.
71. *Irish Times*, 3 April 1972.
72. Taylor, *Provos*, pp. 138–9.
73. Ibid., pp. 137–8.
74. Kelley, *The Longest War*, pp. 180–1.
75. Andrew Mumford, 'Covert Peacemaking: Clandestine Negotiations and Backchannels with the Provisional IRA during the Early "Troubles", 1972–76', *The Journal of Imperial and Commonwealth History*, vol. 39, no. 4, 2011, pp. 637–8.
76. Taylor, *Provos*, p. 142.
77. Ibid., p. 135; Adams, *Before the Dawn*, p. 205.
78. Mike Davis, *Buda's Wagon: A Brief History of the Car Bomb*, London 2007, pp. 53–60.
79. Taylor, *Provos*, p. 134.
80. Davis, *Buda's Wagon*, p. 10.
81. Malachi O'Doherty, *The Telling Year: Belfast 1972*, Dublin 2007, p. 204.
82. *Starry Plough*, no. 5, July–August 1972.

6. Roads Not Taken

1. *Operation Banner*, paras 106, 226–7.
2. English, *Armed Struggle*, pp. 162–4.
3. Bishop and Mallie, *The Provisional IRA*, pp. 265–6.
4. *Irish Times*, 24 September 1973.
5. Republican Clubs, *Where We Stand: The Republican Position*, Dublin 1972, p. 14.
6. Ibid., p. 7.
7. *United Irishman*, February 1973.
8. NAUK CJ/4/193.
9. Patterson, *The Politics of Illusion*, p. 159.

10. *United Irishman*, July 1973.

11. Gerry Foley, *Problems of the Irish Revolution: Can the IRA Meet the Challenge?* New York 1972. In the US, Foley belonged to the same party as George Breitman, whose pamphlet on the African-American struggle had been a touchstone for Michael Farrell at the time of the Burntollet march.

12. Hanley and Millar, *The Lost Revolution*, pp. 257–8.

13. *United Irishman*, January 1973.

14. Ibid., April 1973.

15. Official Sinn Féin, *Document on Irish Liberation Submitted to World Congress of Peace Forces*, Dublin 1973.

16. *Intercontinental Press*, 23 October 1978.

17. *Unfree Citizen*, 28 January 1974.

18. Michael Farrell and Phil McCullough, *Behind the Wire*, Belfast 1973, p. 13.

19. *Republican News*, 27 June, 25 August 1973.

20. Adams, *Before the Dawn*, pp. 215–16.

21. *Unfree Citizen*, 15 April 1974.

22. Kelley, *The Longest War*, p. 205.

23. *Republican News*, 8 March 1975.

24. Conway, *Southside Provisional*, p. 183.

25. Brian Feeney, *Sinn Féin: A Hundred Turbulent Years*, Dublin 2002, pp. 273–4.

26. PRONI CAB/9/J/90/10.

27. Patterson and Kaufman, *Unionism and Orangeism*, pp. 148–9.

28. Patterson, *Ireland Since 1939*, p. 226.

29. Dean Godson, *Himself Alone: David Trimble and the Ordeal of Unionism*, London 2004, p. 32.

30. Patterson and Kaufman, *Unionism and Orangeism*, p. 139.

31. Figures from the CAIN database of conflict-related deaths.

32. Martin Dillon and Denis Lehane, *Political Murder in Northern Ireland*, London 1973, p. 286.

33. Margaret Urwin, *A State in Denial: British Collaboration with Loyalist Paramilitaries*, Cork 2016, pp. 56–9.

34. Ibid., pp. 90–3.

35. Godson, *Himself Alone*, pp. 55–60.

36. Conway, *Southside Provisional*, pp. 178–9. The British police tortured six men into signing false confessions admitting responsibility for the bombings: the 'Birmingham Six' later became the focus of intense political controversy, along with other Irish victims of judicial malpractice, and were finally released in 1991.

37. Taylor, *Brits*, pp. 177–9.

38. Niall Ó Dochartaigh, '"Everyone Trying", the IRA Ceasefire, 1975: A Missed Opportunity for Peace?' *Field Day Review*, vol. 7, 2011.

39. David McKittrick and David McVea, *Making Sense of the Troubles*, London 2012, p. 131.

40. *Irish Times*, 21 December 1974.

41. Ibid., 11 February 1975.

42. Bishop and Mallie, *The Provisional IRA*, pp. 282–4.

43. Anne Cadwallader, *Lethal Allies: British Collusion in Ireland*, Cork 2013, pp. 142–3.

44. Ibid., p. 117.

45. Ibid., pp. 306–7.

46. Taylor, *Brits*, pp. 184–6.

47. *Irish Times*, 20 October 1975.

48. Ibid., 2 December 1974.

49. Seamus Costello Memorial Committee, *Seamus Costello 1939–77: Irish Republican Socialist*, Dublin 1982, p. 58.

50. *Starry Plough*, April 1975.

51. Hanley and Millar, *The Lost Revolution*, p. 284.

52. Between December 1974 and May 1975, the *United Irishman* published an extended political travelogue taking readers through the highlights of East European state socialism. It denounced the Hungarian revolt of 1956 as a 'last-ditch stand' by 'fascist and right-wing elements who tried to turn back the clock of history', and claimed that there was 'very little opposition' to the Soviet invasion of Czechoslovakia twelve years later: 'In fact many Czechs supported it.'

53. *Irish Times*, 14 December 1974.

54. *Starry Plough*, April 1975.

55. *Irish Times*, 15 March 1975.

56. *Hibernia*, 31 October 1975.

57. *Irish Times*, 14 December 1974, 7 April 1975.

58. Jack Holland and Henry McDonald, *INLA: Deadly Divisions*, Dublin 2010, pp. 109–11.

59. *Irish Times*, 15 March 1975.

60. NAUK CJ/4/2774.

61. Patterson, *The Politics of Illusion*, p. 164.

62. *Irish Times*, 25 February 1975.

63. Ibid., 28 February 1975.

64. Holland and McDonald, *Deadly Divisions*, pp. 57–9.

65. *Irish Times*, 7 March 1975.

66. Ibid., 9 April 1975.

67. Ibid., 7 April 1975.

68. Ibid., 29 April, 1 May 1975.

69. Hanley and Millar, *The Lost Revolution*, pp. 402–3.

70. *Hibernia*, 31 October 1975.

71. *Starry Plough*, December 1975.

72. Ibid., January 1976.

73. Ed Moloney, *A Secret History of the IRA*, London 2007, pp. 146–7; Hanley and Millar, *The Lost Revolution*, pp. 315–17.

74. *Irish Times*, 14 November 1975.

75. Ibid., 6 November, 14 November 1975.

76. Ibid., 5 November 1975.

77. English, *Armed Struggle*, pp. 171–2.

78. *Irish Times*, 12 August 1972.

79. *United Irishman*, November 1975.

80. Seán Swan, *Official Irish Republicanism 1962–1972*, Dublin 2008, p. 401.

81. McGarry and O'Leary, *Explaining Northern Ireland*, pp. 161–6. While Clifford was BICO's main authority on Ireland, another member of the group, Bill Warren, became well-known on the intellectual left for his writings on the development of global capitalism.

82. Godson, *Himself Alone*, pp. 29–30, 53.

83. Paul Bew, Henry Patterson and Peter Gibbon, *The State in Northern Ireland: Political Forces and Social Classes*, Manchester 1979, pp. 18–19, 221.

84. Sinn Féin the Workers' Party, *Statement on Northern Ireland*, Dublin 1979.

85. Workers' Party, *The Current Political Situation in Northern Ireland*, Belfast 1983, p. 5.

86. Hanley and Millar, *The Lost Revolution*, pp. 401–21.

87. McAliskey, Johnnie White and their associates set up a short-lived group called the Independent Socialist Party after leaving the IRSP. The new organization identified a basic problem for any movement that tried to mobilize support on an all-Ireland basis: 'Most Irish workers were born and bred in a partitioned country. Their problems they see as directly related to the state in which they live. Cork workers will be hard put to tie up their housing problems with the sectarian murders in Belfast.' Independent Socialist Party, *The Independent Socialist Party: An Introduction*, Dublin 1977, p. 5.

88. Holland and McDonald, *Deadly Divisions*, pp. 126–7.

89. *Irish Times*, 11 October 1977.

90. Derek Dunne and Gene Kerrigan, *Round Up the Usual Suspects: The Cosgrave Coalition and the Kelly Trial*, Dublin 1984, p. 190.

91. Moloney, *Voices from the Grave*, p. 193.

92. *Irish Times*, 17 October, 20 October 1980.

7. The Broad Front

1. *Republican News*, 18 June 1977.
2. *Unfree Citizen*, September 1976.
3. *Republican News*, 11 September 1976.
4. Gerry Adams, *Peace in Ireland: A Broad Analysis of the Present Situation*, Belfast 1976, p. 13.
5. Peter Taylor, *Beating the Terrorists? Interrogation in Omagh, Gough and Castlereagh*, London 1980.
6. PRONI CENT/1/5/5.
7. *Unfree Citizen*, March 1976.
8. Ibid., July–August 1977.
9. 'Appendix 4: Staff Report, 1977', in Liam Clarke, *Broadening the Battlefield: The H-Blocks and the Rise of Sinn Féin*, Dublin 1987, p. 253.
10. *Republican News*, 17 June 1978.
11. NAUK CJ/4/2376. One of the foreign guests at the conference was the Greek Trotskyist Michalis Raptis, better known in far-left circles as Michel Pablo – although as Brian Trench noted, 'few of the delegates can have had an idea of the historical resonance of his name': Trench, 'Provisional Pot-Pourri', *Magill*, 1 November 1978. Pablo's record as an arms-smuggler and sometime adviser for Algeria's FLN guerrillas would have interested the Provos more than his role in the controversies of the Fourth International.
12. John Horgan, *Irish Media: A Critical History since 1922*, London 2001, pp. 148–9.
13. *An Phoblacht/Republican News*, 23 June 1979.
14. Moloney, *A Secret History of the IRA*, pp. 185–6.
15. *An Phoblacht/Republican News*, 10 February 1979.
16. Jim Gibney, interview, 31 August 2015.
17. *An Phoblacht/Republican News*, 9 August 1980.
18. Eamonn McCann, *War and an Irish Town*, London 1980, p. 176.
19. McCann, *War and an Irish Town*, pp. 175–6.
20. *An Phoblacht/Republican News*, 10 May 1980.
21. Ed Moloney, 'The IRA', *Magill*, 30 September 1980.
22. *An Phoblacht/Republican News*, 3 November 1979.
23. Patterson, *The Politics of Illusion*, p. 222; Murray and Tonge, *Sinn Féin and the SDLP*, p. 152.

24. *An Phoblacht/Republican News*, 3 November 1979.
25. Ibid., 10 November, 3 November 1979.
26. Moloney, 'The IRA'.
27. *Republican News*, 31 January 1976.
28. *Unfree Citizen*, March 1976.
29. *Republican News*, 8 April, 1 April 1978.
30. Vincent Browne, 'There will be no more ceasefires – the Provisional IRA', *Magill*, 1 August 1978.
31. 'Appendix 4: Staff Report, 1977', in Clarke, *Broadening the Battlefield*, pp. 251–2.
32. Bishop and Mallie, *The Provisional IRA*, pp. 320–3; Moloney, *A Secret History of the IRA*, pp. 157–61.
33. Moloney, 'The IRA'.
34. Ed Moloney, '"We have worn down their will"', *Magill*, 30 September 1980.
35. Adams, *Before the Dawn*, p. 266.
36. *Republican News*, 25 February 1978.
37. NAUK FCO/87/976.
38. *An Phoblacht/Republican News*, 19 April 1980.
39. *Unfree Citizen*, July–August 1977.
40. *Socialist Republic*, February 1978.
41. *Starry Plough*, February 1978.
42. *Socialist Republic*, March–April 1978.
43. Adams, *The Politics of Irish Freedom*, pp. 75–6.
44. *Republican News*, 4 February 1978.
45. F. Stuart Ross, *Smashing H-Block: The Rise and Fall of the Popular Campaign Against Criminalization, 1976–82*, Liverpool 2011, pp. 51–2.
46. *Republican News*, 2 September 1978.
47. Ross, *Smashing H-Block*, p. 53.
48. *An Phoblacht/Republican News*, 19 May 1979.
49. *An Phoblacht/Republican News*, 2 June 1979.
50. People's Democracy, *Prisoners of Partition: H-Block/Armagh*, Dublin 1980, p. 9.
51. *An Phoblacht/Republican News*, 16 June 1979.
52. Ibid., 30 June 1979.
53. Ross, *Smashing H-Block*, p. 61.
54. *An Phoblacht/Republican News*, 27 October 1979.
55. Ross, *Smashing H-Block*, p. 61.
56. A group of female IRA prisoners in Armagh prison soon joined them under the leadership of Mairéad Farrell. The protest in Armagh had a major impact on the Irish feminist movement, which divided along

pro- and anti-republican lines: Christina Loughran, 'Armagh and Feminist Strategy: Campaigns Around Republican Women Prisoners in Armagh Jail', *Feminist Review*, no. 23, June 1986. The broad front in support of republican prisoners became the National H-Block/Armagh Committee in response.

57. Gerry Foley, 'Bernadette and the Politics of H-Block', *Magill*, April 1981.
58. Taylor, *Provos*, pp. 235–6.
59. *An Phoblacht/Republican News*, 28 March 1981.
60. PRONI NIO/112/196A.
61. PRONI CENT/1/10/25.
62. *Irish Times*, 8 May 1981.
63. PRONI CENT/1/10/25.
64. *Starry Plough*, April 1981.
65. Ross, *Smashing H-Block*, pp. 164, 177.
66. PRONI CENT/1/10/36A.
67. People's Democracy, *From Reform to Collaboration: The History of Gerry Fitt*, Belfast 1981.
68. *An Phoblacht/Republican News*, 30 May 1981.
69. Ibid., 16 May 1981.
70. Ibid., 15 August 1981.
71. PRONI NIO/12/197A.
72. PRONI NIO/12/254.
73. PRONI NIO/12/202.
74. Ibid.
75. Ibid.
76. *An Phoblacht/Republican News*, 8 August 1981.
77. Ibid., 29 August 1981.
78. Ross, *Smashing H-Block*, p. 144.
79. *An Phoblacht/Republican News*, 29 August 1981. Carron's by-election victory later became the focus of bitter controversy when Richard O'Rawe, who had been press officer for the prisoners during the hunger strike, claimed that the outside leadership turned down an acceptable deal when six of the ten hunger strikers were still alive. According to O'Rawe, they wanted to avoid a settlement before the Fermanagh–South Tyrone vote took place: O'Rawe, *Blanketmen: An Untold Story of the H-Block Hunger Strike*, Dublin 2005.
80. *Irish Times*, 29 August 1981.
81. PRONI CENT/1/10/32.
82. PRONI NIO/12/202.
83. *An Phoblacht/Republican News*, 10 October 1981. An INLA statement made a similar boast: 'We now have a new generation of young

people who were brought into the struggle during the hunger strike, and have brought new life into the INLA.' *Starry Plough*, August 1982.

84. *An Phoblacht/Republican News*, 5 September 1981.
85. PRONI CENT/1/10/86A.
86. *Socialist Republic*, October 1982.

8. War by Other Means

1. PRONI CENT/1/11/51A.
2. PRONI CENT/1/11/59.
3. Michael Farrell, 'The Provos at the ballot box', *Magill*, 1 June 1983. Farrell had to move south in the early 1980s to escape the threat of assassination: UDA sources reported that his name was next on their list of targets after Bernadette McAliskey. He went on to become a distinguished lawyer and human rights campaigner.
4. PRONI CENT/1/12/8, CENT/1/12/19.
5. Farrell, 'The Provos at the ballot box'.
6. Michael Farrell, 'We have now established a sort of Republican veto', *Magill*, 30 June 1983.
7. Michael Farrell, 'The Armalite and the ballot box', *Magill*, 30 June 1983.
8. Brendan O'Brien, *The Long War: The IRA and Sinn Féin*, Dublin 1999, p. 113.
9. Farrell, 'We have now established a sort of Republican veto'.
10. Ibid.
11. Martin Collins, ed., *Ireland After Britain*, London 1985, p. 17.
12. Ken Livingstone, 'Why Labour Lost', *New Left Review*, July–August 1983.
13. PRONI CENT/1/12/2A.
14. Rowthorn and Wayne, *Northern Ireland*, pp. 115–19. The rate for Protestant men was only slightly worse than the UK average.
15. O'Brien, *The Long War*, pp. 127–8.
16. *Irish Times*, 8 August 1983.
17. Ibid., 23 May 1984.
18. Ibid., 15 November 1983.
19. Ibid., 20 April 1984.
20. Ibid., 13 June 1984.
21. Ibid., 19 June 1984.
22. Ibid., 22 June 1984.

23. Gene Kerrigan, 'The IRA has to do what the IRA has to do', *Magill*, September 1984.
24. Ibid.
25. Taylor, *Brits*, pp. 219–20; O'Brien, *The Long War*, pp. 107–11.
26. Bishop and Mallie, *The Provisional IRA*, pp. 413–14; Moloney, *A Secret History of the IRA*, pp. 244–5; O'Brien, *The Long War*, pp. 129–30.
27. *Irish Times*, 29 December 1984.
28. Taylor, *Brits*, p. 265.
29. *Irish Times*, 23 November, 20 November 1984.
30. Ibid., 1 May 1985.
31. Ibid., 4 November 1985.
32. O'Leary and McGarry, *The Politics of Antagonism*, pp. 221–9.
33. PRONI ENV/37/1.
34. *Irish Times*, 15 January 1986.
35. PRONI CENT/1/17/38A.
36. Danny Morrison, *The Hillsborough Agreement*, Belfast and Dublin 1986, pp. 8–9, 15.
37. O'Brien, *The Long War*, pp. 130–1; Clarke, *Broadening the Battlefield*, pp. 234–5; Moloney, *A Secret History of the IRA*, pp. 287–8.
38. Skirting the edge of self-parody, Adams later claimed that reports of the Convention's move came 'suddenly and unexpectedly' to him: Gerry Adams, *Hope and History: Making Peace in Ireland*, Dingle 2003, p. 46.
39. *Irish Times*, 15 October 1986.
40. Sinn Féin, *The Politics of Revolution: The Main Speeches and Debates from the 1986 Sinn Féin Ard-Fheis*, Dublin 1986, pp. 26–7.
41. The Unionist leader David Trimble used the term 'sleekedness' to convey his intense dislike and distrust of Adams: Godson, *Himself Alone*, pp. 398–9. Ironically, Trimble's preference for McGuinness, the other half of Sinn Féin's peace-process double act, aligned him with many IRA Volunteers.
42. Kevin Toolis, *Rebel Hearts: Journeys within the IRA's Soul*, London 1996, pp. 294–8.
43. Sinn Féin, *The Politics of Revolution*, pp. 6, 7, 10, 8, 12.
44. Ibid., pp. 14, 4, 6.
45. Ibid., p. 20.
46. O'Brien, *The Long War*, pp. 336–7; Moloney, *A Secret History of the IRA*, p. 289.
47. Sinn Féin, *The Politics of Revolution*, pp. 13–14.
48. *United Irishman*, July 1976; Workers' Party, *Security in Northern Ireland*, Belfast 1989, p. 6.

49. Workers' Party, *The Workers' Party and the Anglo-Irish Agreement*, Dublin 1986, pp. 3–4; Workers' Party, *The Socialist Perspective on Northern Ireland and the Anglo-Irish Agreement*, Dublin 1986, p. 10.

50. Workers' Party, *The Current Political Situation in Northern Ireland*, p. 5.

51. O'Leary and McGarry, *The Politics of Antagonism*, p. 205.

52. Jonathan Tonge, *The New Northern Irish Politics?* Basingstoke 2005, p. 89.

53. PRONI CENT/1/12/24.

54. Hanley and Millar, *The Lost Revolution*, pp. 524–6, 536–7.

55. Sinn Féin, *The Politics of Revolution*, p. 8.

56. *Irish Times*, 23 May 1984.

57. Sinn Féin, *The Good Old IRA: Tan War Operations*, Dublin 1985, p. 3.

58. Townshend, *The Republic*, p. 370.

59. Sinn Féin, *The Good Old IRA*, p. 3.

60. Ibid., p. 2.

61. O'Brien, *The Long War*, p. 129.

62. Figures from the CAIN database.

63. Moloney, *A Secret History of the IRA*, p. 21.

64. Eamonn Mallie and David McKittrick, *The Fight for Peace: The Inside Story of the Irish Peace Process*, London 1997, p. 48.

65. Moloney, *A Secret History of the IRA*, p. 22.

66. Ibid., pp. 22–32.

67. Ibid., p. 22.

68. Mallie and McKittrick, *The Fight for Peace*, p. 48.

69. O'Brien, *The Long War*, p. 141.

70. Kelley, *The Longest War*, pp. 376–7.

71. *Starry Plough*, November–December 1983.

72. Vincent Browne, 'Inside the INLA', *Magill*, August 1985.

73. Irish Republican Socialist Party, *An Historical Analysis of the IRSP: Its Past Role, Root Cause of Its Problems and Proposals for the Future*, Dublin 1987, p. 3.

9. Down a Few Rungs

1. *Irish Times*, 13 June 1988.

2. Ibid., 4 April 1988.

3. Adams, *The Politics of Irish Freedom*, p. 154.

4. *Irish Times*, 14 November 1983.

5. Adams, *The Politics of Irish Freedom*, p. 128.

6. Adams included Coughlan's critique of the Anglo-Irish Agreement in his bibliography for *The Politics of Irish Freedom*.

7. *Irish Times*, 23 June 1986.

8. Ibid., 6 November 1986; Murray and Tonge, *Sinn Féin and the SDLP*, p. 88.

9. Gerry Adams, 'A Bus Ride to Independence and Socialism' (1986), in Adams, *Signposts to Independence and Socialism*, Dublin 1988, p. 17.

10. Ross, *Smashing H-Block*, p. 180. For the same reason, traditionalists like Jimmy Drumm looked on the new members with suspicion, fearing they would begin to raise questions about the armed struggle itself: Henry Patterson, *The Politics of Illusion: Republicanism and Socialism in Modern Ireland*, London 1989, p. 198.

11. 'Sinn Féin Document No. 1', 17 March 1988, in *The Sinn Féin–SDLP Talks, January–September 1988*, sinnfein.ie/files, accessed 22 July 2018.

12. 'SDLP Document No. 1', 17 March 1988, in ibid.

13. 'Sinn Féin Document No. 2', 19 May 1988, in ibid.

14. *Irish Times*, 6 September 1988.

15. Gerry Adams, *A Pathway to Peace*, Cork 1988, p. 60.

16. *Irish Times*, 26 September 1988.

17. Ibid., 28 November 1988.

18. Ibid., 9 January 1989.

19. Ibid., 18 January, 30 January 1989.

20. *Fortnight*, May 1989.

21. *Irish Times*, 30 January 1989.

22. Ibid., 19 June 1989.

23. *Fortnight*, December 1987.

24. *Irish Times*, 30 September, 6 October 1989.

25. Jim Gibney, 'A Liberating Philosophy', *An Réabhlóid*, December 1989–February 1990.

26. *Irish Times*, 22 January 1990.

27. Ibid., 3 February 1990.

28. Moloney, *A Secret History of the IRA*, pp. 334–5.

29. *Irish Times*, 5 February 1990.

30. Ibid., 9 November 1984.

31. Kader Asmal and Adrian Hadland, *Politics in My Blood: A Memoir*, Johannesburg 2011, pp. 65–6.

32. Niall Ó Dochartaigh, 'The Longest Negotiation: British Policy, IRA Strategy and the Making of the Northern Ireland Peace Settlement', *Political Studies*, vol. 63, no. 1, 2015.

33. *An Phoblacht/Republican News*, 16 November 1989.
34. PRONI NIO/10/9/13A.
35. *Irish Times*, 8 November 1989.
36. Ó Dochartaigh, 'The Longest Negotiation', p. 210.
37. *Irish Times*, 17 November 1990.
38. Adrian Guelke, 'The Political Impasse in South Africa and Northern Ireland: A Comparative Perspective', *Comparative Politics*, vol. 23, no. 2, January 1991, pp. 158–9.
39. *An Phoblacht/Republican News*, 25 June 1992.
40. Ibid.
41. Moloney, *Voices from the Grave*, pp. 425–7.
42. Sinn Féin, 'Towards a Lasting Peace in Ireland', in O'Brien, *The Long War*, p. 412.
43. *Starry Plough*, vol. 1, no. 2, 1991.
44. Sinn Féin, 'Towards a Lasting Peace', p. 411.
45. Adams, 'A Bus Ride to Independence and Socialism', pp. 13, 15.
46. Sinn Féin, 'Towards a Lasting Peace', p. 409.
47. Murray and Tonge, *Sinn Féin and the SDLP*, pp. 122, 146.
48. Adams, *Hope and History*, p. 81; Martin Mansergh, 'The Background to the Peace Process', *Irish Studies in International Affairs*, vol. 6, 1995, p. 153.
49. 'Draft 2: A Strategy for Peace and Justice in Ireland', in Mallie and McKittrick, *The Fight for Peace*, pp. 411–13.
50. 'Draft 3: Document sent to John Hume and the Irish government by the republican movement, February 1992', in ibid., p. 414 (emphasis added).
51. 'Draft 5: June 1992 Sinn Féin draft', in ibid., p. 416 (emphasis added).
52. Ibid.
53. O'Brien, *The Long War*, pp. 290–1.
54. Adams, *Hope and History*, p. 112.
55. *Fortnight*, September 1988.
56. Figures from the CAIN database.
57. *Irish Times*, 27 January 1992.
58. Toolis, *Rebel Hearts*, pp. 198–9.
59. *Irish Times*, 24 December 1992.
60. Ibid., 4 March 1993.
61. After his release from prison in 1995, Morrison remained a vocal supporter of Gerry Adams but did not resume his position in the Sinn Féin leadership team, concentrating on a new career as a writer.
62. Danny Morrison, *Then The Walls Came Down: A Prison Journal*, Cork 1999, pp. 96–7.

63. Ibid., pp. 234–5.

64. Ibid., p. 263.

65. Ibid., p. 241.

66. Ibid., pp. 289–90.

67. Ibid., p. 289.

68. Ibid., p. 291–2.

69. Ibid., p. 293.

70. Martyn Frampton, *The Long March: The Political Strategy of Sinn Féin, 1981–2007*, Basingstoke 2008, pp. 86–7.

71. Figures from the CAIN database.

72. *Irish Times*, 9 September 1993.

73. Taylor, *Loyalists*, p. 234.

74. Ibid., pp. 217–19, 231–2; David Lister and Hugh Jordan, *Mad Dog: The Rise and Fall of Johnny Adair and 'C Company'*, Edinburgh 2004, pp. 188–9, 193.

75. *Irish Times*, 23 March 1990, 9 September 1993, 2 October 1993, 8 November 1993; Adams, *Hope and History*, pp. 84–91.

76. Cobain, *The History Thieves*, pp. 198–200.

77. *Irish Times*, 30 January 1992, 4 February 1992.

78. Cobain, *The History Thieves*, pp. 188–90.

79. Mark McGovern, 'Inquiring into Collusion? Collusion, the State and the Management of Truth Recovery in Northern Ireland', *State Crime Journal*, vol. 2, no. 1, Spring 2013; '"See No Evil": Collusion in Northern Ireland', *Race and Class*, vol. 58, no. 3, January 2017.

80. Eamonn McCann, *War and Peace in Northern Ireland*, Dublin 1998, p. 131.

81. *Irish Times*, 2 April 2004.

82. Ibid., 26 April, 3 May, 10 May 1993.

83. Ibid., 30 June 1993.

84. Ibid., 2 October 1993.

85. *Sunday Tribune*, 7 November 1999.

86. *Irish Times*, 28 October 1993.

87. Ibid., 25 October 1993.

88. Mallie and McKittrick, *The Fight for Peace*, pp. 173–5.

89. Sinn Féin, *Setting the Record Straight*, Dublin 1993, p. 26.

90. *Irish Times*, 26 April, 3 May, 22 September, 8 October 1993.

91. Ibid., 9 September 1993.

92. *An Phoblacht/Republican News*, 14 October 1993.

93. Mallie and McKittrick, *The Fight for Peace*, pp. 213–31.

94. O'Brien, *The Long War*, pp. 295–6.

95. 'Draft 5: June 1992 Sinn Féin Draft', p. 414.

96. 'Joint Declaration 1993', in O'Brien, *The Long War*, p. 421.

97. Eamonn Mallie and David McKittrick, *Endgame in Ireland*, London 2001, p. 162.

98. Godson, *Himself Alone*, p. 115.

99. Gerry Adams, *Free Ireland: Towards a Lasting Peace*, Dingle 1995, pp. 216–17.

100. In contrast, the events of 1989–91 hit the Workers' Party hard, with the bulk of its parliamentary group in Dublin breaking off to form a new organization, Democratic Left.

101. Gibney, 'A Liberating Philosophy'.

102. Morrison, *Then the Walls Came Down*, pp. 30–1.

103. Feargal Cochrane, 'Irish-America, the End of the IRA's Armed Struggle and the Utility of "Soft Power"', *Journal of Peace Research*, vol. 44, no. 2, 2007.

104. *Fortnight*, October 1996.

105. *An Phoblacht/Republican News*, 7 July 1994.

106. *Irish Times*, 25 July, 28 July 1994.

107. Mallie and McKittrick, *The Fight for Peace*, pp. 293–4.

10. Endgame

1. 'TUAS Document: Summer 1994', in Moloney, *A Secret History of the IRA*, pp. 598–601.

2. Adams, *Free Ireland*, p. 229.

3. Ibid., pp. 230–1.

4. Eamon Collins, *Killing Rage*, London 1997, pp. 225–6, 231–2.

5. McCann, *War and Peace in Northern Ireland*, pp. 154–5.

6. Moloney, *A Secret History of the IRA*, pp. 426–7; Adams, *Hope and History*, pp. 181–3.

7. 'TUAS Document', p. 601.

8. Jonathan Powell, *Great Hatred, Little Room: Making Peace in Northern Ireland*, London 2008, p. 82; *Sunday Times*, 31 October 1999.

9. *Fortnight*, September 1994.

10. *Irish Times*, 29 August 1995.

11. *Fortnight*, January 1996.

12. *Independent*, 21 November 1994.

13. *Irish Times*, 12 July 1995.

14. Ibid., 31 August 1995.

15. Kevin Bean, *The New Politics of Sinn Féin*, Liverpool 2007, pp. 174–5.

16. *Irish Times*, 31 August 1995.
17. O'Brien, *The Long War*, pp. 347–54; Moloney, *A Secret History of the IRA*, pp. 438–41.
18. *Irish Times*, 5 April 1996.
19. O'Brien, *The Long War*, pp. 357–8.
20. *Irish Times*, 23 November 1996; O'Brien, *The Long War*, pp. 366–7; Moloney, *A Secret History of the IRA*, pp. 445–54.
21. O'Brien, *The Long War*, p. 369.
22. Chris Ryder and Vincent Kearney, *Drumcree: The Orange Order's Last Stand*, London 2001, pp. 163–75.
23. O'Brien, *The Long War*, pp. 370–1.
24. Ryder and Kearney, *Drumcree*, pp. 133–4, 136, 247–8, 283, 295.
25. Mallie and McKittrick, *The Fight for Peace*, p. 382.
26. *Irish Times*, 31 May 1997; Adams, *Hope and History*, pp. 290–1.
27. O'Brien, *The Long War*, pp. 353–4.
28. Trimble's inner circle of advisers included two alumni of the Workers' Party, Paul Bew and Eoghan Harris, who had shared his youthful enthusiasm for the 'Orange Marxism' of the British and Irish Communist Organization.
29. Moloney, *A Secret History of the IRA*, pp. 475–9; O'Brien, *The Long War*, pp. 378–80.
30. Taylor, *Loyalists*, pp. 240–1.
31. O'Brien, *The Long War*, pp. 384–5.
32. Powell, *Great Hatred, Little Room*, pp. 9–13, 79–80.
33. Michael Cox, Adrian Guelke and Fiona Stephen, eds, *A Farewell to Arms? Beyond the Good Friday Agreement*, Manchester 2006, pp. 496–507, 511–12.
34. Mallie and McKittrick, *Endgame in Ireland*, pp. 259–77.
35. Godson, *Himself Alone*, pp. 327–37.
36. Powell, *Great Hatred, Little Room*, p. 104; Godson, *Himself Alone*, pp. 330–1; Adams, *Hope and History*, p. 365.
37. O'Brien, *The Long War*, p. 386.
38. *Fortnight*, June 2000.
39. 'Gerry Adams Presidential Address to Sinn Féin Ard Fheis 1998', 10 May 1998: sinnfein.ie, accessed 9 August 2018.
40. Moloney, *A Secret History of the IRA*, pp. 480–3.
41. 'Gerry Adams Presidential Address'.
42. Tonge, *The New Northern Irish Politics?*, pp. 34–5.
43. O'Leary, 'Mission Accomplished?' p. 235.
44. Collins, *Killing Rage*, pp. 219–20, 295–6.
45. Anthony McIntyre, *Good Friday: The Death of Irish Republicanism*, New York 2008, p. 88.

46. Paul Dixon, 'Guns First, Talks Later: Neoconservatives and the Northern Ireland Peace Process', *Journal of Imperial and Commonwealth History*, vol. 39, no. 4, November 2011.

47. Moloney, *A Secret History of the IRA*, pp. 494–5.

48. Ibid., pp. 505, 510–11.

49. Powell, *Great Hatred, Little Room*, pp. 314, 24–5.

50. Ibid., pp. 162–3.

51. Moloney, *A Secret History of the IRA*, p. 574.

52. Powell, *Great Hatred, Little Room*, pp. 204, 220–1.

53. The preface to Dean Godson's monumental biography of David Trimble, *Himself Alone*, thanks George W. Bush's speechwriter David Frum and the Iraqi politician Ahmed Chalabi, along with more familiar figures on the British conservative scene such as Michael Gove and Boris Johnson. In a paper for an Israeli think tank with close ties to Likud, Godson bemoaned the reluctance of Blair's government to use the 9/11 attacks 'as an excuse to engage in a crackdown on its own insurrectionists'. He also deplored the idea that Northern Ireland's unionist majority would be permitted to leave the UK if they so desired: 'The British state is well-nigh unique in advertising, quite openly, that it does not really mind if it is dismembered.' Dean Godson, 'Lessons from Northern Ireland for the Arab-Israeli Conflict', *Jerusalem Viewpoints*, no. 523, 1–15 October 2004.

54. Moloney, *A Secret History of the IRA*, pp. 510–11.

55. O'Brien, *The Long War*, p. 391.

56. Powell, *Great Hatred, Little Room*, pp. 192–3, 203.

57. *Fortnight*, January 2000.

58. Ibid., May 2002.

59. *Irish Times*, 25 January 2003.

60. Ibid., 25 April 2003.

61. Moloney, *A Secret History of the IRA*, pp. 543–4.

62. Ibid., p. 556.

63. *Sunday Tribune*, 30 January 2000.

64. Adams, *Hope and History*, p. 106.

65. Godson, *Himself Alone*, pp. 524–32, 605–7, 614–16, 629–31.

66. Steven King, 'In from the Cold: The Rise to Prominence of the Democratic Unionist Party Since 2003', *Irish Review*, no. 38, 2008, pp. 6–7.

67. Sinn Féin, *The Politics of Revolution*, pp. 8, 11.

68. Bean, *The New Politics of Sinn Féin*, p. 151.

69. Ryder and Kearney, *Drumcree*, pp. 245–9.

70. Powell, *Great Hatred, Little Room*, p. 132.

71. Ibid., passim.
72. *Irish Times*, 25 April 2003.
73. Bean, *The New Politics of Sinn Féin*, pp. 199–202.
74. *Sunday Tribune*, 1 October 2000.
75. Tonge, *The New Northern Irish Politics?* p. 258.
76. *Irish Times*, 14 May 2004.
77. Tonge, *The New Northern Irish Politics?* pp. 230–3.
78. Cobain, *The History Thieves*, pp. 205–7.
79. *Irish Times*, 23 January, 29 January 2007.
80. Ibid., 10 May 2002.
81. Gerry Adams, *The New Ireland: A Vision for the Future*, Dingle 2005, pp. 40–8
82. *An Phoblacht*, 17 May 2007.
83. Ibid., 15 March 2007.
84. *Irish Times*, 20 February 2006.
85. Ibid., 30 April 2007.
86. Ibid., 2 June 2007.
87. Murray and Tonge, *Sinn Féin and the SDLP*, p. 261.

Epilogue

1. Bean, *The New Politics of Sinn Féin*, pp. 172–3.
2. Ibid., p. 177.
3. For political developments since 2008, see Daniel Finn, 'Ireland on the Turn?', *New Left Review* 67, Jan–Feb 2011, and 'Irish Politics Since the Crash', *Catalyst*, vol. 1, no. 2, Summer 2017.
4. *An Phoblacht*, 7 June 2008.
5. Eoin Ó Broin, *Sinn Féin and the Politics of Left Republicanism*, London 2009. For a more detailed assessment of Ó Broin's work, see Daniel Finn, 'Republicanism and the Irish Left', *Historical Materialism*, vol. 24, no. 1, 2016.
6. Ó Broin, *Sinn Féin and the Politics of Left Republicanism*, pp. 292–95.
7. Ibid., pp. 296–7.
8. Ibid., p. 303.
9. Seán Ó Riain, *The Rise and Fall of Ireland's Celtic Tiger: Liberalism, Boom and Bust*, Cambridge 2014.
10. 'Gerry Adams Presidential Address to Sinn Féin Ard Fheis 2009', 21 February 2009: sinnfein.ie, accessed 17 August 2018.
11. Paul Murphy et al., 'Principles for a Left Alternative', *Irish Left Review*, 28 May 2015. Sinn Féin also faced an electoral challenge in

Northern Ireland from one of those groups, the People Before Profit Alliance. Nearly half a century after he first stood for election as a Labour candidate in Derry, Eamonn McCann won a seat for People Before Profit in the 2016 Assembly election.

12. *Belfast Telegraph*, 9 March 2015.
13. Stathis Kouvelakis, 'Syriza's Rise and Fall', *New Left Review* 97, Jan–Feb 2016.
14. *Irish Times*, 15 November 2017.
15. David Gordon, *The Fall of the House of Paisley*, Dublin 2009.
16. *Irish Times*, 26 August 2015.
17. Patrick Radden Keefe, 'Where the Bodies Are Buried', *New Yorker*, 16 March 2015.
18. Corbyn, John McDonnell, Tony Benn and Ken Livingstone are the only British politicians that Gerry Adams speaks of with any great affection in his memoir *Hope and History*. The excavation of Corbyn's relationship with the Provos took a comical turn in the 2017 general election, when right-wing activists claimed to have found proof that he attended the funeral of Bobby Sands. The scruffy, bearded figure standing behind Adams in the photograph was in fact Jim Gibney.
19. Ó Broin, *Sinn Féin and the Politics of Left Republicanism*, p. 308.

Index